G e r m a n y

land

Rhine

Wesel

Gelilern

Wachtendonck

Emmerich

Cleves

Linnich

Middachten
Arnhem Velp
Doorwerth
Didam
Wageningen Huissen
Nijmegen
Venlo
Roermond
Limbricht
Maastricht
Papenhoven
Obbicht
L i m b u r g

Meuse

Liège

Maas

Sint Andries
Crèvecoeur
's Hertogenbosch
Eindhoven
Hasselt

B r a b a n t

Tilburg
Landen

d r e c h t

Lek
Nieuwpoort
Gorinchem

Waal
Geertruidenberg
Bommelerwaard

Aarschot

B e l g i u m

Gouda
Rotterdam
Rhoon
Dordrecht
Breda
Louvain

's Gravenmoer

Delft
Overschie
Hellevoetsluis

N o o r d

Bergen-op-Zoom

Brussels

Antwerp

Mechlin

Scheldt

Z e e l a n d

Middelburg

Flushing

The Bentincks

THE
BENTINCKS

The History of a European Family

Paul-Emile Schazmann
translated by Steve Cox

Weidenfeld and Nicolson   *London*

ISBN 0 297 77087 X

Printed in Great Britain by
Butler & Tanner Ltd, Frome and London

Contents

Illustrations

Acknowledgments

I HAVE TO THANK all the libraries, state archives and private individuals who have allowed me to consult their books and documents, in particular the Library of the British Museum (Manuscripts, Printed Books, Prints and Drawings); Arnhem Library; the Royal Library of The Hague; the State Archives of Arnhem; Leyden University Library; the Bibliothèque Nationale, Paris; the Swiss National Library in Berne, especially its international and intercity lending service, whose help has been invaluable; the Public and University Library, Geneva; the Municipal Libraries of Basel, Berne, Lausanne and Zurich; Count Ortenburg of Middachten Castle; Baron and Baroness Bentinck of Schoonheten; Mr and Mrs van Brauwere of Amerongen Castle; Mr and Mrs de Vogel-Bentinck, The Hague; Baron and Baroness de Vos-van Steenwick, Dutch Ambassador in Berne, owner of the manor of Diepenheim, birthplace of H. W. Bentinck; and Mr Victor F. W. Cavendish-Bentinck.

The chapter devoted to the late Baron Adolphe Bentinck could not have been written without the kind assistance of his widow, Baroness Gaby Bentinck-Thyssen-Bornemisza, who first had the idea for this book, after having had her attention drawn to the author's study of the Bentinck family in the *Revue d'histoire littéraire*, Paris, 1937.

I also wish to express my gratitude to those who knew Adolphe Bentinck as a friend and colleague and who willingly recalled his activities on behalf of European unity: The Right Hon. Edward Heath, then Prime Minister, who granted an interview at 10 Downing Street; Lord Gladwyn; M. Couve de Murville, former Prime Minister of France; M. Gaston Palewski, then President of the French Conseil Constitutionnel; M. Yves Cazaux, President of the Société des gens de lettres, Paris; and M. François Didier-Gregh, who was Adolphe Bentinck's colleague in the Secretariat-General of NATO in Paris. Further details and tributes to the work of the latest of the Bentinck diplomats came in a number of written communications, in particular from Joseph Luns, President of the NATO Council, and from Admiral Philippe de Gaulle.

My thanks are also due to Sir George Weidenfeld, who was a friend of Adolphe Bentinck and took an immediate interest in the publication of this book. Miss Jenny Ashby has been a careful, competent editor, and Mr Steve Cox has translated my French into English.

P-E. S

To the memory of Adolphe Bentinck

Jan c1372
|
Gerrit c1377
|
Hendrik †1431
|
Hendrik c1444
|
Hendrik †1502

Jan 'de Olde' †1545 Sander 'de Bolde' 1461-1547 Hendrik 'de Beste' †1538˙ VELDE

Adolf †1548 Carel †1553 William Zuylen †1621. Willem †1576 Jan

Alexander 1548-82 Philip BERENKAMP Eusebius †1584 Hendrik †1600

Carel †1645 OBBICHT   Hendrik †1639 Eberhard †1647
|
ALLER   Berend 1604-68 BREKLENKAMP

Hendrik 1640-91 Eusebius Borchard 1643-1710 Anne Villiers O Hans Willem 1st Earl of Portl
| | SCHOONHETEN
Agnes Bentinck O Willem 1673-1747   Henry 1st Duke of Portland 1682-1˙
        |
     Berend 1703-73   Margaret Cavendish Harley O William 2nd Duke of Portlà
             CAVENDISH- I BENTINCK
Dietrich 1741-1813 Wolter Jan Gerrit 1745-81 Dorothy Cavendish O William Henry 3rd Duke of I
| DIEPENHEIM & SCHOONHETEN
Rudolf Floris Carel 1785-1857   William Henry 4th Duke of Portl

Hendrik 1817-79   Berend Willem 1821-54 George 1802-48 William John Cavendish Sc
| 5th Duke of Portland 180C
Rudolf Floris Carel *1867 Rudolf Floris Carel *1847 Constant Adolf
| |
Adolphe Bentinck.-Thyssen 1905-70 Anne Gerhard Wolter *1874

       Rudolf Floris Carel *1913

  Christian Friedrich Anton 1734-68

Willem Gustav Friedrich 1762-1835 Jacoba Helena van Reede-Ginckel O Jan Carel 1763-1833

  Willem Friedrich Christian 1787-1855 Mechtild of Waldeck-Pyrmont Carel Anton Ferdinand 1792-18

     Hendrik Carel Adolf.Friedrich *1846 Willem Carel Philip Otto 1848-1˙
            | ALDENBURG-BENTIN˙
          Willem Friedrich Christian Hendrik 1880-19

   Enrico Gaetani dell'Agricola d'Aragona O Sophie Mechtild Marie *1924

Except in rare instances, living
members of the family are not shown.
†died
*born
O married

Alard 'de Leste'

Laurent

BONSEVAL

549-1709 O Jane Martha Temple
┌───────────────────┐
Charles John 1708-79   William 1st Count of the Empire 1704-74
'26-1762
d 1738-1809
68-1854   William 1774-1839   William Charles Augustus 1780-1826   Frederick 1741-1826
┌──────────────────┐   │
Arthur 1819-77   George Augustin 1821-91
│   │
William John Arthur 6th Duke of Portland *1857   William *1856
│   ┌──────────┴──────────┐
William Arthur 7th Duke of Portland *1893   Ferdinand *1888   Victor Frederick *1897

                John Albert 1737-75
Sir James
Hawkins Whitshed O Sophie Henriette   William 1764-1813
Hendrik Jan Willem O Renira Antoinette   George William Pierrepont 1803-86
                    Hawkins 1796-1878
            Godart Jan George 1857-1916
                    ┌──────────────────────────────┐
            Christian Arthur Reynoud 1885-1964   Godard Adriaan *1887
                    George Leon Alexander de Brauwere O Louise Adrienne Jacoba *1923
rel zu Ortenburg O Isabelle Adrienne *1925

Who are the Bentincks, Cavendish-Bentincks, and the Dukes of Portland?

'We must and will be amicably and definitively associated as among knights, squires and burghers.'

Treaty signed and sealed by Engelbert Bentinck, 1408

'Now we see the purpose of Bentinck's travels among several Protestant princes.'

King James II to Sophia of Hanover

'I am going to serve my King as I have always done.'

H.W. Bentinck, Earl of Portland, to Queen Mary

'It is reported from Holland that the Prince of Orange is well aware that there is likely to be an invasion. . . . He has sent the Earl of Portland.'

Jean Racine, at the siege of Namur, to his wife

'The Earl of Portland then added that in his personal opinion it was in the interest of the whole of Europe that the Spanish succession should not be garnered by one of my grandsons.'

Louis XIV to the Count of Harcourt

'Provided you will make war when I do! For this is what you have not done, although I will not reproach you for it. . . .'

Maria Theresa to Willem Bentinck

'What a surprise it would have been for them if they had seen the Duchess of Portland, whose herbalist I have the honour to be, climbing on rocks where I had difficulty in following. . . .'

Jean-Jacques Rousseau

'I don't know who this M. Bentinck is. . . .'

Napoleon I

'William Cavendish-Bentinck who never forgot that the end of government is the happiness of the governed.'

T. B. Macaulay

'All the questions with which he had dealt were colossal questions.'

Benjamin Disraeli, Lord George Bentinck

'Adolphe Bentinck was a skilled, an admirable diplomat. He had very good judgement. He justly inspired confidence.'

Edward Heath

1 ⚬ The Bentincks Seal the Truce of 1377 and the Pact of Confederation of 1418

HE LINE of the Bentinck family can be traced back in unbroken succession to the Middle Ages, or more precisely to the mid-fourteenth century, through a history in which each generation has played its part, some in minor, others in major roles. Their existence first comes to light when they receive a mention in a parchment or append their seal or signature to a deed; in later days their descent appears on baptismal registers and official records. There may still be documents lying in unclassified archives that would establish a definite link between earlier, thirteenth-century representatives of the name[1] and those of later periods.

The study of successive generations of Bentincks over more than five centuries soon reveals that there exist in certain cases parallels between the actions of the family and the destiny of their country, whose history they have reflected both in Europe and overseas. As far back as feudal times they exemplify the close interdependence of the different parts of Europe. Sometimes they have produced personalities strong enough to make their mark on the history of one or several nations. In their finest moments – and here their past is etched indelibly on that of the Netherlands, England and Europe – they have been the supporters and artisans

of the conquest of liberty within a setting of statutory and constitutional order, showing that same constancy that one of them
wished to see re-established in the eighteenth century as it had
existed in Roman times.[2]

By studying the history of one family which has continuously
reflected its times we shall see that Europe has been the product,
not of chance, still less of a grinding determinism, but of continual exertions which are not extinguished with the individual.

The name of Bentinck or Benting appears in the thirteenth
century in the same region where a century later we shall locate
the family whose history and special traits are the subject of this
book. Bentinck first occurs as the name of a soldier of the territories
of Overijssel or Gelderland, in the east of present-day Holland.
He bore the Latinized forename of Wicherus. Some genealo-
gists have considered Wicherus the ancestor of all the Bentincks,[3]
while others have accounted him purely legendary. In fact the
relationship between Wicherus Bentinck and Jan Bentinck, sometimes presumed to be his great-grandson, is unproven.

On the other hand, Jan Bentinck is indisputably an ancestor of
all the Dutch and English branches of the family. Wicherus
Bentinck did exist, however, and was not just a soldier, as one
contemporary document indicates; he appears as a witness for
the Bishop of Utrecht, Willebrand van Oldenburg, in the foundation deed of an important town in Overijssel, then in the Bishop's
territory. By this deed, dated 1230,[4] the former village of Zwolle,
on the border of Gelderland and Overijssel, received the rights
and privileges of a town.

So towards the middle of the thirteenth century we find our-
selves in a town close to the Ijssel, the northern arm of the Rhine
delta before it emerges into the Zuidersee, in a locality so flourish-
ing because of its commercially favourable position and the energy
of its inhabitants that it had been able to go to the assistance of the
Bishop, by providing the money and manpower to fortify his
castle and sustain his war against the sandy, less fertile province of
Drenthe.

The new-born town of Zwolle surrounded itself with walls built with the willing aid of the neighbouring peasantry, who could now take refuge against outside attacks by sheltering in the suburbs. Zwolle prospered, trade grew, relations were established with the north of Germany, then in the fifteenth century the town joined the powerful brotherhood of the Hanse. In 1495 the Emperor Maximilian conferred upon it the status of a free town of the Empire and the right to mint money. It is worth noting that years later the Bentincks sought to link their family name not with imaginary heroes reputed to have fought in the Crusades or in famous tournaments but with the witness to the granting of that charter.

Two generations separate Wicherus Bentinck from the certain founder of the family, Jan Bentinck. His father and grandfather have been improbably identified as Helmich and Willem Bentinck, the latter presumed to be the son of Wicherus. Since the relationship remains unproven we shall not linger on it, but the fact that Jan Bentinck suddenly appears in numerous documents of the later fourteenth century as master and lord of estates in Gelderland and Overijssel shows that the Bentinck family had for some time enjoyed a position superior to that of many minor lordlings.

Soon we shall find descendants of Jan Bentinck all over this part of middle Europe, the north of the former Lotharingia, from the Zuidersee to Deventer, Arnhem, Nijmegen and further to the east, Utrecht, on the main lines of communication with the south along the rivers Moselle, Rhône and Scheldt and above all the Rhine.

According to a deed of 1385,[5] Jan Bentinck held land in Gorssel, south of Deventer, and in Dommeren, still closer to Deventer, in the part of Salland near Raalte. Here, in a region which was independent both of the German states and of France, the Bentincks sank their deepest roots and still reside. Soon they were to branch out to the Veluwe, near the Zuidersee, on the confines of the Veluwemeer, now an arm of the sea separated from the great lake by the polders of Flevoland. None of their estates gave its name to the Bentinck family as a whole, presumably because they started off with too much property in too many different places. There were Bentinck van Schoonhetens, Bentinck van Rhoons, but Bentinck has always remained the patronymic of the family in general.

There is said to have been a chateau Bentinck, situated between Deventer and Zutphen, which belonged to a man called Gerrit Bentinck in the fifteenth century and which was sold to Dietrich Stakebrant in 1455.[6] I shall not venture to say that the Bentincks owe their name to the seigneury. It appears more likely that the owner gave his own name to the estate, as occasionally happened elsewhere – at Broglie in Normandy, for example.

The first Jan Bentinck held an ecclesiastical post at Heerde,[7] in the eastern part of the Veluwe, on the main highway which runs from the Rhine to Nijmegen, then northward to Arnhem and Apeldoorn, skirting Deventer to the west, and goes on through Zwolle to reach Friesland in the west and Groningen in the east.

The countryside in which we find the first Bentinck knights has none of the rugged heights which buttressed the almost impregnable castles of France and the Germanic towns. Their protection was a moat or a ditch, crossed by a drawbridge; no lord could extend his holdings very far. It is the multiplicity of the domains and manors situated in heathlands or on forest borders which distinguishes the Bentinck properties even at this early date.

In 1377 Jan Bentinck was admitted to the knighthood of Gelderland.[8] The Gossen Bentinck who gained the same distinction was not his son, as the Dutch guide to the nobility still claimed in 1910. Eight years later, two years before his death, when Jan drew up a document sharing out his estates, Gossen is mentioned as a relative but is not listed among the children of Jan's two marriages, as was the Hendrik Bentinck who was to carry on the family line. Nor, contrary to what has been claimed, were Jan or another member of the family, Gerrit, present as witnesses to the marriage of the Duke of Gelderland to Catherine of Bavaria. The marriage contract bears neither their name nor their seal.[9] Their absence need not perturb us, since the union managed to prosper without the attendance of the Bentincks at the impressive wedding ceremony.

Another document does, however, call attention to the activities of Jan Bentinck, his blood relation Gossen and the third Bentinck, Gerrit. This is the general peace treaty signed on 6 January 1377 by Jean de Châtillon, Count of Blois, by the Grace of God Duke of Gelderland and Count of Zutphen, and by Matilda.[10] The signatures of the three Bentincks appear on it as do those of other knights and burghers from the High and Low Veluwe, from Bommelerwaard and from towns such as Huessen, Hardewijck, Elburg and Hattem.[11]

The treaty to which Jan, Gerrit and Gossen appended their signatures and arms (the moline cross for the Bentincks) represented an attempt to end the continual quarrels and wars of succession that raged in the Low Countries and in Gelderland in particular. The truce was short-lived, however, and a succession of wars first established the house of Egmont in Gelderland in 1423 and finally led to Charles the Bold of Burgundy purchasing Gelderland and Zutphen in 1471.

How did these dynastic struggles affect the Bentincks? We must remember that in the Middle Ages national feeling as we know it in our own time did not exist; subjects did not necessarily feel themselves injured by a change of sovereign, or rather of suzerain, and great families such as the Bentincks continued to administer their estates relatively undisturbed. Towards the end of the fourteenth century and throughout the fifteenth a number of records show them helping their neighbours, supporting monasteries and promoting the rule of justice and peace. Indeed, at this time the Bentincks embodied the two great tendencies of late feudalism, the spirit of Christendom and of chivalry.

Although the title of knight was not hereditary and demanded a long period of preparation, numerous generations of Bentincks belonged to the institution of chivalry. They risked much on behalf of liberty: their arms, azure with silver moline cross, are a symbol of their faith and hope rather than a reminder of a crusade or a pilgrimage to the Holy Land (for knights were not

Don Quixotes or paladins, as the romantic writers would have us believe). And very early on we can distinguish their spirit of solidarity and sense of continuity.

Some two years before his death in 1387 Jan Bentinck, who had also inherited estates in Olst and Terwolde, both on the bank of the Ijssel, north of Deventer, ensured his descendants' inheritance by a deed.[12] He had already given land to the poor in Bursen, in the parish of Terwolde.[13]

We come now to Jan's grandson, Hendrik Bentinck, knight of Gelderland, lord of Arensberg, future site of the manor of Berinkhuisen or Berenkamp, near Wapenveld, not far from Heerde.[14] This was the residence of the Bentincks of the Berenkamp branch. This Hendrik, benefactor of the monastery of Hulsberg, is not to be confused with several subsequent generations of Hendrik Bentincks. He developed domains between Hattem and Heerde and donated a piece of land called Ellenhoorn which played an important part in the foundation of the monastery in 1407.

The outlook for Gelderland and Overijssel was anything but tranquil at the start of the fifteenth century. Matters came to a head when Gulik V of Juliers asserted claims over Gelderland on behalf of his mother. These lords and their vassals clashed. Town rivalries multiplied: Deventer and Zutphen each wanted a monopoly of shipping on the Ijssel; Kampen and Zwolle each wanted to fob off the costs of defence on the other. Finally, in May 1418, a large number of representatives of the knighthood and towns of Gelderland and the county of Zutphen held a meeting. These included several Bentinck knights, the sons and grandsons of Jan Bentinck. After long deliberations they decided to unite to protect their rights and defend their property, declaring that they would do their utmost to avoid all quarrelling and warfare. Neither the rule of common law nor the burghers' privileges were to be eroded. Where rights had been diminished they would help each other to regain them, and in the face of any threat they would come to one another's assistance.

This solemn document[15] was copied four times on parchment, with minor variations. The contributing parties, divided into four groups after the regions bearing the names of the capitals, Nijmegen, Roermond, Zutphen and Arnhem, appended their signatures to the manuscript of their respective countries. The Arnhem parchment is signed by Engelbert Bentinck among others, and the seal of the moline cross, in green wax, hangs alongside those of his peers. The first of the signatories was Henric van Middachten, whose chateau was later to belong to the Bentincks, when they became allied to the van Reedes who owned it for some time. Engelbert Bentinck was one of the sons of Jan Bentinck and the uncle of Hendrik Bentinck, benefactor of the Hulsberg monastery and ancestor of the Bentinck family.

The pact that they signed expressly provided in each copy that no modifications or additions were to be made on the original parchment, so as to preserve its full integrity. New inclusions were to be contained in letters referred to as *transfixes*, which were to be cut out of the principal document. Thus the parchment attesting to the pact would not be smudged, holed, crumpled or stained and thus invalidated. On the same evening as the settlement, 3 May 1418, such a *lettre transfixe* was drawn up as an extension to the Arnhem pact by a number of knights and town dignitaries, among them the grandson of Jan Bentinck and nephew of Engelbert, 'Henrich Bentinck'.

This document, in whose decisions one Bentinck took an active part and another became immediately associated, testifies to the great influence already achieved by the lesser nobility and the burghers. From then on they were to be collaborators in the maintenance of their own independence against any abuse of power, devoted to their country and, with some reservations, to their duke.

Engelbert and Hendrik Bentinck swore with the others 'In the name of the Almighty who loves his people and leads them in the path of justice and fidelity'. As the historian Sismondi writes,[16] the spirit of chivalry gave rise to a legacy more glorious and heroic than all the wonders of adventure novels, for this legacy was liberty. At the same time it is a patrimony common to a large part of Europe, since, although Sismondi refers to this phenomenon in connection with Italy, we find it in the Low Countries. Switzerland already had its own pact, signed on 1 August 1291, embodying the same spirit of liberty.

By this pact groups which had hitherto been separated came together. Since the knights of the four capitals and the smaller towns and urban authorities now united each time any of them found their rights threatened and defended themselves vigorously against injustices and the claims of other lords, neither the Bishopric nor the external power of the Juliers and Egmonts could gain any serious hold in Gelderland.

Hendrik Bentinck died in 1431. His son, also named Hendrik, became a judge at Heerde in 1435, having made his home there. It was a moment when efforts to reach an understanding between the Duke and the town administrations were under special strain. The Duke of Gelderland had also managed to fall out with the knights by trying to obtain money against pledges and by making excessive demands. At the end of 1435 the capital towns and the knights together with the lesser towns demanded to take over the administration of the fiefs and the common and municipal law, and the control of dikes, and asked for assurances on the safety of the roads and waterways, respect for ancient rights to mint money, the surrender of domanial property and a formal guarantee of an equitable jurisdiction.

Demands on such a scale were unacceptable, and a diet met at Nijmegen in 1436. It was attended by Hendrik Bentinck and his brothers Johan and Helmick. In the presence of these three Bentinck knights, and with their participation, the pact of 1418 was solemnly renewed; it was confirmed once again in 1441.

The Nijmegen diet of 1436 had reinforced the position of the lords and the towns against that of the Duke, though they never took advantage of him when external dangers made his situation critical. When Gerard II, Duke of Juliers, made war on Jean II of Egmont, who had married Marie of Gelderland, Hendrik Bentinck was there as envoy of the town of Elburg, despite his

differences with the Duke. At the battle of Linnich on St Hubert's
Day, 3 November 1441, when the Duke of Gelderland was
defeated, Hendrik Bentinck was taken prisoner and had to be
ransomed.

This Hendrik Bentinck, the second knight of that name, comes
to notice again in 1468, on the occasion of the reconciliation
between the Duke of Gelderland and Count Jean de Meurs
before his death in 1477. He and his wife owned property at
Welsum, now a hamlet opposite Olst, on the left bank of the
Ijssel. His love of liberty, order and justice was expressed at the
diet of 1436: he had been a careful administrator of his lands and
had responded to the call when a town had need of him or when
he could help his suzerain to make peace. The second Hendrik
Bentinck was a worthy represenative of his family.

In the next generation the three sons of Hendrik took part in a
far-reaching modification of the politics of Gelderland and its
neighbouring provinces. The defeat and death of Charles the
Bold at the battle of Nancy in 1477 did not immediately bring
about the decline and annexation of Burgundy by France. Mary,
daughter of the Duke of Burgundy, married Maximilian of
Austria, and she and the Archduke became suzerains of Gelderland
by the decision of his father, Emperor Frederick III. William of
Egmont's efforts to rebuild his power bore little fruit, and he
received hardly any support, except from Arnhem, which he had
invaded and subdued. The forces of his ally the Duke of Cleves
were meagre, however, and his soldiers were themselves besieged
at Arnhem.

Realizing that they could not defend themselves against an
attack by Maximilian, the Gelderlanders cast about for help from
the Duke of Brunswick-Lüneburg and the Bishop of Münster
and held parleys with the King of France on 25 January 1480 at
Bar-le-Duc. But neither the Bishop nor Louis XI sent help when
Maximilian attacked. Towns fell one after another.

Hendrik III Bentinck, a man of substance who owned the
manors of Berenkamp, Loo and Oosterhof, the domain of Manen,

at Epe, and a house in Hattem, was one of the last to surrender to Burgundy. No one could then have predicted how fast Gelderland would regain its independence, thanks to Charles of Egmont, who found a loyal aide in Hendrik Bentinck. In 1492 Charles gathered an army and managed to reconquer his father's heritage with the help of France. In return for his loyalty Hendrik Bentinck received the life suzerainty of Berinkhuisen in 1494.

One of the sons of Hendrik was dubbed Jan de Olde (the old) because he was the eldest of four brothers and a sister. He received the freehold of Het Loo, near Apeldoorn, and on the death without issue of his son Adolf in 1548 it passed to his sister Adelheid Bentinck and her husband Phillipp van Varick.[17] Here in 1685 William III of Orange built the chateau of Het Loo, which is today the summer residence of Queen Juliana of the Netherlands.

A year before his death in 1501 Hendrik Bentinck arranged to divide his many estates among his children. Jan de Olde received not only Het Loo but also Oosterhof and the Bentinck house in Hattem. Oosterhof was a thriving farm on the east side of the little town of Rijssen on the road running east from Deventer to Amelo. Rijssen's charter as a city dated from 1243; its markets and warehouses had for long made it one of the main commercial staging-points of the Bishop of Utrecht.

Some years after the death of Hendrik, Jan de Olde Bentinck became Master of the Hunt in the household of Duke Charles of Gelderland. His name crops up now and then as the Duke's special envoy to the town councils. Some of the Duke's towns were occupied by the troops of Margaret of Austria when Philip II was trying to regain the northern Netherlands for Spain, and in 1511 Hattem found itself under the command of Philip van Reck, an officer in the service of Spain. Hattem, which lay in the far north of Gelderland, only seven kilometres from Zwolle, was a particularly well-fortified stronghold, as well as a Hanse town. It enjoyed an almost impregnable natural position, being situated on a bend in the river, bordered by a dike and enclosed by trenches topped by walls. The entrance was by way of a gate through a square tower.

Knowing what was at stake and eager to see the town restored to its suzerain, Jan Bentinck resorted to a ruse. He was familiar with the town and had no trouble in finding out that van Reck kept a mistress there. He made an approach to her and offered a reward of eight thousand gold florins to her lover if he would surrender the town to two Gelderland captains, Willem van Rossen and Henri de Meerveld. Once the town had been retaken by this new kind of Trojan Horse invented by 'a certain Jan Bentinck',[18] other larger cities, especially Utrecht, plucked up their courage and resisted the Spanish forces.

Charles of Egmont had no children, and when, towards the end of his life, he wanted to cede Gelderland to France the States-General objected. A year before his death during a diet at Nijmegen, which Jan de Olde Bentinck attended as representative of the knights of the Veluwe, he appointed the Duke of Cleves to succeed him. William of Cleves found it no easy task to defend Gelderland. He succeeded for a while with the help of France, but Jan Bentinck was still alive when in 1543 the Emperor Charles v came in person to the Low Countries and compelled William of Cleves to give up the four quarters of Roermond, Nijmegen, Zutphen and Arnhem. They now became part of the Spanish Netherlands, under Habsburg rule. Jan de Olde's son Adolf was present at the conclusion of the treaty, and the Generality thus formed lasted until the Union of Utrecht thirty-six years later, in which Jan de Olde's grand-nephew Alexander was instrumental as envoy of the court of Gelderland. In doing so Alexander aligned himself with the Orangist party in opposing Alexander Farnese, later Duke of Parma, when he was threatening the independence of Gelderland in the name of Philip ii of Spain.

One of Jan de Olde Bentinck's brothers, Hendrik, called 'de Beste' (the best), created a collateral branch of the Bentincks: these were the van Veldes, so called because Hendrik de Beste had acquired the domain of Velde from his father-in-law Lerinck.

One noteworthy descendant was his grandson, also a Hendrik, also a knight. He was a judge in Arnhem before his appointment as bailiff of the High Veluwe by the Duke of Alba in 1572.

The Duke, who was governor of the Low Countries under King Philip II of Spain, never succeeded in reducing the rebels gathered around the Prince of Orange and left for Spain the year after he appointed Hendrik bailiff. Hendrik held his office in the confused period that followed the Duke of Alba's departure. In 1579, Philip II sent Alexander Farnese to the southern provinces. He was a far better diplomat than the Duke of Alba and could appeal to people's hearts and minds. Hendrik Bentinck now became a captain in the royal army of the Spanish Netherlands, governor of Venlo and a member of the knighthood of the Veluwe, which, however, no longer enjoyed the splendid independence of the era of the Nijmegen diets which his ancestors had attended. By his second marriage Hendrik Bentinck had a son, Marteen, whom we shall encounter in Limburg at the chateau of Obbicht when he married the daughter of Anne van Vlodorp and Philip Bentinck.

On Hendrik Bentinck's third marriage, to Sophie van Morebeck, heiress to the seigneury of Breklenkamp, near Denekamp, began the now extinct branch of the Bentincks of Breklenkamp. Their grandson Gerhard Adolf Bentinck built the manor of Breklenkamp.

We now return to another brother of Jan de Olde and Hendrik de Beste: this one is Sander, called 'de Bolde' (the bold). Sander inherited the estate of Berenkamp from his father and also bought from Gisbert van Aller in 1501 the domain whose name he bore. The Duke of Gelderland granted Sander Bentinck the suzerainty of Aller and also bestowed various posts on him. He became collector of the marriage tax and master of the ducal kitchens, which were well stocked with the finest products of the hunt. The extent of Sander Bentinck's estates is breath-taking: Pas and Sclick, in addition to Berenkamp and Aller, lands as far away as the outskirts of Diedam and the seigneury of Udenhof. He also owned Schoonderbeck, which he ceded to the Duke of Gelderland in return for an annual allowance. His wife, Johanna van Zuylen, was the daughter of Willem van Zuylen van Anholt, a judge at Hengelo.

Sander's son Carel was lord not only of Aller and other estates but also of Berinkhuisen, the old Bentinck property which came to him at the death of his cousin Hendrik. He also owned the family house at Arnhem. He married the daughter of Olever van Hackfort, of the chateau of that name at Vorden, near the town of Zutphen and the manor of Velde. It is this manor that gave its name to the Velde branch of the family, from which the present-day Bentincks are descended. Although the chateau of Hackfort caught fire in the late sixteenth century, two towers and some ruins remain.

Carel Bentinck was a receiver and judge in the Veluwe. He had several sons, among them Alexander and his younger brother Philip. They became supporters of two powerful rival coalitions which they tried in vain to reconcile: the northern provinces grouped around William the Silent and the southern provinces which stayed faithful to Spain.

Before examining the fertile careers of Carel's two sons we must mention an offshoot created by his brother, Willem Zuylen Bentinck (d. 1621), who took his second name from the maiden name of his mother Johanna. His first marriage was to the daughter of Andries Schimmelpenninck, his second to Sophia Eijssen, daughter of Hendrik Tiejssen, who came from Emmerich, in the Rhineland, not far from the Gelderland frontier. The marriage took place at Nijkerk, and one of their descendants, Lambert Berend Bentinck, knight of the Veluwe, was head of the dikes at Wageningen on the Rhine, west of Arnhem in the direction of Utrecht.[19]

To return to the sons of Carel Bentinck, Alexander, lord of Aller and Berinkhuisen, was a magistrate at Arnhem, the capital of the whole of Gelderland. The deputies of the seven provinces of the north had their seat at Utrecht and Alexander Bentinck, Elbert van Leeuw, who had Latinized his name as Leoninus, and Reinier Clant, represented Gelderland at the assembly.

The moves towards a reconciliation between the Netherlands and Spain at Breda in 1575, at Geertruidenberg in 1577 and at Cologne in 1579 had all foundered in the face of Philip II's intransigence. The Bentincks, whether they were in the northern provinces or in the Spanish Netherlands, wanted to maintain unity between north and south, the unity of what was called the Generality of the Netherlands. At the same time they set as much store by their independence as had their ancestors in the earliest days of the knights of Gelderland. That liberty was irreconcilable with the Spanish occupation.

Negotiations began at Utrecht on 28 November 1578. Most of the deputies had come from Holland, Zeeland and Friesland. The States of Gelderland were still opposing a separate alliance and tried to prevent John of Nassau from signing. He was in possession of Dillenburg but at the same time governed Arnhem on behalf of Gelderland. William the Silent had advised him to suggest the Utrecht conference. In the early new year of 1578 they learned that Alexander Farnese was threatening the northern quarters of Gelderland, and when on top of that came the news that the southern states of the Netherlands had already signed the Union of Arras among themselves they realized that the Generality of the States of the Netherlands had had its day.

On 12 January, John of Nassau arrived in Utrecht to join his envoys, among them Alexander Bentinck, who participated in the solemn measure of 23 January 1579 which placed William the Silent as Stadtholder at the head of the seven provinces of the northern Netherlands and enabled them to form a federation of states, the Republic of the United Provinces, on 26 July 1581 and to sanction the deposition of Philip II as their sovereign. The dream of Maximilian and Charles V had been destroyed. The northern Netherlands, where the province of Holland was to play a leading role, no longer had anything but a theoretical connection with the Empire, and their independence was finally recognized at the end of the Thirty Years' War by the Treaty of Westphalia.

At the time when the Netherlands divided, neither of the two new parts as yet envisaged a final rupture. Even within provinces and families there were those who hoped for a *rapprochement*. Gelderland was split. Among the sons of Carel Bentinck, Alexander belonged to the United Provinces, while Philip was a colonel in the army of the Spanish Netherlands. The behaviour of these two brothers, each convinced that the Generality must survive, but on the basis of opposing principles, is symbolic of the sorry situation in which Gelderland then found itself.

Philip Bentinck became governor of Venlo in 1586, and the town of Geldern was given up to him by its governor, Patton, who had come over to the Spanish side.[20] In 1590 he fell into disgrace with the Spanish government which was represented by the administration of Alexander Farnese.

It was not in Philip Bentinck's character, as a worthy descendant of the knights of Gelderland, to turn his coat because he had suffered underhand treatment. He went into dignified retirement with his wife Alverta in the chateau of Obbicht, in her seigneury in Limburg. Born Alverta van Vlodorp, and widow of Carel van Bronkhorst-Batenberg, she came of Limburg stock through her mother, Ann van der Donck, and had lived in Gelderland, the country of her father Willem van Vlodorp. Philip Bentinck had had the chateau rebuilt in 1585 on the remains of the old house destroyed by the Spaniards to punish his wife's first husband, Carel van Bronkhorst, for becoming a Protestant.

Philip owed his titles of lord of Obbicht and Papenhoven to his fine estates in Limburg. He had also become bailiff of the land of Montfort and as such tried to restore peace between the southern provinces, including his native province of Gelderland, then partitioned in two, and the seven United Provinces of the new Union created at Utrecht in 1579.

After the disgrace and death of Farnese and the short, cruel administration of his successor, the Count of Fuentes, the Infanta Isabella and her husband, Archduke Albert of Austria, became sovereigns. They ran into considerable difficulties, in spite of the brilliant inauguration of their reign in the Brussels Palace in 1598 and in 1600 called a meeting of the States General of those

provinces which had remained loyal to Spain. The States of
Gelderland had not been forgotten, and so it came about that
among the deputies appointed from Gelderland to go to Brussels
was Philip Bentinck.

Philip Bentinck reached Brussels at the beginning of April,
before the other members of the States of Gelderland, on private
and military business. He lodged in the 'Gulden Kasteel', accompanied by five servants. He and his colleagues from the southern
provinces recognized that their situation was poor compared with
that of the Orangist United Provinces. Maurice of Nassau, who
had become leader of the United Provinces after the assassination
of his father William the Silent, had been successful in the field
and, taking advantage of a hard winter which had frozen the
rivers, had surprised the town of Wachtendonck in Gelderland.
In March he seized the fort of Crèvecœur and proceeded to lay
siege to the fort of Sint-Andries. On top of that, the army was
being weakened by mutinies and the inhabitants of Antwerp were
in revolt; the agricultural situation was critical because the
peasants were no longer sowing for fear of plundering
soldiers.[21]

It was in the midst of this disastrous situation that the States
General of the South assembled. The sittings began on 28 April
1600, were suspended on 24 July, resumed on 2 September and
terminated on 9 November.

The opening session took place in the Brussels Palace, in the
room which had witnessed the abdication of Charles v. Archduke
Albert and Isabella presided. They took their position on a dais,
the Infanta to the right, the Archduke to the left. Their court,
knights of the Golden Fleece, provincial governors and members
of the collateral councils, stood near them.

The 160 members of the States occupied the middle of the hall.
About half of the deputies were from Brabant and Flanders, and
all of them were chosen by the States themselves, men of high
quality and the greatest authority, prudence, judgement and
application. By a note in the margin of the convocation, Albert
of Austria had entered an emendation according to which they

were to be 'easy, tractable people, to be swayed by what will be proposed to them'.[22]

The deputies from Gelderland had been unable to produce credentials or warrants, since they represented only one part of the province, but that did not prevent the States General from designating Philip Bentinck as one of the three members of the diplomatic mission to be sent to Holland, a mission that might have changed the course of European history.

After several sessions the majority decided to ask the Archdukes for permission to conclude a peace or truce with the provinces of the Union of Utrecht. Some dissenting provinces, especially Artois, did not want a peace which, they feared, would allow Calvinism into their territories.

On 31 May the States General chose the deputies to be sent to Holland. They elected Gerard de Hornes, Baron de Bassigny, member of the States of Brabant, and Philip Bentinck, lord of Bicht and member of the States of Gelderland. When they asked the States of Flanders to name a third deputy themselves, they designated Hendrik Codt, pensionary of Ypres.[23]

The provinces of these three deputies had expressed their opinion by vote in full session of the States General that peace must be sought, but on terms. The deputies from Brabant had proposed talks with the United Provinces to give them the chance to join the others 'by means of a good peace'. Those from Flanders wished to conclude a peace treaty without prejudice to the authority of the Archduke but at the same time to look into the measures necessary for the country's military protection. They wished Their Highnesses to reconsider the numbers of their soldiery. Philip Bentinck belonged to the Gelderland contingent, which wanted to go much further towards the Orangist position and expressed the view that Albert and Isabella should publish a general pardon. Those who did not share the Catholic religion and wanted to live in the north should be free to do so, provided that they made no trouble and swore their loyalty. The deputies from Gelderland were the only ones to ask for the town offices, citadels and castles to be manned and guarded 'by natives, and for

B

foreigners to serve only in the country', thus raising the thorny problem of the Spanish occupiers.[24]

At last the letter 'to the men of Holland and Zeeland' was ready, approved by the Archduke and translated into Flemish, and it was decided that the three deputies appointed to deliver it were to leave on Thursday 8 June and go first to Antwerp. On 10 June, 'G. Hornes; Philips Van Bentinck, Heere tzo Bicht; Hendrick de Codt' signed a letter addressed from Antwerp by the noble lords deputy of the States General assembled at The Hague, asking them for a passport and a herald.[25]

On 16 June three hundred ships and fourteen thousand foot-soldiers headed by three thousand horsemen of the United Provinces were threatening Flanders. All hope hinged on the negotiations.[26]

Just as the Brussels deputies were arriving the Hollanders took offence about the signature of the letter that preceded them; it read 'deputies of the States General'. They claimed that only the United Provinces were entitled to this description and insisted that the Netherlands should be rid of Spanish domination. The states of the United Provinces were also perturbed to learn that the Brussels assembly was subject to the authority of the Arch-duke. Gerard de Hornes returned to Brussels to consult the assembly of the southern provinces, while Bentinck and Codt waited in Antwerp. On 28 June the three deputies requested a meeting again, pointing out that the questions of the expulsion of foreigners and the payment of war damages could then be settled. The instruction given to Philip Bentinck and the other two envoys did in fact leave them free to hold talks with the States of Holland once they had delivered the letter from the States General.[27]

Meanwhile the armed struggle continued. Albert and Isabella left for Ghent and counter-attacked near Nieuport. The States General of the United Provinces had moved to Ostend for a closer view of the military operations and it was there that they received the second letter from the three southern deputies. The site of the conference was arranged for Bergen-op-Zoom.

The two delegations arrived practically simultaneously and

were lodged together in the magnificent Gothic building known
as the Cour du Marquis. Philip Bentinck and his two colleagues
were greeted by Johan van Oldenbarneveldt, Santen and de
Renesse representatives of William the Silent for the seven
United Provinces. There were sixteen delegates from Holland,
plus a clerk. The conference opened the next day in the great hall
of the Cour du Marquis. Codt made known the contents of the
letter from Brussels, offering to enter into friendly communication 'to find means for peace and concord' and to rescue the
country from the sufferings of civil war which had afflicted them
so long.

The reply was made by Oldenbarneveldt, a skilful negotiator
impelled by a fierce love of liberty to oppose the hold of the
Archduke and the Spaniards, just as later he resisted the domestic
ambitions of Maurice of Nassau – so condemning himself to the
scaffold. He dealt principally with the wrongs and cruelties for
which he held the rule of Spain responsible. The southern states
had let slip a golden opportunity to restore liberty after the death
of Philip II two years previously, when they had allowed the
Spaniards to strengthen their hold and to take command of the
main towns and fortresses. These objections echoed those put
forward in the States General of Brussels by the deputies from
Gelderland – yet Bentinck and his companions had to be content
with maintaining that the departure of the Spaniards would be
better settled by a sound peace than by force of arms.

Evening brought no resolution of the two points of view. The
Hollanders' last word had been that nothing more could be done
without first consulting their principals. At the same time they
handed the envoys from Brussels a letter commending the welfare
of the Netherlands.

Gerard de Hornes, Colonel Bentinck and Pensionary Codt left
Bergen-op-Zoom at once. They had reached Brussels again by
23 July and presented their report at a session of the States
General on the next day. Philip Bentinck also reported that the
United Provinces had been on the point of organizing themselves
into cantons on the Swiss model, recognizing no sovereign prince,

but that the Gelderlanders and Zeelanders had broken off the discussion for fear that the people might also want to set themselves above the nobility. Nor would the neighbouring princes tolerate such a republic.[28]

The reply from The Hague on the proposal to negotiate peace according to the offers made at Bergen-op-Zoom had still not arrived by late September, and the Archduke refused to permit the three deputies to write to remind the United Provinces of a duty that needed no reminder.

The war dragged on for nine years, the Bentinck brothers, Philip and Alexander, each maintaining their allegiance. Not until 1609 did Oldenbarneveldt, who had met Philip Bentinck in 1600 at Bergen-op-Zoom, at long last manage to conclude the twelve-year Truce of Antwerp with the Spaniards. This enabled the United Provinces to live in peace according to the principles established thirty years before at the Union of Utrecht, sealed for Gelderland by, among others, Alexander Bentinck, Philip's own brother.

Alexander Bentinck had died in 1607, and one of his sons, Carel Bentinck, who acquired the seigneuries of Aller and Berinkhuisen and became burgomaster of Arnhem, was to cast Arnhem's vote for the peace in 1609. In the year of Alexander's death, Philip Bentinck visited Brussels in May as one of the delegates from the quarter of Roermond to discuss the submission of a new report favouring negotiations with the States General.[29]

Philip Bentinck had twice found himself in disgrace, once with the King, once with Roermond, but he had always found his feet again and had always kept in touch with his family on the other side. In the year of his brother's death he was not afraid to visit Nijmegen and Arnhem in the north. He obtained authentic versions of various documents concerning his own family, in particular the statute of the former chancellory of the town of Arnhem. The town of Nijmegen gave him copies of parchments concerning the Venlo deed granted by Duke Charles of Gelderland, the letter from Duke Arnold confirming the oath-giving ceremonies between the bannerets, knights and towns in 1423, 1436 and 1441, attended by his Bentinck ancestors, and the contract between Duke Charles and the province, all documents which had bearing on his family and ancestors.

The line of these two brothers became extinct in the eighteenth century, though not before showing signs of brilliance. Philip's branch owned considerable estates and seigneuries in Limburg and the south of Gelderland and finally emigrated to the duchy of Juliers, where one member became president of the knights of Juliers in 1689.

Philip Bentinck's wife, Anne van Vlodorp, had a daughter by her first marriage, Petronella van Bronckhorst, who in 1590 married a grand-nephew of Philip, Marteen Bentinck, an officer in the army of the Spanish Netherlands. While Philip was the grandson of Alexander, called de Bolde, Marteen was descended from his brother Hendrik de Beste. This Hendrik had several sons, one of whom, Willem, lord of Velde, became the ancestor of all the present-day Bentincks, the dukes of Portland, counts of Varel and Kniphausen and barons of Gelderland and Overijssel.

As for Alexander, his marriage to Adelheid van Buckhorst produced two sons, Carel and Willem, and four daughters, one of whom married Jacob Schimmelpenninck van der Oye.

Carel Bentinck, town magistrate of Arnhem, was burgomaster seven times between 1609 and 1643 and counsellor at the court of Gelderland. As spokesman for the quarter of Arnhem he attended the States General of 1609 at the conclusion of the Truce of Antwerp. In addition to his political activities, he was also curator of the Academy of Harderwijk, where Linnaeus and Boerhaave were students. Several of his descendants were knights of the Veluwe. Goswin Gerhard Bentinck, born in 1712, held important posts in the Veluwe, Arnhem and at the university of Harderwijk. He married the daughter of Baron Godard Adrian van Reede, who belonged to the family of one of the companions of William III of Orange.

The waning of feudal times brought no decline in the Bentincks' spirit of initiative, which proved extraordinarily vigorous in the course of the following centuries. Despite their membership of high political circles and their service at court they never lost their love of their native lands, the hunt and horses, canals, windmills and old manors.

2   A Gelderlander in the Capital of Flemish Burgundy

WE HAVE TRACED some of the activities and achievements of three Bentinck brothers, Jan de Olde, Sander de Bolde and Hendrik de Beste, and their ancestors, descendants of the knights of Gelderland who signed the general peace of 1377 and the first treaties of confederation of 1418 and 1436. Before turning to the roles of the descendants of Hendrik the Best we shall catch a glimpse of the colourful life of the fourth and youngest brother, Alard, called 'de Leste' (the last).

Alard Bentinck spent a happy childhood in his parents' fine houses at Berenkamp, Het Loo, Oosterhof and Manen, meeting-places for the nobles of Gelderland and Overijssel. It was his brothers, however, who were to inherit all the seigneuries (Hattem and Oosterhof, in northern Gelderland, for Jan; Berenkamp for Sander; Manen, on the Apeldoorn–Zwolle road, for Hendrik), and Alard had to make do with the family house in Arnhem, which he sold, fortunately to a member of the family.

When Margaret of Austria, the daughter of the Emperor Maximilian and Mary of Burgundy, set sail in 1497 from Flushing for Burgos to join Don Juan of Castile, Alard Bentinck was a member of her retinue. Margaret had married Don Juan by proxy two years previously, at the age of fifteen, in the church of St Peter in Mechlin.

The little Princess had been introduced to the arts and had acquired the charm and wordly wisdom which were to stand her in good stead in the thick of difficult negotiations during her unconsummated marriage to the French Dauphin, which he broke off to marry Anne of Brittany. Her mother had died young, and her father never paid her much attention except as a pawn in the game of alliances. Yet she had been fortunate with her companions – first with her French nurse, Anne of Beaujeu, the stern daughter of Louis XI, then with Madame de Segre, whose husband was Margaret's grand chamberlain.

Other counsellors of the new Infanta of Castile included important figures such as Jean of Bourbon, lord of Rochefort, who wrote an account of the voyage; Philip, son of the Marquis de Bade; Diego de Guevara and Louis Barangier, the tireless secretary who personally wrote every letter she dictated for more than twenty years. Barangier and Alard Bentinck became friends, and we shall find them together in Burgos, Pont-d'Ain and Mechlin.

On 3 April 1497 Alard was present at the dazzling ceremony which joined the glowing young Princess to the pallid Infante. Exactly six months later he attended Don Juan's funeral. The contemporary historian Philip de Comines wrote: 'I never heard tell of greater mourning . . . .' Alard returned with the widowed Infanta this time through France. They reached Ghent in time for Margaret to become godmother of the future Charles V, son of her brother Philip the Handsome.

Two years later Alard Bentinck was at Pont-d'Ain, near Bourg-en-Bresse, with Margaret, now Duchess of Savoy by her marriage to Duke Philibert. Although she now surrounded herself mainly with Savoyard counsellors, Alard Bentinck remained attached to Margaret and became a valued member of the court of Savoy. Like Margaret, Duke Philibert had been brought up in Amboise. In addition to Savoy his territory included his states in Italy, a part of present-day Switzerland, Bresse, Bugey and Gex, so

it is not hard to imagine the variety of political and diplomatic
figures who surrounded the sovereigns in Pont-d'Ain either as
residents or as visitors. Alard Bentinck's career had brought him
within nothing short of a fortified palace. As well as military and
political advisers the little court of Pont-d'Ain also attracted
artists, poets and musicians.

Luckily for him, Alard Bentinck's tasks kept him clear of
hunting, too often a fatal pastime for the family of Margaret, for it
removed her devoted Philibert after four years' happy marriage.
Her grandmother, Mary of Burgundy, had succumbed when her
horse threw her; her father-in-law had died after a reign of only
two years from the after-effects of a broken arm suffered while
hunting at Chazay. In his turn, the morning after a brilliant
gathering of foreign lords and a ball, Philibert set out hunting on
a sultry summer day in 1506, despite Margaret's fears. He drank
too much cold water and died ten days later.

Maximilian's brave daughter was an inconsolable widow and
refused a number of marriages, among them to the King of
England. She would have preferred retirement, but the death of
her brother Philip the Handsome compelled her to accept the
regency of the Netherlands, one of the Habsburg territories, a task
in which she received great support from the brilliant team of
advisers who had accompanied her. Though still young, Alard
Bentinck and Barangier were among her most long-standing
companions. The tasks of Margaret's household were no
sinecure in the palaces of Mechlin, where she settled her court.

On Margaret's return to the Netherlands in the year of
Philibert's death, the lord of Chièvres and Jean Micault, lord of
Watervliet, acquired for her the town house situated on the
present-day rue de l'Empereur, near the church of St Peter and
St Paul, in the heart of the city of Mechlin. Margaret of Austria
arrived on 7 July 1507 with her nephew Charles (the future
Charles v) and her nieces, the children of Philip the Handsome.
They were to live opposite her in the Cour de Bourgogne, once
the palatial residence of Margaret of York.[1]

Opposite the Cour de Bourgogne were the main buildings of

Margaret's town residence, restored in the late Gothic style and decorated for her with Renaissance alabaster. Alard Bentinck worked there until Margaret's death, supervising one of the most impressive households of his day, in which tapestry-makers rubbed shoulders with butlers, pantlers, cellarers, confectioners, pastry-makers and fruiterers.[2]

Most of the counsellors who were Alard Bentinck's colleagues in the Regent's household had also belonged to Philibert's court at Bourg-en-Bresse and Pont-d'Ain. They included Gorrevod, squire to the Duke of Savoy, who became a knight of the Golden Fleece in Burgundy and whose portrait still illuminates one of the stained-glass windows in Brou; Louis de Balliant, Lord of Verboz; and Gui de la Baume, one of whose sons was the last Bishop of Geneva, immediately before the Reformation.

In Margaret's household music was a popular post-prandial entertainment. As well as the Regent's tabor and viola players, the choristers of the church of St Rombaud sometimes came to sing at her table, or an organist might find himself playing the spinet.[3] Margaret received and encouraged two of the greatest composers of her times, and Alard Bentinck must have listened to the creations of Pierre de la Rue, cantor of the court of Burgundy, a polyphonist in the purest Netherlands' manner, who dedicated seven of his thirty-one masses to Margaret, and to Josquin des Prés, the greatest of the French polyphonists. Josquin was appointed dean of Condé sur l'Escaut by the Emperor Maximilian and was in constant touch with the Regent's court at Mechlin. In summer, when the barred windows of the Hôtel in the rue de l'Empereur were opened, Alard Bentinck could hear the peals of bells above the singing from the church.

Thanks to the tranquillity of her household Margaret was able to devote all her mental resources to the government of the Netherlands, exercising a relative tolerance in an age of religious wars. She concluded the Treaty of Cambrai, known as the Ladies' Peace, with the Duchess of Angoulême and Louise of Savoy in 1529. Agriculture and the arts made great strides under her administration. Thinkers of genius such as Thomas More and

Erasmus stayed in her capital, and she received Lucas Cranach the Elder in 1508 and Albrecht Dürer in 1521.[4] Her portrait was painted by van Orley and Mabuse. In this court, Alard Bentinck went about his business – though not always without incident!

Once, when a squire jostled him under the pretence of helping him stay on his feet after a gathering of several court retainers, the quarrel turned sour. According to a judgement of 28 August 1516 our master Alard called the squire a 'rogue', and the man set about revenging himself for the insult 'armed with a long dagger'. Bentinck managed to regain his quarters and the squire received the mild sentence of eight days' house arrest.[5]

Alard set great store by the education of his son Laurent, the offspring of his marriage to Johanna Esther van Bygaerden, which he entrusted to the mother-in-law of Margaret of Austria's secretary, Barangier, widow of a President of the Council in Bresse. She did her best for him. While still young he learned French, a universally useful language, and was introduced to important people. When Thomas Wolsey, adviser successively to Henry VII and Henry VIII of England, made several visits to the Netherlands, Alard Bentinck had no difficulty in persuading him how useful his son might be, and Laurent Bentinck therefore became the secretary of one of the most powerful men in England. As cardinal, Archbishop of York and Lord Chancellor of England Wolsey was an immensely powerful man. He suffered a sudden disgrace, however, and died in 1530, so that Laurent Bentinck was back at the court of Mechlin with his father when Margaret of Austria died later in the same year. Like many members of his family who worked closely with great chiefs of state, Laurent had to develop great aplomb and self-control, for Wolsey was a hard, arrogant man.

Alard Bentinck had another son, Philibert, named after the Duke of Savoy, as well as three daughters. Of the two younger daughters, one married a bailiff from Enghien, the other became a nun in the abbey of Jericho in Brussels. The eldest, Margaret, married into the famous family of Carondelet,[6] from the Franche-Comté; her husband, Philippe Carondelet, was one of the eleven children of the Grand Chancellor of Burgundy, from whom he inherited the seigneury of Champvans.[7] One of Margaret Bentinck Carondelet's brothers-in-law became archbishop of Palermo in 1520, though he never went there, another became the head of Margaret's privy council. A third, Ferry, was governor of Viterbo and Charles v's ambassador at the court of Rome before returning to the Franche-Comté; there he built the abbey of Montbenoit[8] near Pontarlier and became its commander. Ferry Carondelet's portrait in marble was placed in the church of St John in Besançon; Fra Bartolommeo's portrait of Claude Carondelet and the tombs of several of his brothers are at Dôle.

On the eve of her death, Margaret of Austria, no longer able to write, dictated a famous message intended for her imperial nephew Charles v: '. . . I leave you your *pays de par deça* [the Flemish provinces], which during your absence I have not only kept . . . but greatly augmented . . . in particular commending to you peace, and especially with the Kings of France and England.'[9, 10] Louis Barangier, Margaret's secretary for over twenty years and close friend of Alard Bentinck, had retired in 1509 and become clerk to the Parlement of Dôle. Margaret's knight of honour Gui de Baume had died in 1516. Laurent de Gorrevod, her chief treasurer, knight of the Golden Fleece and Marshal of Burgundy, had left the Regent for Charles v and died at Barcelona in the same year as his former mistress. Mercurin de Gattinara, who came from Piedmont and was with Margaret first at Bourg, then at Mechlin, where he was president of her privy council, retired to a Carthusian monastery near Brussels before becoming Grand Chancellor of the kingdom of Castile and finally, shortly before he died, a cardinal.

Alard Bentinck had met many great cultural figures during his career with Margaret of Austria. Her town residence had been restored by the famous architect Rombaud Keldermans, who in 1515 added the gallery of the inner courtyard, the ceremonial stairway and the entrance lodge. Erasmus, admired by both north and south in the Netherlands, by Margaret as well as by William the Silent, finally left to live near his publisher in the

Rhineland town of Basel. Lemaire des Belges, poet and historio-grapher of Margaret of Austria, spent eight years at the court and left fine descriptions of both its public and its private life; this he disclosed by pretending to quote the words of his parrot, called the 'green lover' after the colour of its plumage.

It was not until years after the death of the Regent of the Netherlands that the architects and sculptors completed the beautiful church of Brou, which she had ordered to be built in memory of her husband Philibert of Savoy and which she never saw.

The counsellors who in her lifetime had accompanied Margaret, daughter of the Emperor of Austria, Infanta of Spain, Duchess of Savoy, Regent of the Netherlands, now escorted her mortal remains. Among them were Antoine de Lalaing, Alard Bentinck and his son Laurent.[11] They left Mechlin on 14 May 1532, followed by a few loyal retainers of the Archduchess. Laurent Bentinck was in charge of providing the horses and the funds. After a month spent travelling through Burgundy and Savoy the funeral cortège reached Brou, where Alard and Laurent Bentinck at last came face to face with this wonder of Flemish architecture, a church built as a unified expression of the flamboyant Gothic style. There Margaret's wish, as expressed in the will which Alard Bentinck had watched her write, was fulfilled: 'We wish to be buried next to the body of our dearest lord and master, Duke Philibert of Savoy, whom God absolve, on his left hand side, and on his right will be the body of the late Madam Margaret of Bourbon.'[12] The living Margaret he had known in Mechlin now lay on a slab of black marble donated by the Bishop of Lausanne.

Alard Bentinck and the other members of the escort, led by Claude de Boisset, once Margaret's legal adviser, professor of canon law and counsellor of the Parlement of Dôle, saw nothing of this last effusion of Gothic art, nothing of the light streaming through the immense windows blazoned with the blue of France, the dark red of Savoy and the gold of the Holy Roman Empire, nothing but the marble image of Margaret, their sovereign, with the nobly disdainful mouth, stubborn chin and gently bowed head, a tender, loyal wife.

3 • *Manors by Canals and Rivers*

W HEN ALARD BENTINCK left the northern provinces which were later to make up the United Provinces he sold the family house in Arnhem to his nephew Adolf Bentinck, the son of his eldest brother Jan Bentinck de Olde. He in his turn inherited the estate of Oosterhof, a fine fortified farm, since restored in the eighteenth century. Adolf Bentinck was also lord of Het Loo, like his father and grandfather. He had been a deputy at the diet of 1543 in the course of which Duke William of Cleves had to renounce the administration of Gelderland and at which Charles V succeeded in having Gelderland attached to the Netherlands. Later part of the province, the southern quarter of Roermond, came under the sway of the Spanish Netherlands while the other three quarters, Nijmegen, Zutphen and Arnhem, joined the United Provinces.

Adolf Bentinck and his wife Margaret, daughter of Goswin van Varick, died without issue, and since Adolf was hereditary master of the hunt of the Veluwe he passed on this profitable post to his brother-in-law Zeger Bentinck, the husband of his cousin Anna Bentinck. Zeger's daughter in turn inherited Het Loo. When the chateau became the property of the Orange family in the following century, William III often invited Hans Willem

Bentinck there in the hunting season and during the wars against Louis xiv. Adolf Bentinck's youngest sister also married one of Goswin van Varick's children.

We have now traced some of the more memorable activities of the now extinct branches descended from Hendrik de Beste Bentinck's brothers: Jan de Olde, father of Adolf, lord of Oosterhof and Het Loo, who died without issue; Alexander de Bolde, founder of the Berenkamp branch which in turn founded the Aller offshoot, in which the Orangist and Spanish Netherlands parties were represented by Alexander and Philip; and finally Alard, founder of the Bonseval branch, faithful companion of Margaret of Austria in Spain, Savoy and Mechlin during the infancy of Charles v.

We now return once and for all to the still thriving branch of the descendants of Hendrik the Best and its numerous offshoots: that of Kemnade, which remained in the service first of Spain, then of France, with no exceptional achievements to its credit; the Breklenkamp branch, already mentioned, which included officers and diplomats in Münster, Trier and Cologne; and the Werkeren branch, nursery of the nobility of Overijssel, including numerous knights and one commander of Maastricht, Lieutenant-General Zeno Arend Bentinck, son-in-law of Jacob Emmery van Wassenaer. His wife, Arnoldine, née van Wassenaer, was the widow of Colonel Willem van Hambroek, who fell before Brussels in 1745. The last Bentinck of this branch, the lord of Werkeren, died before the end of the eighteenth century, on 10 December 1800. He rests in the church of St Michael in Zwolle.

A nephew of Eberhard Bentinck, founder of the branch from Breklenkamp, on the River Dinkel near Singraven, was Philip Hendrik Bentinck, who in turn founded the Wolfrath branch. He was chamberlain and master of the hunt to the Duke of Juliers as well as Grand Master of the Hunt in the county of Neubourg. He died in 1658. His son Johann Wolfgang Wilhelm von Bentinck von Wolfrath was chamberlain to the Duke of Juliers in his turn, then bailiff of Millen and Borne, and lived until 1674.

His wife, Elisabeth van Breyll, had brought him as a dowry the seigneury of Limbricht, in Limburg, close to the chateau of Obbicht which had been rebuilt in 1585 for Philip Bentinck, the negotiator of Bergen-op-Zoom. Philip's son, Franz Nicolaus von Bentinck, chamberlain of the Prince Elector of the Palatinate, was sworn in to the diet of Juliers in 1676. His son, Adrian Constantin Ferdinand Bentinck, lord of Wolfrath and Limbricht, born in 1699, became a privy counsellor of the Palatinate and a knight of the order of the Lion.

A last representative of the Wolfrath branch, Maximilian Bentinck, was also chamberlain of the court of the Palatinate and a knight of the order of the Lion. He sold the seigneury of Wolfrath in 1801. Having been president of the chamber of the court of Juliers, Cleves and Berg – then nothing more than a province of the Prussian Lower Rhine – he died childless in 1823. Two of Maximilian Bentinck's brothers, Friedrich-Wilhelm-Joseph and Carl, were high-ranking officers, the former in one of the Palatinate's dragoon regiments, the latter as an Imperial captain. They left no descendants.

The Bentincks must have been delighted on many occasions when the birth of a new family member was announced, could they have known what he was to make of this life, perhaps with the help of favourable circumstances but not without obstacles and reverses to surmount. The branch whose history we now confront followed the example of a long line of direct and collateral ancestors and produced men whose stature matched the exceptional events of their times. It was known from the first as the Velde branch and harks back to Hendrik de Beste, Jan de Olde's brother.

Hendrik the Best was said to have seen the future Charles v during his childhood in Brussels. His wife Catherine, née Lerinck, had inherited the manor of Velde from her brother. Hendrik's son Willem thus became lord of Velde, a fine woodland region in the neighbourhood of the village of Warnsfeld, not far from Zutphen.

In 1577, a year after the death of Willem Bentinck, his eldest son Eusebius I Bentinck became lord of Velde. He had commanded the royal troops at Kampen in 1572 and had married Sophia van Ittersum in 1570. Their son Willem renounced the lordship of Velde in favour of his brother Hendrik, embraced a military career and was killed during the lengthy siege of Wachtendonck by Spanish forces in part commanded in this sector by Willem's cousin of the Aller branch, Colonel Philip Bentinck, lord of Obbicht, of whom we have heard much.

Eusebius I's second son Hendrik, who became lord of Velde, held several other seigneuries which had belonged to the van Ittersums: Werkeren, Schoonheten and Diepenheim. He in his turn gave up Velde in favour of his sister, wife successively of Florenz, then of Goswin van Buckhorst. So the Bentincks left the county of Zutphen and the seigneury of Velde; with Hendrik's three sons they formed the branches of Schoonheten, Diepenheim and Werkeren.

We have already spoken of the Werkeren branch and its alliance with the van Wassenaers. We shall meet the Wassenaer family again among the descendants of Hans Willem Bentinck, Earl of Portland. As for the wife of Lieutenant-General Zeno Arend Bentinck, commander of Maastricht, she was the widow of the Colonel Willem Hambroek who fell outside Brussels in 1745, and I mention him because his mother was born Mechtild Anna Bentinck, of the branch of Schoonheten and Diepenheim. The sister of this Mechtild Anna Bentinck was to marry her cousin Willem Bentinck, lord of Schoonheten, nephew of Hans Willem Bentinck, Earl of Portland. This Willem was the author of a remarkable work on *The Constancy of the Romans*. When his first wife died he married Wilhelmina Judith Agnes Bentinck, of the Werkeren branch. Thus Willem Bentinck, the son of Eusebius Bentinck and Elisabeth van Brackel, united the Diepenheim and Schoonheten offshoots and added that of Werkeren. It is he who is the ancestor of all the members of the present-day Dutch branch of the barons Bentinck.

Since they were all in good health and of good stock, consanguinity was no drawback to these marriages among cousins, most of whom were fairly distant in any case, any more than were the repeated marriages of the Bentincks to heiresses of the same van Ittersum family, starting with the first Eusebius Bentinck, grandson of Hendrik de Beste. The van Ittersums were to contribute elements both of stability and of greatness to the family.

Hitherto the Bentinck knights had struggled above all for the independence and unity first of Gelderland, then of the Netherlands, both politically, as members of deputations, and militarily, by fighting for their ideal of peace. But this ideal could not be realized without a sound economic base, and the inhabitants of the Netherlands and the Rhineland responded to their geographic position by creating cities trading along the great waterways and across the sea to England and the Baltic. Livestock soon came to play a vital economic role. In the land of polders which cover part of Overijssel, sheep produced wool, the raw material of the cloth industry, thanks to which the towns connected to the agricultural manors were able to compete with Antwerp and England. The van Ittersums, allied with the Bentincks, owned a great deal of land near the mouth of the Ijssel and from Zwolle onwards. As far back as the early fifteenth century a Jan van Ittersum was lord of Werkeren, Voorst and Nyenhuis, which subsequently became Bentinck possessions, and of det Hoof in Zwolle. Jan van Ittersum was an influential figure in Zwolle, where he drew up the town register and founded the chapel of Saint-Laurenius.

In the same period, Wolphert van Ittersum lived at Gerner, which still belonged to Wolf van Ittersum when Hendrik Bentinck married his daughter Elsabé in 1591. Wolf van Ittersum's son Rudolf lived at Diepenheim, which was to play a great part in the history of the Bentinck family.

This Hendrik Bentinck, husband of Elsabé van Ittersum, was the son of Eusebius and Sophia Bentinck, née van Ittersum. He was lord of Werkeren, another van Ittersum property in the fifteenth century, and of Diepenheim and Schoonheten, as well as being bailiff of Ijsselmuiden, at the mouth of the Ijssel near Kampen, where his father had commanded the royalist forces.

Thus the most vigorous and eminent branches of the Bentinck family first came to prominence in Gelderland, especially in Arnhem, then spread out and held important positions in the Veluwe and later took root further north, in the neighbouring province of Overijssel, whose future was closely linked with that of Gelderland. When Willem Bentinck renounced the lordship of Velde the Bentincks left their huge manor and moved closer to the trading towns of the Hanse, near the Ijssel. Deventer, close to Hendrik Bentinck's estates at Diepenheim and Schoonheten, sent its merchants into northern Europe, England, the reaches of the Loire and La Rochelle, where they exchanged wood and cor n for salt and wine.

The Baltic towns had granted Deventer prior rights to sell their cloth from their vast flax meadows. The Overijssel lands produced butter, bacon and rye. The fairs of Deventer supplied the duchy of Gelderland, the county of Cleves with Wesel and Emmerich, and, further south, the duchy of Juliers.

On the death of Hendrik Bentinck, husband of Elsabé van Ittersum, his property near Zwolle and Deventer was divided among his three sons, Eusebius II, the elder, who was lord of Schoonheten and became a colonel in the cavalry and a knight of Overijssel; Wolf Goswin, who received the domain of Werkeren (we have already mentioned his second marriage to his cousin Anna van Haersolte, herself the daughter of Christina Bentinck of the Aller branch); and Berend, lord of Diepenheim.

Schoonheten later reverted to Berend's son Eusebius Borchard, ancestor of all the barons Bentinck.

During the sixteenth century Deventer remained the meeting-point of the Dutch maritime regions, the Lower Rhine and Saxony. Competition from Antwerp and Bruges had weakened. But Deventer lacked shipyards, had little provision for warehousing products against lean years, and was unable to adapt to the money market as did Amsterdam. Silt had made the Ijssel less easily navigable than the Waal. Products from Bergen had to be moved on small river boats. During the third quarter of the sixteenth century internal wars made the situation of the region even more difficult. The town remained loyal to royal rule in 1572; in 1578 Rennenberg conquered it for the states of The Hague; in 1587 an officer of the forces under Leicester, sent by Elizabeth of England to help the rebel provinces against the Spaniards, betrayed Deventer into the Duke of Parma's hands. The city was finally retaken by Maurice of Orange in 1591.

By that time the Bentinck properties in Overijssel lived not off their feudal connections but by their contribution to the country's economy. Diepenheim was no longer one of the temporal possessions of the Bishop of Utrecht. The Deventer fairs provided an outlet for goods until Amsterdam took up the trade in corn and rye on a larger scale, trading with the Baltic towns, England, Scotland, Ireland, the Rhine, the Meuse, and Spain and Portugal. There was even a time when Cologne obtained its corn from Danzig and Königsberg via Amsterdam, where the warehouses in the big port made it possible to maintain supplies when they were scarce elsewhere.

When Berend Bentinck, youngest son of Hendrik Bentinck van Ittersum, finally made his home at Diepenheim, the nearby town of Deventer still retained its character as a transit point between the Ijssel and the canal which follows the course of the ancient walls and had not expanded beyond its medieval fortifications or become an enormous commerical centre like Amsterdam.

The date and place of Berend Bentinck's birth are unknown, and even the year, probably 1604, is uncertain. Since his father was already lord of Diepenheim, as well as of Schoonheten (which was closer still to Deventer), and bailiff of Ijsselmuiden and Salland, it is clear that he was a native of the Dutch province of Overijssel, where he spent his life. From Diepenheim he paid visits to Deventer, where he held the office of dean. Later he became a deputy to the States General at The Hague.

Berend Bentinck certainly spent part of his youth in France. In 1624 he was a student at Blois, where a great many Protestants were living. While still a young man he was appointed bailiff of Deventer, and on 21 December 1638 he married Anna van Bloemendaal, daughter of Hans Hendrik van Bloemendaal, who was bailiff of the fortified town of Vianen, twenty-one miles from Utrecht. Vianen was still a fief of the van Brederodes, who had opposed Margaret of Parma and Cardinal Granvelle during the uprisings against Spain.

Berend had been a deputy in the diet of the States General at The Hague for three years when he married. His wife was only sixteen. We do not know if she ever saw Vianen again, for from then on the young wife lived in the country at Diepenheim.

When Berend Bentinck inherited Diepenheim, the chateau must have been barely habitable, particularly in view of the refined tastes of the century of Rembrandt. Yet ten years had passed since the marriage at Olst of Berend and Anna van Bloemendaal, and four children had been born, when the happy parents decided not to restore the vanished old chateau but to build a mansion. Their fifth child, Hans Willem, was born there the following year, in 1649. Their daughter Eleonora Sophia was then five years old and Hans Willem's three brothers were older still. After him four more girls were born in quick succession.

The house has changed little since it was built except for the monumental gateway opening on to the front terrace. This outer gate was built thirty-seven years later, in the year of Berend's death, as if with him gone the little chateau needed greater material protection. His elder son and heir Hendrik must also have been expecting more troubles after the period of peace that had followed the Thirty Years' War. But Hendrik could not know that his grandson Hans Willem, as a member of the immediate entourage of William III of Orange, would be closely linked with the preliminaries of the conflict and the defence of the Netherlands against foreign invasion. The porch at Diepenheim still displays the arms of the new owner, Hendrik tot Diepenheim and of his wife, Ida Magdalena van Ittersum tot den Luttenberg – the moline cross and the donkey's head with its two long ears that resemble those parts of the shears used for clipping sheep, the prime source of the van Ittersums' wealth.

At Diepenheim the Louis XIV style makes itself keenly felt. The hipped roof of the older Dutch dwellings has given way to an attic. While the wings are brick, the central part is grey sandstone. The façade is decorated with half-columns, though not ordered, as they would have been during the Renaissance. On the right stands a small outbuilding; there was probably another on the left, which has since disappeared. There is every indication that the Amsterdam architect Philips Vingboons played some part in the building. Some historians believe him to have been the designer, but there is no definite proof. Vingboons' activities in the region seem to confirm the supposition, however. He built several houses in the village of Diepenheim and the pilastered façade of the lateral wing of Deventer Town Hall.

The new home of Berend Bentinck and his family is pierced by high barred windows whose bars are now painted white. The small first-floor balcony has a glazed door surmounted by the twin arms of the Bentincks and van Bloemendaals, the moline cross to the left, a wallflower to the right. In the pediment, an *œil-de-bœuf* contains a further example of the Bentinck moline cross, and the mansards on each side of the roof reflect the influence of Louis XIV's architect Mansart, recalling the windows of the so-called Gaston of Orleans wing (designed by Mansart) of the chateau of Blois, where Berend Bentinck had studied.

Broad meadows where cattle browsed reached from the back of the house to the forest's edge. Horses graze in the fields; the Bentinck children made their acquaintance young and had as good an eye for horseflesh as their ancestors in the heyday of chivalry.

When Berend Bentinck invited a few lords of the neighbouring manors and chateaux or influential burghers from the towns of Overijssel or Gelderland to the reception rooms at Diepenheim, the conversation must have hinged mainly on prices and markets and in particular on the domestic policy of the Netherlands.

It was from Diepenheim that Berend Bentinck set out for the

town of Deventer, to attend the collegiate church of St Lebuinus, where he was dean of the chapter. Berend may have been taught by Gualterus, rector of the school of Latin, who in 1619 created the still readable inscription on the dome – 'Trust God – watch – ponder – act boldly' (*Fido Deo – vigila – consule – fortis age*). When he took his children to church on Sunday they must have read these maxims – words worth living by – high on the tower from which the thirty bells chimed out the music of one of the finest of the Dutch carillons. Seventeen of the bells still survive. (The pretty church of Diepenheim, with its warm tones of red brick, was built ten years after Berend's death, when his son Hendrik, lord of Diepenheim, was a knight of Overijssel, bailiff of the Twenthe and a colonel in the cavalry.)

It was from Diepenheim too that from 1635 onwards Berend Bentinck used to set out on horseback or by coach to attend the Diet of the States General, together with other knights of Gelderland. In January 1655 he must have passed through Deventer on his way to The Hague, when he joined a deputation which included the town's burgomaster, Johan van der Beeck. They were defending the rights of the nobility of Overijssel by trying to reach an agreement to end the disunity which accompanied the appointment of heads of delegations, as well as the procedure to elect the Stadtholder. They felt that the provincial deputies should have more say in these matters.

The nobility of Overijssel and Gelderland were anti-Orangist at first, and in the time of William II of Orange they maintained that power had only been temporarily vested in the Stadtholders of the Orange family. After the death of Frederick Henry of Orange-Nassau in 1647 the deputations of the States General to which Berend Bentinck belonged attempted to oppose William II of Orange, son-in-law of Charles I of England, who wanted to resume the war against Spain and the Cromwellian republic in England. William's death by smallpox at the age of twenty-four changed the situation. All the Orangist hopes now rested on a new-born child, the future William III of England. It was Jan de Witt, who became Grand Pensionary in 1643, who took

control of the policy of the United Provinces. Louis XIV's
continental expansion was creating a new danger which de Witt
failed to recognize in time. At the Hague Diet of 1655 Berend
Bentinck, understanding that the first threat would be to the
eastern Provinces, went over to the Orangists. Thus one of the
principal representatives of the old Velde branch of the Bentincks
embraced the ideal of the United Provinces, created by William
the Silent and John of Nassau at the Assembly of Utrecht in 1578.

4 ☙ The Struggle for the Existence of the United Provinces

BEREND BENTINCK's house at Diepenheim had been built for little more than a year when on 20 July 1649 Anna Bentinck, née van Bloemendaal, gave birth to Hans Willem Bentinck in a Europe recently restored to peace by the Treaty of Westphalia. A baseless old superstition has it that when a house is built death enters in. Here the opposite was the case. A particularly healthy child made his appearance. Throughout his life he showed his outstanding physical and moral capacities, no matter how great the difficulties he faced.

Overijssel had a less privileged position than in the days of his grandfather Eusebius, who had kept Werkeren and acquired a large number of other lands and seigneuries. Gelderland and Overijssel were struggling to recover from the Spanish wars, and elsewhere the wars of religion had not assisted the flow of merchandise.

Trouble and strife must have alternated in the beautiful house of Berend Bentinck and his numerous family. His wife had been sixteen when they married; it cannot have been an easy job to rear her nine children. In the Netherlands the wife's duties were very time-consuming. Absolute cleanliness was the rule, domestic staffs were small, and masculine assistance not available, because

the men had other work to do. Even with the kind of maid-
servant who could be treated as one of the family, many
children were often left to themselves. The wife did not have the
spare time to accompany her husband to diets and political
assemblies in other towns or on private business trips. Only on
Sunday did the whole family go out to church, which was usually
very austere and Calvinist, with no interior decoration.

Yet judging by the paintings of the time, home life was anything but joyless and uncomfortable. The parquet floors and
panelling gave the rooms beauty and intimacy, and clocks and
paintings hung on the walls. Sometimes on fine summer feast
days the big table was taken outside the house, and everybody
sat round it under the trees.

In the (contemporary) painting in the chateau of Middachter
depicting Hans Willem Bentinck's mother, she is no longer
young; she wears her hair scraped back under a dark cape and
sits up very straight over strong hips. The mouth is sad rather
than bitter, the eyes dark-ringed by fatigue, but kindly and
seeming to ask a question. And now many problems were set by
the family whose pivot she was. For as long as we have known
them, the traditions of the Bentinck family have always been
passed on by the men – their independence of mind, their abilities
as organizers and peace-makers, their attachment to worldly goods
and particularly to the land, in so far as they serve the community
or will prove useful to future generations. It is the mother who
inculcates the human qualities in each generation, not only by
bringing children into the world but by her example and guidance.

If the portrait of Anna Bentinck, chatelaine of Diepenheim at
the time the manor was rebuilt, does not express the grace which
emerges in Netscher's portraits of her grand-daughters, her tapering
hands retain a rare distinction. She holds them with the same
nobility as her grand-daughter, the sister of the first Duke of
Portland, Lady Mary Bentinck, wife of the Earl of Essex. It is
partly from his mother that Hans Willem Bentinck derives the
rather starchy distinction of his mature years and still more the
spirit of devotion, which he took to its highest limit.

All the evidence suggests that Hans Willem Bentinck's mother gave him instruction, examples and great affection – even if it was rather severe, as was required by the Calvinist educational principles of the day, and diluted among several brothers and sisters. It was his sister Eleonora Sophia, five years his senior, who gave him a kinder, freer affection, closer to a boy's needs. We have no evidence of this from his earlier youth, but we can reconstruct it from Hans Willem's later emotional life, discreet as it was, when he had become the closest colleague of William III of Orange, Stadtholder and King of England. When Hans Willem's wife Anne fell very ill while he was taking part in the march on London with the Prince of Orange it was Lady Eleonora, his sister, who was with her; when his wife died it was Eleonora who was there in her dying moments and who took care of her children until Hans Willem could send for them; when Hans Willem was in fear of death in his turn,[1] it was to Eleonora that he entrusted his interests with unconditional confidence, in a letter expressing his last wishes. Considering that at the age of fifteen he left Diepenheim, his parents and all his brothers and sisters, to return only on very rare and solemn occasions, there can be no doubt remaining that during his childhood and early youth he grew deeply attached to the young Eleonora.

Hans Willem's childhood was austere, solitary, reserved and with little contact outside the stern family circle. We do not know of childhood friends, and later in life he always had difficulty in establishing relationships other than those required by his profession, whether as diplomat or soldier.

Hans Willem's brothers Eusebius and Hendrik both belonged to the knighthood of Overijssel. Hendrik administered the Twenthe at the same time as controlling the domain of Diepenheim after his father's death and married the daughter of Zeher van Ittersum, of the same family as his grandmother and great-grandmother. His father-in-law, lord of Luttenberg, not far from Schoonheten, was a cavalry major and was killed at the siege of Saint-Omer in 1677. Hendrik Bentinck became a cavalry colonel in his turn.

Eusebius inherited the seigneury of Schoonheten from his uncle in 1666. He became burgomaster of Maastricht, which had joined the United Provinces in 1632, and of Hasselt, a dependency of the bishopric of Liège, whose numerous Protestants were often at odds with the Bishop.

Hans Willem was an expert on horses and on their use in battle and military campaigns. His success, and that of his troops, in one of the great battles of history has been attributed to his handling of the cavalry. Riding, open-air exercise – probably winter skating on the frozen canals – badly heated schools and freezing bedrooms toughened the young Hans Willem's constitution and enabled him to stand the most extreme cold and the hardships of irregular campaigning, when there was no shelter at night.

The school taught reading and writing; French was the principal written language, for Dutch was still split into a number of dialects, despite attempts to develop it as a literary language. Arithmetic was important in a region where trade, fairs, buying and selling were crucial,[2] and Hans Willem Bentinck turned out to be a good keeper of accounts, both for himself and for the private treasury of the crown.

Hans Willem was barely fifteen when, in 1664, he was called away from the family home at Diepenheim, from his parents and elder brothers. One brother, Eusebius Borchard, spent all his life at Diepenheim; his beloved sister Eleonora, the future Baroness van Ittersum, lived in Nijhuisen. He also left his sister Isabella, whom he saw again in London when her husband Alexander Schimmelpennick van der Oye became ambassador of the States General. He said farewell for ever to his sister Anna Adriana, who married a lord of Amerongen, the chateau which later became the residence of the counts Bentinck, her descendants; to his ten-year-old sister Agnes, who became a canoness at Almelo; and to his youngest sister Johanna Elisabeth. He only made flying visits to Diepenheim after that, though he stayed there for a few days four years later, when his father died.

During the last years of his life Berend Bentinck had grown increasingly convinced of the importance of the house of Orange in the independence of the United Provinces. After the death of his father William II, the young Prince of Orange had to be helped to become Stadtholder of Holland in his turn. The young Prince's mother was a Stuart, the sister of Charles II of England; the Stuart restoration after Cromwell's Commonwealth strengthened the position of his nephew William III of Orange.

Although Grand Pensionary de Witt had obtained a secret act of exclusion forbidding the Prince to hold the posts of commander-in-chief and Stadtholder, the States General named William III of Orange 'a child of the State' and gave him as a residence a wing of the former chateau of the counts of Holland, which adjoined the hall where the States held their sittings. It was here that Berend Bentinck had been a deputy, and it was here one day in 1664 that the young Prince of Orange saw the arrival of a young page of fifteen, not at all brash, but rather timid and astonished when he was introduced to the orphan Prince. The prince lived with his grandmother, the dowager, widow of the Stadtholder Frederick Henry, born Countess of Solms, and a tutor, Frederick of Zuylenstein, bastard grandson of Frederick Henry.

The young Prince already had a kind of miniature court composed of the sons of Dutch noblemen: a first gentleman in waiting, a first squire and a first steward. Now he had been given a page, in the person of Hans Willem Bentinck, who was also to be given military training with him; in this his experience with horses would stand him in good stead.

After his mother's death Jan de Witt deprived the little Prince of all his English supporters, who were dismissed from the chateau of The Hague. He was treated like a schoolboy once more but allowed to keep a young page. De Witt also managed to get rid of William's tutor and uncle, the Count of Nassau Zuylenstein who was married to an English wife; he had been like a grandfather to him. The whole policy of the Grand Pensionary consisted of removing from The Hague the friends of England who tended to favour the accession to the stadtholderate of this new William of Orange, nephew of Charles II and of the Duke of York, the future James II.

Yet the people of the Netherlands, particularly at The Hague, did not forget what they owed to the Orange family, remembering the time of William the Silent and his son Maurice of Nassau, who had established the United Provinces' independence of Spain and the House of Austria. The Dutch also remembered Frederick Henry, second son of William the Silent and third Stadtholder of Holland, Zeeland, Utrecht and the provinces of Gelderland and Overijssel. It was these memories that had bound the Bentincks to the Princes of Orange, on whose behalf they now began to exert their exceptional qualities and loyalty.

To judge by his letters, William's education does not seem to have been very extensive and Hans Willem Bentinck easily outdid him, particularly in spelling. Perhaps there was an attempt to enforce the teaching of French, to avoid English influence. William's French tutor was a man called Samuel Chappuzeau, whose birthplace has been wrongly identified as Geneva by some biographers. He was in fact born in Paris though he did study in Geneva. A rather spineless character, Chappuzeau is mainly remembered nowadays for editing the great traveller Tavernier's account of his visits to Persia and as author of *L'Europe vivante*. He did not stay long enough to teach the Prince good French but he may have had some influence on his European ideas.

During those youthful years at The Hague Hans Willem Bentinck acquired a civilian and military education which prepared him to support the Prince of Orange in the enormous tasks and responsibilities that awaited him and which he in part foresaw. Knowing of the dangers surrounding the young Prince, who carried the hopes of all young men who wanted the Netherlands to be independent, Hans Willem Bentinck learned not to disclose his master's plans or ambitions. William III of Orange also knew how to keep his own counsel: like his great-grandfather before him, he might well have been nicknamed the Silent.

Hans Willem Bentinck had distinguished himself in the horse guards ever since arriving at The Hague. Four years after starting out as a page, ensign Bentinck was carrying the Orange standard in the guard company whose sergeant-major was Adam van der Duyn, lord of s'Gravenmoer.

When Hans Willem Bentinck's father died in 1668, William of Orange wrote him a moving dispatch in his own hand. The Prince told Hans Willem that he felt himself 'so much your friend that I take everything that happens to you as if it were happening to myself'. He promised to do his utmost to show his affection and to share in his family's affliction.

In that same year Adam van der Duyn, who was ten years older than Hans Willem Bentinck, became colonel commanding the horseguard regiment of Holland and eastern Friesland. When, six years later, he became quartermaster general of the cavalry in 1674 the States General appointed Bentinck to form a new company. At the same time he was appointed a colonel in the guard. In 1683 he became commander of the guard in his own turn as sergeant-major general, the post s'Gravenmoer had held when Hans Willem was starting as an ensign.

That Hans Willem had in one sense been disinherited, not for any personal failing but because the economic situation in Overijssel did not allow all the sons of large families to be provided with seigneuries, did not displease his master. No matter: he too would have his estates and titles. But in order for Hans Willem to fulfil all the requirements of his prince, he also had to serve his apprenticeship in diplomacy and domestic and foreign policy.

Late in 1670 came the opportunity for the Prince of Orange to make a visit to his uncle, Charles II of England, who seemed to be attached to him and had shown him affection since his father's death by coming to The Hague. William III had inherited property in England on his mother's death, and he decided to visit it, taking Hans Willem with him. The Dutch visitors received a worthy welcome, particularly in the universities. Bentinck listened to the speeches from the authorities and the Prince's reply in Cambridge, and he himself received the degree of LL B *honoris causa*. Oxford's reception was still more impressive. On the evening of 19 December the Netherlanders walked in procession between two lines of academics bearing flaming torches, while the bells of the church of St Mary pealed. They visited the botanic gardens, one of the curiosities of the age, a counterpart of the Leyden gardens. There too they listened to a number of speeches in English, Latin and Dutch and were welcomed into the cathedral church by Henry Compton, son of the Earl of Northampton, who was in charge of the religious education of the Princesses Mary and Anne. During this visit the Prince and four members of his entourage, including Hans Willem Bentinck, received doctoral degrees.[3]

Yet the twin aims of the Orangists who accompanied their prince to Whitehall were not achieved. The Prince did not obtain any of his mother's estate, and although Parliament was not hostile to a rapprochment between England and the Netherlands it knew nothing about the secret Treaty of Dover concluded more than six months previously between Charles II and Louis XIV, which set out plans for the destruction of the United Provinces. The Stuart king had also agreed to support Louis's claims in the matter of the Spanish succession and to proclaim himself a Roman Catholic.

Jan de Witt had attempted to take advantage of the Prince of Orange's absence to undermine his standing with the States of Holland by spreading the rumour that his allegiance to Charles II was greater than to Holland. On their return the two young men found themselves alone in the palace of The Hague and prey to the underhand anti-Orangist campaign being waged by the Grand Pensionary.

Hans Willem Bentinck had learned more during that English visit than from formal lessons. He knew now that a man could only rely on himself and his own honest intentions, whether he were the Prince of Orange and great-grandson of William the Silent or the descendant of the proud free knights of Gelderland and Overijssel, whose motto was to fear nothing but dishonour. A cautious waiting attitude was necessary until the time came in February 1672 when, barely a year after that fruitless visit to England, the Prince of Orange was appointed Captain-General of the United Provinces: at that time the Netherlands were threatened with total loss of independence.

Hans Willem now became the Prince of Orange's standard-bearer, ready for every kind of exertion, deprivation or sacrifice on his behalf. He was eager to help William III to uphold the rights of the United Provinces and was soon to help him to re-establish them in England. Hans Willem Bentinck could only discern a little of all this at the time, but his actions were to be an extension of the treaties signed by his ancestors and sealed with the Bentinck moline cross.

For his own part the Prince of Orange had no one whom he could trust as completely as Bentinck. At the time when he came to The Hague as the Prince's page and during the years that followed, none of those who subsequently became the Prince's chief supporters could be numbered among his friends. Several were even known partisans of the Grand Pensionary, Jan de Witt. Thus, among the older men, Gaspar Fagel, a native of Haarlem, was a late adherent to the cause of William III of Orange. While clerk to the States he was in favour of the policy which excluded the Prince of Orange from the stadtholderate and from command of the army. He even accepted the Eternal Edict legalizing William's disqualification. It was only when Louis XIV invaded Holland, after the bloody siege of Maastricht by Turenne, that he realized the danger of Jan de Witt's policy and refused to recognize the States General's desire for peace with France at any price.

Gaspar Fagel died in office as Grand Pensionary of the States of Holland in the stadtholderate of William III of Orange. He was succeeded by Antonius Heinsius, who remained Grand Pensionary until after the death of the sovereign. He was originally pensionary of Delft, his home town, and as such opposed William III's foreign policy. It was only after being sent as an envoy to France that he realized how great a danger Louis's ideas of universal monarchy were to the Netherlands.

Godard van Reede-Ginckel, born in the chateau of Amerongen in the province of Utrecht, knight then knight commander of the Teutonic Order of the Netherlands, joined the Prince of Orange

C

when he was appointed leader of the army and served under him as a colonel at Seneff. Amerongen later came into the hands of the counts Bentinck, the most direct Dutch descendants of Hans Willem.

Hans Willem Bentinck was therefore the sole confidant of the Prince of Orange for many years. The principles established at Utrecht in 1579, when Alexander Bentinck represented Gelderland, and recognized in the Binnenhof at the Hague Palace on 26 July 1581, were upheld in the United Provinces once they were rid of foreign invasion. These principles were similar to the declarations which were the basis of the constitutional monarchy established in England in 1689. As early as the age of William the Silent, the Stadtholder declared that he was the servant of his subjects 'in order to govern them under law and reason'.

All this was only a remote possibility, a dream on the horizon for the Orangists. Yet they made no attempt to cover their faces and wait for a friendly wind to bring back the sun to a land ravaged by a foreign power. They stood up against the ruthless policy of France, all the more so because Louis xiv was the ally of King Charles ii of England. That the United Provinces had insulted Louis was mere pretext.

Meanwhile the Netherlands, more immediately exposed than the distant Electorate of Brandenburg, had to turn their urgent attention towards defending themselves in the summer of 1672. To fight pitched battles against an enemy superior in numbers and commanded by experienced tacticians such as the Grand Condé, Luxembourg and Turenne, and likewise to defend towns fortified in the Middle Ages against the onslaughts of military architects schooled in modern methods was to be exposed to large-scale successive defeats and massacres from which the country would never recover. The moats around each separate castle, the rivers, moats and canals which encircled towns and villages, and the stretches of water near the farms, could all be forded with the equipment available to the enemy.

In a famous speech given in July 1672 William iii refused to place the States under the protection of France and England, who promised him the administration of the proposed double protectorate. Through his refusal he mobilized the popular will to keep the United Provinces free of outside control, now that Spain had finally abandoned that role.

If water, the great natural force whose presence pervades the Netherlands, were not enough to ensure the defence of each individual centre of armed resistance, the answer was to multiply that same force by releasing it throughout the group of provinces: not simply to have castles with drawbridges but to make the whole area of the States into a single giant moated fortress by opening sluice gates whose secrets and interconnections with the canals and rivers were known only to Dutchmen born and bred.

Even the winter, on which Louis xiv and his marshals had been relying to transform the treacherous element into a layer of ice allowing troops to pass, proved exceptionally mild, coming to the rescue of a brave populace which had sacrificed its fields and crops, part of its flocks and herds and its own welfare to its independence. Behind the waves of the flood which the Dutch had been fighting for thousands of years, they organized for defence. The numbers of the Orangists had grown considerably, to the point where occupied Gelderland and Overijssel, once the least willing to accept the idea of the United Provinces, now provided the Prince's most zealous supporters. Their contingents fought fiercely under the flag of William of Orange, carried by one of their own knights, Hans Willem Bentinck.

The almost frost-free winter weakened the French. Marshal Luxembourg was almost drowned when the ice gave way beneath his horse; the Grand Condé, surprised at Seneff by the troops of John Maurice of Nassau and Godard van Reede, just managed to win the battle but afterwards beat a retreat; Turenne had his hands full fighting the Elector of Brandenburg and was killed by a cannon ball in the battle of Salsbach in 1675. Meanwhile diplomatic activity was working in favour of the Prince of Orange in the greater part of Europe.

During this period we find Hans Willem Bentinck sometimes

with the Prince at The Hague, sometimes on the estate of Sorgvliet which was a gift from William in 1674, and had been created by the Dutch national poet Jacob Cats, who had died there fifteen years previously.

Often too the demands of war drew Bentinck into military campaigns. In his *Journal* the Dutch historian Constantijn Huygens refers to Hans Willem Bentinck as an infantry captain. In 1672, when the Prince of Orange was placed in command of the entire Dutch army after the death of Jan de Witt, Bentinck was appointed major. What Bentinck learned as major, in part once again under the command of Zuylestein, was to be very useful to him later on, particularly during the campaign in Ireland. In the war against the French cavalry played a distinctive part: instead of being drawn up in battle order, the mounted troops were dispersed and kept ready to support the infantry.

Away from the battlefield, Bentinck was master of the Prince's wardrobe. Through his work in the palace and his friendship with William III he was always the first to hear of political developments. In late February 1674 the English Parliament forced Charles II to make peace with the Netherlands, so putting an end to a pointless and particularly atrocious war, the more so since the King was William III's own uncle. The bishoprics of Münster and Cologne soon followed suit, thereby terminating the continual strife among neighbouring regions in which the Bentincks had taken part time and again, ever since the battle of St Hubert in 1444.

Although the peace was still fragile, events were now taking a far more favourable turn than two years before, when John Maurice of Nassau, commander-in-chief of the Dutch forces, painted the situation in the gloomiest light in his letters to the Prince of Orange.

Yet suddenly an unexpected force threatened to bring William's career to an early end: the delicate frame was racked with fever, his overtaxed brain was tortured by headaches, red blotches, then purulent spots broke out on his skin. Smallpox set the Prince of Orange on the same road travelled by his mother ten years before.

William would have faced this terrible threat alone if Hans Willem Bentinck had not intervened.

Once again the Prince and his former page were alone in the chamber by the entrance to the Binnenhof where William lay shivering and vomiting on his bed, covered with the pustules which were undermining his resistance. Yet the sick man was well covered, the blazing fire was kept alight night and day, and he never went thirsty, taking his draughts only from his friend, for fear that an attempt might be made to poison him under cover of his illness. His former page never left him for a moment and even went purposely close to him in the hope of taking the disease on himself and away from the feverish patient, of dying that the Prince might live.

When Hans Willem had saved William III, after a desperate struggle and with the help of Providence, he himself was shivering with fever and his legs could hardly carry him. He too took to his bed with smallpox and it was some time before he recovered.

The times were too hostile for a long convalescence. The anti-Orangists, who had hoped for the death of William and his close adviser, soon found them more valiant than before and had to fall back on tainted weapons in the form of the foulest kinds of slander. In June 1675, only a few weeks after his grave illness, Hans Willem Bentinck received marching orders. For the horseguard regiment the instructions were to cross the Demer at Aarschot, not far from Louvain and Mechlin, in the Spanish Netherlands. The infantry and cavalry were to join them by various routes at the bridge over the Demer, where the quartermasters would wait for the quartermaster-general.

At this point we must remember that Louis XIV had never given up his ambition to occupy the Spanish Netherlands and thus gain a stranglehold on the United Provinces. Despite the Treaty of Breda and the triple alliance between England, Holland and Sweden, intended to check Louis, Charles II remained secretly allied to the French monarch. When Charles finally tried to compel his new chief minister Thomas Osborne, Earl of Danby, to sign a new alliance with France when Parliament had not met for two years, the struggle for power between Parliament and the King had reached its height. Charles received large sums from the French crown and offered in exchange to sign a reciprocal agreement by which neither he nor the French king would conclude any treaty of alliance on the Continent without consulting the other. By the same agreement he also promised to dissolve Parliament if he had to break the alliance with France and pledged himself not to support the Netherlands.

As long as Charles II reigned, and James II (then the Duke of York) after him, the situation in England looked insoluble. Would it be possible when Charles II died to prevent his brother from ascending the throne? And if James II did become King would Parliament succeed either in exercising its rights or in making him abdicate? Who would take the succession after James II? If it were to be James II's daughter, who unlike her uncle and father had kept her reformed religion, would she be capable of standing up for herself against the influences which had set the Stuart kings at loggerheads with Parliament? If she married a prince, as might be expected, with what country would Princess Mary contract such an alliance?

These were the kinds of question beginning to be asked by some English politicians uneasy about their country's future and that of Europe. Among these was Sir William Temple, the English ambassador at The Hague. A friend of Holland, where he had studied, he had also lived in Paris, Madrid, St Malo and Brussels. In his native town of Dublin he had become a member of the Irish Parliament at an early age, settling in England after the prorogation of that assembly. His sister came to run his household, and later she looked after their niece, Jane Martha Temple, which gave Hans Willem the opportunity to meet her.

Lady Temple was a close friend of Lady Villiers, Princess Mary's governess, and had occasion to talk to the Prince of Orange about his cousin Mary. Soon top-secret discussions were taking place on Hans Willem Bentinck's estate at Sorgvliet about the charming wife that Mary might make for William III. There was less risk of eavesdroppers at Sorgvliet than in the Prince's own sumptuous house. Whereas the English ambassador was concerned with finding a future monarch willing to provide constitutional guarantees for the deliberations of Parliament, William III of Orange wanted to tighten links with England so as to gain respect for the Netherlands and security for the United Provinces, without concluding a peace at any price with Louis XIV, which would look like a capitulation. For that purpose he required an absolutely trustworthy envoy, and his choice naturally fell upon Hans Willem.

So Bentinck, who then held the rank of major, was suddenly summoned away from the army, at the moment when the struggle on the ground had abated, and the Dutch were aiming simply at maintaining the integrity of the Netherlands. In June 1677 Bentinck received orders to go to England with precise instructions whose content he was told not to disclose. He was to present himself to Charles II and if possible to draw him out on a number of points, the first two of which would determine whether it was necessary to go into the rest. We still have the notes made by Bentinck on the purpose of his London mission. The crucial points were:

1. Find out from His Majesty Charles II how His Highness William III ought to govern, both during the continuation of the war and in the event that peace should be made.
2. That His Highness is persuaded that His Majesty desires peace, and that in spite of the reasons which could make His Highness prefer the continuation of the war, he has no aversion to peace, and that in this matter he will very willingly submit to the King's will, and that on the contrary he wishes that this war could be terminated thereby, but has great difficulty in believing that after such great advantages France would resolve to grant peace on acceptable conditions.[4]

By 11 June the Prince of Orange thought that his envoy would have reached London; in fact unfavourable winds had kept his ship two nights and three days at sea. After arriving at Margate Bentinck took the mail coach and reached the English capital the following evening. He wasted no time before paying his respects to the King and the Duke of York. At the time of this first meeting, which took place in public, the King did not dwell upon any political question, but Bentinck was able to write to the Prince of Orange that His Majesty had evinced great satisfaction with His Highness's conduct in terms of affection and tenderness which should in his view, give complete satisfaction.[5]

Since the latest news received at the Prince's headquarters in Antwerp, however, there had in the space of a few days been considerable changes in the state of the quarrel between the English crown and Parliament. Lord Shaftesbury had failed in his attempt to have Parliament dissolved in the hope that after elections the Chambers would contain more lords and members favourable to his policy of toleration towards the Presbyterians, and he and his supporters had been imprisoned in the Tower of London.

In spite of the prorogation of Parliament the King had burned his fingers and decided against taking chances with foreign policy in future. After three days Bentinck wrote to the Prince that the King and his brother the Duke of York (who had negotiated the secret treaty with France) had refused to discuss the first point in his instructions, thus refraining from giving advice on European policy. On the question of war or peace, Bentinck had the impression that the United Provinces' ambassador in London, Conrad van Beuningen, had shown his hand too bluntly: by disclosing that William of Orange had no intention of ending the war with France on unfavourable terms the ambassador had put the King on the defensive. Bentinck wrote to the Prince that without overstepping his orders or broadening the discussion, and without giving away that he was acting on instructions, he would do his best, short of a definite commitment, to prevent the King from making unacceptable proposals 'which you would reject so flatly that it would disoblige him and render my journey completely useless'.[6]

The Duke of York also attended these meetings. From his journal, published later under the title of *Mémoires de Jacques II*,[7] we have a fairly accurate record of Charles II's attitude and the replies he made. According to York, the Prince of Orange had sent Mr Bentinck, 'the man he most trusted, to make His Majesty great protestations of service and obedience and to assure him that he would put himself completely in his hands and follow his advice and guidance relative to peace and war'.

The two accounts are a perfect fit. Bentinck for his part says that he hoped that Charles would be heedful of the Prince's honour and ask him nothing that was contrary to it.[8] From then on it seems that the King was unwilling to be compromised. The Duke of York's account says that Charles stated that he would always hold his nephew, the Prince of Orange, in high esteem, both on his own merits and in the interests of the unity of the royal family. He then told Mr Bentinck that he should see His Majesty's reluctance to undertake a foreign war only as a natural consequence of concern for his own preservation. It would be asking for the ruin of the royal family to venture on a war in the present state of its affairs – magazines were empty, the fleet unready, and Parliament so ill disposed that it was all he could do to maintain domestic peace. Once His Majesty was committed to a foreign war the necessity of sustaining it would put him in Parliament's hands; what might it not attempt, what advantage might the republican party not take of an opportunity so favourable to its plans?[9]

The second point of Hans Willem Bentinck's instructions referred to whether the King wanted his nephew to make an immediate peace with France on terms which could only be unfavourable or whether it would be better to hold out for more favourable circumstances before concluding an armistice, although the United Provinces were threatened with the occupation of part of Flanders. If England were to reach an understanding with France and then refuse to support the United Provinces the cause of the Prince of Orange would become very critical.

In his talks in Whitehall Hans Willem Bentinck had had no success at all in changing Charles II's secret political aims, as expressed in his secret treaties with Louis XIV, or the aims of the Duke of York, his elder brother's heir. This was not the chief object of his mission, however, since he had been instructed not to press the point. He had fulfilled his task by informing Charles II and James of William of Orange's preoccupations and so had prepared the ground for the Prince to call upon the King, at the same time indicating that it was pointless to offer him compromises incompatible with his honour.

The Prince of Orange waited impatiently for Bentinck's return, which would bring more information than letters about 'the good union and correspondence which the King and the Duke wish to maintain with Your Highness . . .'.[10] In addition to his dealings with Charles and James, Bentinck was to probe the attitude of the English Parliament, which unlike Charles II was anxious about Louis XIV's territorial expansion.

Before Bentinck's return the Prince of Orange sent him another dispatch mentioning the arguments to be driven home at Court. He concluded with the mysterious sentence: 'Meanwhile do not forget G. or the promises you have made him.' And the letter was signed with the same 'G', for Guillaume. Perhaps this was a reference to William Temple's plans for the marriage of William III, of which the first written mention was in a letter from William Temple to the Prince of Orange dated 22 February 1674.[11] This casts further light on one of the other instructions noted by Bentinck before he left The Hague: 'After the Royal House I am to see . . . the Treasurer.'[12] This was Thomas Osborne, Earl of Danby, to whom Lady Temple had already confided her plans.

William III had taken some time to accept the idea of the marriage and wanted to know about the girl's personal qualities first. He had already tried to find out from Sir William and Lady Temple whether Princess Mary was capable of bearing his occasionally difficult temperament. He was also afraid that in view of the strife between King and Parliament his marriage to Princess Mary might be interpreted as proof of his sympathy for the policy of Charles II and the Duke of York and was far from suspecting that there were in fact Parliamentarians who wanted not only to bring Holland and England together by the marriage but to provide for a succession which would avert the absolutism of the Stuart house.

After Hans Willem's return to The Hague the Prince of Orange no longer hesitated to press his suit. In October of the same year, 1677, he landed at Harwich and went straight to Newmarket, where the King then was, and at once discussed the proposals for keeping Flanders intact when peace was made with France.[13]

Events now moved in quick succession. On 17 October William obtained the King's consent. On the next day he asked the Duke of York for his daughter's hand, which was reluctantly granted three days later. The Duke immediately informed his daughter at the Palace of St. James. The marriage took place a fortnight later in Mary's apartments, too soon to send to Paris for robes worthy of the ceremony. Bentinck took part in the preparations and had the task of buying the jewels which were William's gift to Mary, at a cost of £40,000.

Mary was only sixteen years old. She wept for two days when her father informed her of her fate. Bishop Compton officiated at the wedding, as he had been present at all the great functions attended by Hans Willem Bentinck in England, ever since the day when he had helped him to follow the Anglican form of worship in Oxford during his first visit to England. It was to Compton that the Duke of York's two daughters, both future Queens, owed the firm faith that upheld them in the course of their arduous lives.

Ten years after her marriage, when her father, now King James II, was under attack for his absolutism and pro-French policy, Mary begged him not to put Bishop Compton on trial for his conciliatory attitude towards dissident Protestants. She also asked him to use his influence with Louis XIV not to annex the United Provinces. It was to no avail, and Mary was converted once and for all to the Orange cause.

Before going on to that troubled period of European history we must revert to the days that followed the marriage of William and Mary and take a moment to observe the deck of the vessel bringing the young couple and their entourage back to The Hague. When bad weather in the Channel abated enough to allow the party to set sail from Margate, Mary left behind many who were dear to her. Her own escorts included her childhood friends Elizabeth and Anne Villiers, the daughters of her former governess Frances Villiers. Many people expressed surprise at the Prince's lack of attention for his bride, but it must have been hard for him to forget the political problems which were awaiting his return, among them the peace settlement, which he would have preferred to delay a little longer in the hope of victories in Hainault. Without wishing to deny that the Prince might have been in love with Mary it must be admitted that reason of State had a lot to do with his union.

Hans Willem now fell in love with Lady Villiers' second daughter, Anne. Anne's father, Sir Edward Villiers, had been a colonel, and her mother was the youngest daughter of the second Earl of Suffolk. Bentinck had first been attracted by Mary's former playmate at Richmond, although she was frail and less good-looking than her elder sister, being drawn by her face and her strong character. Anne Villiers now brought him all the feminine graces that had been absent from the life of the adviser, the envoy, the army officer. They were married in February the following year.

Just after the wedding Hans Willem had to rejoin the army and fought hard in the murderous battle of Saint-Denis, at which Marshal Luxembourg failed to take Mons.

Some days later, on 10 August 1678, the peace of Nijmegen was signed with France. The treaty was initialled in the town where Hans Willem Bentinck's ancestors had sat in the diets which brought independence to Gelderland and the county of Zutphen. It restored the occupied towns to the United Provinces and re-established the peace and independence of the Netherlands, as had been the intention of the Peace of Westphalia thirty years previously.

When he was away from the army in the following years Hans Willem lived at The Hague and on his estate of Sorgvliet, surrounded by tree-lined walks, ponds and the woods that reached to the nearby North Sea. A year after the wedding the Bentincks had their first child, a girl, followed two years later by a son, Willem. When he learned of the birth, the Prince of Orange heard at the same time that Hans Willem was ill and invited him to his estate near Arnhem, where he was stag hunting. But Hans Willem recovered soon and did not need the services of the royal physician to make a good recovery.

The Bentincks' first son was only ten years old when he died, while his father was on an important mission to Berlin on behalf of the Prince of Orange. It was he who broke the sad news to him in a letter: '... poor Willem ... it will cause you much sorrow to learn that he died yesterday evening, and I assure you that it has deeply affected me; I do not doubt that you will submit to the divine will as a good Christian must; I pray God to preserve your family from such misfortunes for many long years ....'

Epidemics and harmful fevers were frequent in Holland at that time, and during the summer of 1679 not only was Hans Willem affected but also his wife, mother and sister. The Bentinck family continued to grow, however. A month before young Willem's death the seventh child was born. With the exception of Henry, born at The Hague in 1682, they were all girls, who later married into great Dutch and English families. It was Henry who secured the line of the English Portlands and Cavendish Bentincks down to this day.

In Holland Hans Willem Bentinck's position was considerable: in addition to his military rank, earned in the hard school of the Prince's uncle Zuylenstein and of van Duyn of s'Gravenmoer, Hans Willem was lord of Dordrecht. This enabled him to become leader of the knights of Holland. William III appointed him bailiff of Breda and Lingen. In 1681 he became forest warden of Holland. Finally, in 1683, he was wealthy enough to buy the seigneury of Rhoon and Pendrecht, near Rotterdam, for 145,000 guilders and the surrounding land for a further 9,000. This gave Hans Willem access to the States of Holland.

Bentinck always remained very attached to this seigneury,

being known abroad as Monsieur de Rhoon. The sculpted slabs in the church there bear funerary inscriptions in rococo lettering to Bentinck's son Willem. There too lies Anne Bentinck, as well as Bentinck's eldest son by his second marriage, another Willem Bentinck, who also became lord of Rhoon and Pendrecht, and an Imperial count, but who lived mainly at Sorgvliet and Leyden.

It was at the Sorgvliet house that the family of Hans Willem Bentinck grew up. Lawns and orange trees, which wintered in the orangery, decorated the terraces in the summer season, and a long avenue of elms built from The Hague to the bell-tower at Scheveningen provided access to Sorgvliet by coach and barouche. The Prince and Mary often used to go there to relax with Hans Willem Bentinck and his wife, Mary's former playmate. The proximity of The Hague, and the absence of the salons and antechambers of the palace, made the Bentinck estate an ideal political meeting-place.

In May 1679 when, because Charles II was in poor health, the question of the royal succession began to be broached in England, the Earl of Sunderland voted for an Exclusion Bill intended to bar the Duke of York from the crown. Sunderland took Henry Sidney into his confidence, and soon Sidney came to Holland to discuss a plan to summon the Prince of Orange to England. The plans debated at Sorgvliet carried all the more weight because Sidney was speaking with the assent of the influential George Halifax, Shaftesbury and William Temple.[14] The news which reached Sorgvliet from England testified to a deep split between the monarchy and the nation as represented by Parliament.

In 1683 a plot to assassinate Charles II and the Duke of York at Rye House near Newmarket misfired, and the ruthless Judge George Jeffreys pronounced sentence of death upon Lord William Russell and Algernon Sidney, who were not the true authors of the plot. Hans Willem Bentinck was sent to London to express William III's congratulations to the King for having escaped death. Unfortunately for the safety of Holland, however,

Charles II remained 'still persuaded of the good intentions of France'.[15]

The tempo of events accelerated from 1685 onwards. Charles II died at the beginning of the year and was succeeded by the Duke of York. The Duke of Monmouth, Charles II's natural son, now came out of exile in Brussels and landed in Dorset in an attempt to oust his uncle. He received no support from the Prince of Orange, who in fact tried to upset Monmouth's plans. The failure of this absurd expedition brought Monmouth to the scaffold. Hans Willem Bentinck found himself once again sent to assure the King of the good wishes of his nephew. William III offered to proceed against any accomplices of Monmouth in Holland, and Bentinck had to persuade James II that there had been no collusion on the part of the Prince of Orange.

In the autumn the political situation remained complex. Louis XIV revoked the Edict of Nantes, under the influence of the Jesuits,[16] and the King's dragoons harassed the Huguenots, many of whom fled to Holland. Numerous malcontents were reaching Holland from England, either expelled by James II or refusing to act contrary to their principles. James took draconian measures to prevent any lessening of his own power, setting a watch on the coastline where landings might take place and replacing Protestant officers liable to support the exclusion of a Catholic king. He also intended to rule without opposition from Parliament and stopped the Commons from either meeting or dissolving themselves, in case subsequent elections should turn out unfavourable to the cause of absolute monarchy.

By 1687 the situation between the King and Parliament was so strained that several influential figures were in favour of replacing James II with the nearest heir, his daughter Mary. In Holland William III was also considering this; only personal feelings argued against setting aside his father-in-law in favour of Mary, for Louis XIV's policies threatened the Netherlands, and James II supported them.

That Mary suffered in this situation is certain but she nevertheless kept her trust in William III, who never stopped loving her despite his infidelities. Fortunately Gilbert Burnet was then resident at The Hague and put all his tact and affection for Holland at the service of William and Mary. Born in Edinburgh, he was on familiar terms with some of the most prominent figures in Scotland, England, France and the Netherlands. In visiting the Netherlands he had found 'a great fund of peace and tranquillity notwithstanding the diversity of opinions, which was due to the mildness of the government and the tolerance which let each man live as he would.'[17] Burnet managed to make William promise to show more affection towards his wife, and Mary, without renouncing her right to the English crown, declared that she would leave administration wholly in William's hands.

In making up his mind to attempt a landing in England, William had to consider the dangers faced by Europe as a whole. By weakening Parliament and preventing it from renewing itself, James II was preventing European union and favouring Louis XIV's policy of supremacy. And the boldest and most eminent of parliamentarians were eager to regain Parliament's legislative power and longing for a sovereign capable of respecting a freely agreed charter.

5 ❦ Hans Willem Bentinck and the Prince Electors

WHEN WILLIAM III was won over to the idea of a well-planned move supported by partners capable of enforcing Mary's rights, he again needed a courageous second of impeccable loyalty – someone with the experience to investigate and make first-hand reports on the reactions he could expect from other nations, from England to the most distant German principalities. His envoy must carry out his orders promptly and send accurate, reliable accounts of his missions; he must be able to keep the matter secret for as long as necessary, even if this meant laying false trails for the inquisitive. Hans Willem Bentinck was the obvious candidate for such a task, particularly since in addition to his other qualifications he knew enough about the character of the Prince of Orange to be able to anticipate his wishes. This emerges in several of Bentinck's letters written at that time, in sentences such as 'I believe that you know him well enough to be aware that generally he does not do things by halves,' or 'You know His Highness's character, which consists of never saying what he does not think.'[1] Bentinck had proved that he was ready to save his master's life at the risk of his own. Now his mission was to be his precursor in the great enterprise which would decide the liberty of Holland, the end of revolutions in England, and the peace of Europe by maintaining the 'countries between' with their trading towns open to all comers, yet self-determining.

As well as the hard-pressed members of the English Parliament who had fled to Holland or made frequent visits, a number of important naval figures appeared there. Arthur Herbert, who had proved himself a brilliant commander against the pirates in the Mediterranean, had antagonized James II by refusing to sign the Test Act. Charles Mordaunt, after fighting the Moors under the orders of Herbert, his uncle, had entered the House of Lords, made a speech attacking the King's policy of intolerance, and came under suspicion of having taken part in the Rye House Plot; Edward Russell, later an admiral and Earl of Oxford, the cousin of the executed Lord William Russell, had left James II's navy after the ruthless elimination of a member of his family.

When the supporters of William III and Mary had clarified their minds about the plan for a Dutch invasion to overthrow James II, the question arose of the security of the Netherlands. They needed protection in the absence of the ships and soldiers who would undertake the expedition across the Channel. On the eastern side a diversion into the Rhineland by Louis XIV's generals could be fatal to the expedition if it meant recalling Dutch troops during the march on London.

Inside Holland the opposition of the burgomasters of Amsterdam had to be overcome. At first it had been impossible to inform the States General of the projected invasion for fear of a leak to the other side; now they hesitated to approve the plan.

In the same year, 1688, two unexpected events further complicated the situation: the birth of a son to James II and Mary of Modena, which came as such a surprise that doubts were raised about the true paternity of the new Prince of Wales, and the death of the old Elector of Cologne. The displacement of Furstenberg, who was devoted to Louis XIV, and the appointment by Pope Innocent XI of Joseph-Clement, Duke of Bavaria, as Prince Bishop of the great town on the Rhine had angered the

King of France, who occupied Cologne. In England, hopes of a Catholic dynasty were revived by the arrival of an heir.

Only rapid action, supported at home in both Amsterdam and The Hague and abroad by neighbouring countries, would offer any hope for the salvation of the Netherlands through an alliance with England acceptable to a free Parliament. Could the Prince of Orange's envoy gain this support in time? Would he persuade the German princes, already alarmed by the presence of French armies on the Rhine, of the imminence of events which closely involved them? There was no time to lose.

Hans Willem Bentinck left The Hague and his ailing wife in the middle of May and crossed the United Provinces by fast post-chaise. He passed through his native Overijssel and travelled through Hanover and Brandenburg to Berlin. The Elector of Brandenburg at once informed him of a plan for the defence of the Rhine and assured him that he was well disposed towards the intentions of his cousin the Prince of Orange.

Talks had taken place in March, before the death of the Great Elector, with one of his generals. The new Elector, Frederick III, confirmed their result, so enabling the negotiations to be extended to the dukes of Brunswick and Wolfenbüttel, the Elector of Saxony and if possible to the dukes of Celle and of Hanover, although the latter had commitments to France.

On the English side, it was also realized that the freedom of Parliament had to be preserved before it was too late. On 30 June 1688 seven determined men signed an invitation asking William III to come to England, disarm James II and guarantee the liberties of the people. It was brought by Admiral Herbert, disguised as an ordinary seaman. The signatories were Henry Sidney, who had spent some time discussing the plan for a Dutch landing in England with William III, Mary and Hans Willem Bentinck at Sorgvliet; Danby, the former Lord Treasurer, who had been one of the first to suggest a marriage between William and Mary and who had joined the party of Sidney and Edward Russell after compromising himself by condemning James II's high-handed treatment of Halifax; Admiral Edward Russell himself, a devotee of the cause of William III ever since James II had had his cousin and brother-in-law beheaded; the Bishop of London, Compton, who had been Mary's religious preceptor and officiated at her wedding; and Richard Lumley, who became a Protestant in 1687 and early in 1688 entered into communication with William's friends. Lumley captured Monmouth in 1685 but later became dissatisfied with James II's policy. Compton's support must have delighted her, and he had already won the hearts of the Prince of Orange and Hans Willem Bentinck with his welcome at Oxford so many years before. He had been suspended from office for refusing to commit an act of flagrant injustice, and Mary had interceded on his behalf with James II, but to no avail. Other signatories were William Cavendish, Earl of Devonshire, who had opposed James II by trying to save William Russell's head, and Charles Talbot, Earl of Shrewsbury, the King's former chamberlain who had since turned against his policies.

These seven declared that the people were so discontented with the Government's treatment of their religion, their liberties and their property rights that at least nineteen out of twenty of the population wanted a change. They stated that they were ready to attend upon William as soon as he landed and to do everything in their power to prepare others.[2]

Hans Willem Bentinck knew that this invitation gave his negotiations special importance. It was not just a matter of one nation's future. England might be sick of James II's arrogance and intolerance, which was keeping members of the reformed Church out of the highest positions, but The Hague's concern was the freedom of the Netherlands and of larger parts of the Continent too, for, with the help of James II, Louis XIV was threatening their independence.

On 16 July 1688 Bentinck dined at Huys ter Bosch, the country estate of the princes of Orange, with William and Mary. In a letter the previous day William had made no mention of fresh orders to leave for Germany. But the assurances given by Frederick III, particularly as regards the contingents promised by the other German princes, were still quite vague. It must have been over dinner at Huys ter Bosch that William III and Bentinck discussed the support likely from the Elector of Brandenburg, who was already committed to provide 12,000 men, the Elector of Saxony, the Dukes of Celle and Wolfenbüttel, and the Landgrave of Hesse-Cassel, Frederick III's brother-in-law.

Eight days after his talk with William and Mary Bentinck was back on the road to Hanover, then on to Celle, the pretty medieval town whose castle was the residence of the dukes of Brunswick-Lüneburg.

The new Elector of Brandenburg sent his personal adviser, Paul de Fuchs, to meet Bentinck. Fuchs had studied in the famous Dutch universities of Leyden and Franeker, in Friesland, and fully supported Frederick William's policy of protecting the Netherlands against any invasion. In 1685 he had been sent to The Hague to discuss the treaty of the League of Augsburg with the States General.

Bentinck's mission depended on two conflicting conditions – speed and secrecy. The Great Elector's envoy had taken a roundabout route, so as not to be recognized and followed. He had taken lodgings in an inn on the outskirts of town. Bentinck did not join him until the day after his arrival, in order not to arouse suspicion by a nocturnal visit.

The Dutchman's first task, after congratulating Fuchs on the accession of the new Prince Elector, was to dissuade him from waiting until James II appointed a Parliament. If the King could pick his own members they would follow his instructions to suppress oath-taking ceremonies, vote funds for his army and navy, and help France to occupy the Protestant countries. Then Bentinck explained the powers granted by the States of Holland to levy as many troops as possible; the French still believed that they were for defence on the Continent. When these units crossed over to England instead, the French would probably try to create a diversion in Holland. The Great Elector could counter the move if he wanted to. Paul de Fuchs had always advised against leaving matters until the French had subdued the

Netherlands. 'The loss of a single country concerns us all,' he had written in the *Diarium Europaeum* in 1673, 'and it is always better to put out the fire in our neighbour's house than to wait for it to reach our own.'

The Elector of Brandenburg's envoy had received very extensive powers to negotiate with Bentinck.[3] The negotiators agreed that an army of about nine thousand men should be mobilized and stationed in the United Provinces, which would provide their pay and upkeep. The Elector's own army was not big enough.

While the two envoys were still in Celle, Fuchs arranged a meeting with the prime minister of Duke Georg Wilhelm of Brunswick–Lüneburg, Andreas Gottlieb von Bernstorf. This wily diplomat had already organized several alliances, and when George of Hanover united his country with Celle by marrying the heiress, Sophia Dorothea, he entered the service of Hanover and became a minister of George, future Elector of Hanover, later King George I of England.

There too secrecy had to be maintained. The talks took place in a garden outside the town, where Fuchs and Bentinck walked so as not to attract attention. It was no problem to show Bernstorf that, if England were governed by King James II and closely allied with Louis XIV, Holland would fall and the German states would be threatened in their turn. The Duke therefore fell in with Bentinck, and an agreement was concluded between the Elector of Brandenburg, the Landgrave of Hesse and the Duke of Lüneburg, a personal friend of the Prince of Orange.

The future Elector of Hanover had concluded a separate peace with the French court and could not enter into a commitment for immediate aid. Gilbert Burnet was, however, known to Princess Sophia of Hanover, daughter of the Prince Elector of the Palatinate and grand-daughter of James I. He had been in touch with her through a French Huguenot called Boncour, who had taken refuge in Hanover. In his *History of My Own Times* Burnet wrote:

It was to acquaint her with our design with relation to England, and to let her know, that, if we succeeded, certainly a perpetual exclusion of

Papists from the succession to the Crown would be enacted: And since she was the next Protestant heir after the two Princesses and the Prince of Orange, if the Duke of Hannover could be disengaged from the interests of France, the succession to the Crown would be lodged in her person. . . .[4]

On his return Bentinck reported the assurances he had gained. These meant that diversionary action against the Netherlands by Louis xiv's generals would be met by concerted action on the part of Frederick iii and a number of Electorates.

In late summer Bentinck made another secret trip to Amsterdam, where the burgomasters were showing less enthusiasm for the expedition than the men at The Hague. The news that William's envoy had brought German help did a great deal to allay the great maritime city's fears for its trade. Louis xiv's blockade of herring was the decisive factor for the two chief magistrats Witsen and Hudden, and when the people of Amsterdam learned of this provocative measure they were won over to the plan to rid England of a King favourable to Louis xiv.

In London James ii was beginning to suspect his son-in-law's intentions, although he had no idea how close the invasion was. On 28 September he wrote to his cousin Sophia of Hanover: 'Now we see the purpose of Bentinck's travels among several Protestant princes.'[5] The Prince of Orange himself had had a final personal meeting with Frederick iii at Minden, on that part of the Prussian frontier closest to the Netherlands.

In October the Dutch fleet assembled at Hellevoetsluis, at the mouth of the Meuse, under Admiral Arthur Herbert. On 26 September William iii wrote instructing Bentinck 'to make it quite clear to Mr Herbert that he is to avoid combat as long as possible, for since the outcome is still uncertain, although our side is stronger, now is not the time to display bravery, or to fight, if it can be avoided.' If anything were to happen to the fleet, all would be lost.

Bentinck went into every detail with Admiral Herbert, arranged another itinerary in case the ships were prevented from leaving the Meuse by adverse winds, and, noting that too few bombs had been loaded for the mortars, told the artillery sergeant-major to take another thousand, to be loaded later.[6]

All the plans for the crossing had passed through Bentinck's hands. He himself had copied out Admiral Herbert's reports for revision by William III – sending 'a few galliots to the English coasts for intelligence'; he had determined the role to be played by the Dutch ambassador in London, van Citters, as an informant; he had realized the importance of getting hold of English pilots who knew every inch of the coast.

Before leaving Holland with his navy and a large part of his army, the Prince of Orange addressed the States of Holland. He thanked them for the help they had granted him ever since they had welcomed him as an orphan boy to the Binnenhof in The Hague, and commended his beloved wife Mary to the States' representatives in case of his own death, a sign of the great risks the expedition was running. But his confidence was reinforced by the knowledge that, thanks to the diplomatic activities of his former page, any attempt at a flanking attack by the allies of James II would run into determined resistance from the neighbours of the United Provinces.

6 ✍ The King for Parliament

STORMS DELAYED the departure of the six hundred ships grouped near the mouth of the Meuse and the Waal. A first attempt to cross was followed by a return to port. Many horses died of suffocation because the weather prevented the port-holes being opened.

While he waited at Hellevoetsluis, Hans Willem Bentinck was growing increasingly worried about his wife's health, now that she was left alone with their five surviving children. But on 26 October he had to rejoin the fleet, and his sister Eleonora van Ittersum gave him some more reassuring news. When the time came to set sail, Hans Willem wrote to Anne: 'Farewell, I beg you to believe that all my life I shall love you with the same passion.'

On the next day the part of the fleet that had been anchored off the Texel left the island to rejoin the rest, but headwinds stopped them sailing westward.

On 30 October Bentinck was tormented by the knowledge that he could not expect news of his wife's condition in the near future. He was on board the *Briel*, at anchor off the mouth of the Meuse, waiting for a high tide to cross the bar. 'There is ground to hope for a good crossing,' he wrote to Anne Bentinck, 'since the wind is quite strong. Today's news from England is very good. God preserve you and restore your health, to the delight of him who will always love you. . . .' This was his last expression of love. Hans Willem never again set eyes on his beloved wife, who was struck down soon afterwards by a fever which it was beyond the doctors' powers to relieve.[1]

At last the fleet put to sea, sailed down the coast to Calais, crossed the Channel and sailed past the Isle of Wight and into Torbay. The Prince's ship, the *Briel*, was the last to set sail. On board were Bentinck; Zuylenstein; Henry of Nassau-Ouwerkerk; the Count of Solms-Braunfeld (a lieutenant-general in the service of Holland); and Arthur Mordaunt, formerly an English commander in the Mediterranean. The *Briel* was commanded by Admiral Willem Bastiaensz Schepers, generally known as Bastiaensz.

During the crossing Bentinck read the reports of Aernout van Citters, the ambassador to London of the States General. His job had been a hard one since the accession of James II. In order to help the revolution which was to overthrow the King he had had to find out about the agreements with Louis XIV, refuse the repatriation to England of the English and Scottish troops in the service of Holland and conceal preparations for the expedition to England.

The Prince's ship landed in Dartmouth Bay, a few miles down the coast from Torbay, and separated from it by hills which came as a surprise to the Dutch soldiers, who were used to flat country. Many of them had been seasick during the voyage, and they made slow progress under a driving rain. From the top of the first hill the Prince and Zuylenstein looked out to discover what kind of welcome the population would give them.

The Prince's secretary, Constantijn Huygens junior, whose father had been secretary to the princes of Orange-Nassau, kept a journal of the expedition. He climbed the hill with Bastiaensz and noticed that Bentinck and s'Gravenmoer were both poorly mounted.[2] Bentinck, the descendant of the knights of Gelderland, brought up at Diepenheim in good bloodstock country, was out of his element.

Although it poured with rain on the first night and they were soaking wet, even the Prince's closest colleagues had no roof over their heads and had to sleep in a soldier's tent. Next day the peasants called out 'God bless you' to the intruders. Many of them had been cruelly punished for letting Monmouth pass and rejoiced at the news that James II was to be overthrown.

The Exeter magistrates were unable to prevent the townspeople from decorating their windows and giving an enthusiastic reception to the motley band. A procession was arranged, and two hundred English gentlemen led the way, accompanied by Negroes from the Guyana sugar plantations, and followed by Swedish cavalry, with swords drawn. Pages waved flags. The Prince sat on a white horse, with a white cockade in his helmet. Count Schomberg followed him, then came the Swiss infantry who had distinguished themselves so signally in Holland and were now treading English soil for the first time. Bentinck, Solms, van Reede, Talmash and Mackay were at the head of their respective regiments.

During the march on London, Bentinck was considered the best informed about the numbers being recruited to the Prince's cause. He was plied with questions. It was not long before news arrived that the people of Plymouth had come over to the Prince under the influence of Admiral Russell; now the frigates carrying the late arrivals could anchor in harbour there.

On 4 December there was an alarm. Huygens learned that Bentinck had set out in the morning with a squadron of four hundred horse and in the afternoon he heard from Zuylenstein that a brigade of three of James II's regiments was approaching. Just when a dangerous clash seemed imminent Bentinck was informed that the royal troops were coming over to the Orangists, together with their leaders John Churchill and the Duke of Grafton. From then on the royalist resistance was broken, Mordaunt having already persuaded the counties of Dorset and Wiltshire not to oppose the Prince of Orange.

A few days after the landing Bentinck had reached Hindon, about six miles from Salisbury, where the Prince of Orange joined his advisers every day. Defectors were flooding in from all sides. Lord Clarendon's son Cornbury, a nephew of James II and a member of Parliament, had already declared his allegiance, and this decision brought many others in its wake. James II was running out of support.

Bentinck was still a mine of information, the centre of many gatherings. On the approach of a delegation from James II everybody consulted him to find out how the question of the Stuart succession would be settled. Bentinck answered that everything would have to be examined by Parliament, in keeping with the statements of the Prince, who meant to stand by them.[3] Those who claimed that the Prince would take the crown by force were slandering him. In an aside to Clarendon, Bentinck also remarked that, while the lure of seizing three realms at once might make a man ambitious, the King set greater store by keeping his word.[4]

The Prince's principles had cost him a great deal of thought. Three months before setting out to England he wrote to Bentinck about the text of his declaration:

I confess that this puts me in frightful difficulties and uncertainties, and that more than ever I have need of divine Direction; you will see that through my conclusion I cast myself completely on the mercy of Parliament, although I am afraid that it cannot be otherwise, and yet it is no small risk to put my fate in their hands. . . .[5]

The Prince of Orange's declaration, prepared with the help of the Grand Pensionary Fagel and translated into English, had been revised by Gilbert Burnet, who was with Bentinck on the way to London. The preamble recalled that in any community strict observance of the law was necessary both for the good of nations and for the security of government. The Prince of Orange had been grieved to find that the fundamental law of a realm to which he was tied by blood (his mother) and by marriage (his wife Mary) had been grossly and systematically violated, under the influence of evil advisers.

The freedom to dispense with Parliament, the Prince continued, had been taken to a point where all legislative power was exercised by the crown. Decisions which conflicted with the constitution had therefore been taken by tribunals whose judges had been continually replaced until all the new magistrates declared themselves ready to obey the crown. The convocation of a legal Parliament might be the effective cure for all these ills, but the nation could not hope to find such a Parliament unless the system were changed.

The Prince rejected any idea of conquest. He solemnly committed himself to calling a legal Parliament. The liberty of Parliament had become the goal of the expedition and was the theme of the banners that the soldiers carried.[6]

At the end of December dispatches from Holland reached the Hindon headquarters; these included the first news from The Hague for several weeks. One letter revealed that Anne Bentinck, the modest, devoted wife of Hans Willem, had succumbed to a fatal fever.

When the news reached Bentinck his beloved Anne was already at rest in the chapel at Rhoon, next to her son Willem. The remains had been taken by boat to Delft and thence to the locality whose name had sometimes been applied to Hans Willem. In a few words which informed 'M. de Rhoon' of his wife's death, the secretary described her final hours, in the presence of Princess Mary, and spoke of a last reconciliation between the dying woman and her sister Elizabeth Villiers, estranged on account of the latter's affair with William. The weeping Princess had promised to take care of some of the children.

According to an account by the Princess of Orange herself, Anne Bentinck had learned of her husband's landing in Dartmouth and Torbay on the eve of her death. On the 20th, Mary was with her when she died:

Madame Bentinck died after a long illness, and though she had suffered much as to her body, yet the Lord had great pity on her soul, in that she had so long a time to prepare for another world. She bore all her illness with much patience, but felt much pain in leaving her husband

and five little children, and although she had led an innocent life yet she lamented loudly having so offended God by her lack of resignation. . . .

I was by her when she expired, and although she suffered for a while, yet she died as gently as if she had but fallen asleep. She was very glad for prayers to be said around her as long as her senses remained with her, and when her speech failed she showed by signs that she knew each person and understood what was said to her. I have no doubt that God has received her soul, and I hope that her death will have such effect on those who were present that we shall be able to learn to number our days and apply our hearts to wisdom. . . .

Anne Bentinck had died after giving life to a large family. Six months later Mary was writing from Kensington that she herself did not rule out all hopes of having an heir after thirteen years of childless marriage:

. . . Humanly speaking there is no likelihood of my being thus blessed after such a long time barren, and I must be content, since man does not see what the Lord sees. He knows why he has refused me that benediction for so long and he knows why he continues to refuse. If the good Lord had given me children I would never have been able to bear, as I have borne, everything which the Lord laid upon me, when my husband undertook the crossing to England, when he went to Ireland last year, and at present in Flanders.[7]

The example of Anne Bentinck inspired Princess Mary with the finest form of resignation – Christian patience.

Anne Bentinck's chief mourner was Hans Willem's brother Eusebius, lord of Schoonheten, himself a widower for several years. The painful days of mourning in the absence of Hans Willem had been tempered by the presence and ministrations of his sister Eleonora, with whom he had spent his childhood at Diepenheim.

Across the Channel, and alone in the midst of the army, Hans Willem had to swallow his tears. Only to a single friend did he confess his weakness and grief at his loss, in the conviction that the man was close enough to him to sympathize with his misfortune. The Prince had always shown him the greatest concern during his wife's long illnesses. During his mission to Germany William

III had written to him three days running with news of his wife
and had entreated him to return when she took a turn for the
worse. Each time he had been moved to tears to see his friend so
anxious when the fever rose again. But we know nothing about
his response to Hans Willem Bentinck's bereavement.

The followers of the Prince of Orange who were with Bentinck
when he received the painful if not unexpected news of his wife's
death had other preoccupations and do not seem to have been
much affected on his behalf. The Prince's secretary, Constantijn
Huygens, who had been with Bentinck continually since setting
sail from the Dutch coast, confined himself to noting in his
journal: 'Monsignor Bentinck receives the news of the death of
his wife.'

On 3 December 1688 Lord Clarendon had driven down from
London to a point close to Salisbury. He left James II very
disturbed by the printed text of William III's declaration, which
was beginning to spread. At the same time he learned that his son
had gone over to the Orangist cause. James II had deprived
Clarendon successively of his position in Ireland and his high
office of Lord Privy Seal. This great lord, the King's own brother-
in-law, came to see the Prince of Orange of his own accord,
without being ordered to do so by the King, in the hope of
reconciling the two parties. He found ambassador Citters in a
Sarum inn and was directed to the Prince's headquarters.

William was already surrounded by a constellation of important
figures. Discovering that Gilbert Burnet was in the house,
Clarendon went to his room only to find that their views were
at variance. Clarendon still believed in the possibility of co-operation between James II and Parliament. For Gilbert Burnet, such a
reconciliation was impossible. In the dining room Clarendon met
Lord Churchill. A discussion began between Clarendon and
Churchill on the latter's reasons for abandoning the King but was
interrupted by the arrival of Sir Henry Capell who had been one
of the strongest supporters of the Exclusion Bill.

After missing the Prince that night, Clarendon returned on the
next day, met Schomberg, the former Marshal of France, who

had joined the Prince of Orange after the revocation of the Edict
of Nantes and was then admitted to see Hans Willem Bentinck.
Clarendon kept a journal too[8] and made as brief a note as Huygens':
'The previous day he had received news of the death of his wife.'

Bentinck congratulated Clarendon on his son's swift support
for the Prince's cause. Then he reassured him about the Prince's
intentions and explained that his declaration was sincere and that
his behaviour had been in keeping with it ever since the landing.
The Catholics had suffered no depredations, and no one claimed
that the Prince of Orange had come to take the crown on his own
account; Parliament would have to offer it.

Clarendon then told Bentinck that if the Prince kept to these
conditions the task of the King's envoys would be an easy one
and declared himself satisfied with their conversation, although
on the next day he complained bitterly to Bentinck that the
Dutch troops were not paying for the accommodation and
transport they had requisitioned. According to Clarendon,
Bentinck's answers were very feeble.[9] For his part, Bentinck
wondered why Clarendon should meddle with questions of
supply and transportation, which were difficult for any army.
Capell had to explain that the country people had approached
Clarendon because he came from the region, having been born
in Wilton, a few miles west of Salisbury.

This was the start of a new era for Bentinck. For twenty-five
years he had served the Prince of Orange; ever since William's
marriage he had been devoted to Princess Mary. But now he had
taken on new tasks, the re-establishment of constitutional rights
in England. The ground he trod now was foreign to him, and
everybody felt entitled to criticize. In his journal, Clarendon even
noted 'Bentinck shews his temper betimes.' Only the Prince of
Orange displayed an incredible peace of mind and maintained a
silence worthy of his great-grandfather.

Events were moving very fast as, in the last days of 1688,
Bentinck reached London, where he was in the immediate
entourage of the Prince. Delegates came from the King and
joined William when they learned that he had fled. James was

stopped by some fishermen, only to be released at once on the instructions of the Prince of Orange. He returned to Whitehall, requested Parliament to ask the Prince into London to avoid bloodshed and fled once again, this time crossing without mishap to France, where the Queen had preceded him.

Though many knowledgeable observers expected the Prince of Orange to seize the crown, he waited, true to his promises, even though he was aware that delay would enable Louis XIV to organize a campaign to restore James. Parliament met and debated, and a Convention made up of both Lords and Commons assembled. William III confined himself to maintaining order in the capital and seemed aloof from the negotiations. He even went so far as to forbid a popular demonstration in favour of his accession to the throne.[10]

Bentinck found it harder to contain his impatience and his feelings. While the Convention was examining the question of the future of the absent King and whether it was possible to declare the throne vacant, Bentinck was working hard to have the kingship entrusted to William III alone. He felt that Mary's husband could not be asked to play the part of a prince consort.[11] Was Bentinck reflecting the Prince's opinion or was he going too far? At any rate he bore the brunt of a violent response from Admiral Arthur Herbert, who insisted that the crown must belong to James II's daughter, not to his nephew and son-in-law. He dragged himself out of the bed where he had been confined with an attack of gout to exclaim: 'I would never have drawn my sword in favour of the Prince if I had suspected him capable of behaving thus towards his wife.'[12]

The Prince reacted by offering to withdraw to Holland. Bentinck, who according to Gilbert Burnet was becoming publicly known as one of the architects of the expedition's success, now made it known to his influential acquaintances that William would be content to share sovereignty with Mary provided that the administration was bestowed on him alone. This solution, which was in keeping with Mary's pledge not to renounce the throne and yet to remain obedient to her husband,

D

was proposed to the Convention by the Earl of Danby, who had been made President of the combined assembly.

The Convention agreed that the throne was vacant by the desertion of James II and decided to offer the crown jointly to William and Mary. It felt that it could not exclude from power the man who had restored the liberty of the nation; that would mean he would become an ordinary citizen should the Queen die before him. It was a condition of the coronation of William and Mary that they accept the Bill of Rights which guaranteed the rights of the nation, represented by a free Parliament.

Nearly twelve years had elapsed since the Duke of York's daughter had married the Prince of Orange and said farewell to her childhood days at Richmond with Anne Villiers, who had accompanied her to The Hague. When the royal party reached Whitehall, so recently the residence of James II, they were surrounded by memories. The thought of his wife, who had died only a few weeks before, made Hans Willem more conscious of his own solitude.

The swearing-in ceremony took place at the Banqueting Hall in Whitehall on 13 February 1689. Lord Halifax, in his capacity as Speaker of the House of Lords, solemnly asked William and Mary to accept the crown of England. The new sovereigns stood beneath a canopy before the vacant throne. Among those present were John Churchill, the future Duke of Marlborough; Hans Willem Bentinck, soon to be Earl of Portland; Gilbert Burnet, who was to become Bishop of Salisbury; Henry Powle, Speaker of the House of Commons; Compton, the Bishop of London; John Somers, principal author of the Bill of Rights; and Lord Danby.

In the presence of the members of the two Houses Lord Halifax came forward, accompanied by the secretary who acted as spokesman. The assembly listened as he read out:

... The said lords spiritual and temporal, and commons ... being now assembled in a full and free representative of this nation ... do ... for the vindicating and asserting their ancient rights and liberties, declare:

1. That the pretended power of suspending of laws, or the execution of laws, by regal authority, without consent of Parliament, is illegal. . . .
4. That levying money for or to the use of the crown, by pretence of prerogative, without grant of Parliament, for longer time, or in other manner than the same is or shall be granted, is illegal.
5. That it is the right of the subjects to petition the King, and all commitments and prosecutions for such petitioning are illegal.
6. That the raising or keeping a standing army within the kingdom in time of peace, unless it is with consent of Parliament, is against the law. . . .

The declaration also provided for freedom of Parliamentary debate, the abolition of excessive fines and cruel punishments and for frequent meetings of Parliament for the reform of abuses and the amendment, strengthening and preservation of the law.

This new constitution placed the monarchy on a Parliamentary basis. Though it reduced the powers of the king considerably, it left room for an ill-defined royal rule, no longer based upon divine right but upon the application of laws and human rights. The provisions for strict respect of the law, the guarantee of a free and legal Parliament and the right to present petitions to the King were taken from William's own declaration, made before his departure for London. The declaration signed by William and Mary was the constitutional expression of the spirit of the Glorious Revolution, which ruled out a republic as contrary to the English tradition but saw absolute monarchy as a threat to the rights of man and the nation.

For Bentinck, the words which rang out in the Banqueting Hall had a special meaning, linked as they were with the causes for which his ancestors had fought.

Just two months after the ceremony in the Banqueting Hall, Hans Willem Bentinck attended the coronation of William and Mary in Westminster Abbey. For the first time in English history, neither of the two was a consort. The King bore all the insignia of royalty received by his predecessors. For the Queen, the jewellers had created a second orb, the symbol of royalty, studded with pearls and precious stones and surmounted by a cross. Carrying these attributes and the Bible, and with a sword at her side, Mary ascended the throne beside the King.[13]

Among the ladies who carried the train was her cousin Lady Henrietta Hyde, niece of James II and Clarendon. The father of 'pretty little Lady Henrietta, the best child in the world' was the Earl of Rochester, who had fought to the last against the throne being declared vacant. Other peers who had voted for a Regency under the little Prince of Wales and who were not expected at the ceremony showed by their presence that they were rallying to the new King. The Bishop of London, Compton, always ready to honour his former pupil, took the place of the absent Archbishop Sancroft.

After William III's coronation, Bentinck, now created Earl of Portland, attended a ceremony together with Devonshire, Ormond and Schomberg at which they received the Order of the Garter. Prince George of Denmark, the husband of Princess Anne, received the title of Duke of Cumberland. Danby became Marquis of Carmarthen. Churchill was dubbed Earl of Marlborough.

It was customary to distribute rewards on such occasions. William III had been very discreet in the honours granted to his Dutch compatriots, but Bentinck was too deserving to be overlooked. He now bore the English title and name of Earl of Portland. The eldest son of Hans Willem and Anne Villiers, who was six years old at the coronation, was afterwards made Duke of Portland by King George I in memory of his father's great achievements, and all the eldest sons of his branch have borne this title to the present day.

Standing in the midst of these noblemen old and new and of the Whigs whose principles were now triumphantly recognized, Portland heard Gilbert Burnet call for God's blessing on the royal couple, asking Providence to give them long life and mutual love and hoping that it might please God to give them obedient subjects, wise counsellors and loyal allies.

7 ❧ Portland in the King's Service

FTER THE CORONATION Parliament continued to concern itself mainly with domestic issues, while William III, often through the medium of Bentinck's correspondence with the King's envoys, had to face difficulties on all sides. In Scotland his advisers were preoccupied by the opposition to the existence of bishops in the reformed Church.

In Holland the attitude of the burghers of Amsterdam was creating problems which had to be settled on the spot. The King sent Bentinck to The Hague early in 1690. The representatives of the oligarchy of Amsterdam, especially Witsen, were afraid of the effects of William's European policy on their trading interests and took their fears out on his envoy. The States forbade Bentinck to sit among them, claiming that his allegiance to the English crown disqualified him. Nevertheless Bentinck buckled down to the thorny question of the nomination of the magistrates appointed annually by the Stadtholder from a list drawn up by the burghers. The row took a long time to settle, and even when things were smoothed over the underlying causes remained.

William was pressing Portland to return; Portland himself thought that the King should join him in Holland. Graver and more urgent problems awaited them both in Ireland, however, for James II had landed with a French force at Kinsale and marched on Londonderry with the Duke of Tyrconnel. William III did not willingly commit himself to a war against his father-in-law in Ireland. A few days before he set out in June 1690 at the head of his troops he said as much to Bishop Burnet. He was torn between his duty to defend England and the feelings that gripped him when he thought about his wife. For her part the Queen feared for the health and safety of William, physically weak, continually racked by bouts of asthmatic coughing and obliged to confront the risks of a hard campaign which might drag on till winter.

At the moment of setting out for Ireland Bentinck unwittingly became involved in a minor family squabble between William III and his brother-in-law, Prince George of Denmark, the husband of Mary's younger sister Princess Anne, the immediate heir to the throne. Prince George wanted to travel at the King's side in the royal carriage. Wanting to avoid any undue ceremonial formality, however, William III decided to give preference to his devoted H.W. Bentinck.[1]

The fate of the two tireless fighters was once again closely linked, this time in a war which was especially tragic for the Irish, because Ireland was merely the battleground. It was clear that if James II were victorious, thanks to the troops made available by Louis XIV, he would not be content with Ireland but would march on London and there resume his previous policy. France in alliance with a Stuart monarch in England would then have every chance of dominating the continent.

By no means all the Frenchmen who fought in Ireland in 1690 were among James II's army. Many on the opposing side were refugees who did not forget that the Stuart king had surrendered the French pastors exiled in Dublin[2] and that he had turned back the refugees who had fled after the revocation of the Edict of Nantes. As for Marshal Schomberg, although French by adoption, he had left France rather than abjure his Protestant faith and fought by the side of William III at the Battle of the Boyne, where he was killed. The Abbé Prévost, author of *Manon Lescaut*, puts these words into Schomberg's mouth: 'After serving successively in Germany and France I am going over into the service of this [English] house; and I do not know that anyone finds fault with my conduct.'[3]

When William III's army took the field in Ireland, where it was opposed by Marshal Lauzun, reconciled for the occasion with Louis XIV, Hans Willem Bentinck had command of an impressive cavalry force. In the murderous battle fought on the River Boyne near Drogheda he used a tactic of his own devising to disperse his horsemen among the infantry instead of charging as a body under the fire of the enemy guns. Lauzun's forces had to retreat.

The Orangists paid dearly for their victory at the Boyne. William III escaped death but was wounded in the hand by a cannon-ball. Lauzun had withdrawn in good order, and his army was still effective. It was only broken the following year, when Athlone was stormed by the Dutchman Godard van Reede, lord of Ginckel and Middachten, who later received the title of Earl of Athlone.

It was an absurd, fratricidal war. Many of the combatants knew nothing of the real reasons (still a bone of contention among historians). Each side blamed the other. The bloody brutality of the fighting left permanent scars. Yet for the English people, its representatives in Parliament and King William III one thing was beyond dispute: they would no longer tolerate an absolutist sovereign supported by a foreign power.

James II's departure for France again was greeted with relief in London and in some parts of Europe. Parliament met in October 1690 and congratulated William III on his personal valour and his victories over the self-confessed enemy of their religion and laws. But soon the news from Holland gave the King cause for concern, for the threat of a French invasion hung over Flanders and all the United Provinces. Fortunately the two Houses assured him that they would restore public order, and he felt free to go to The Hague.

The King left London on 16 January 1691 accompanied by several great English lords – Compton, the Bishop of London, the Dukes of Norfolk and Ormond and the Earls of Devonshire, Dorset and, of course, Portland. The escorting fleet was made up of twelve large vessels, seven yachts and a number of other ships. The winds were unfavourable, and it took four days to come into sight of the Dutch coast. Coming in closer they saw mountains of ice forming promontories into the sea.

The captain wanted to put back to England, but the King refused and ignoring the advice of his entourage transferred into a small boat, accompanied only by Bentinck, Ouwerkerk, Dorset, one servant and seven rowers. For eighteen hours the seamen fought against cold, ice and fog. Waves kept breaking over the boat and soaking their clothes, which froze stiff. 'The fog poisoned their brains and lungs and froze their hair and faces.'[4]

At daybreak the island of Goeree offered a refuge, and they sheltered in the cabin of a fisherman who recognized them. The King could have changed his clothes but did not want to linger, so two sailors took him in their arms and carried him into the boat which finally reached Orangie-Polder, at the mouth of the Meuse, in great danger of being sunk by floating ice.

The people rejoiced at the news of the King's arrival, the more so since it had been rumoured that he was dead. Preparations for a triumphal welcome had been made for some time, but nobody had expected him to arrive in the depths of winter. The King would have preferred to avoid all ceremonial but acquiesced in view of the care and expense involved. The avenue joining the town to the Bentinck estate at Sorgvliet was ideal for a solemn procession, and triumphal arches were designed by Roman de Hooghe and executed by Nicolas Chevalier, designer of the decorations on the façade of the town hall at Deventer.

After a few days everything was in readiness. In spite of the recent death of his wife, who would have been at the centre of the reception, Bentinck gave a dinner at Sorgvliet to the whole court. It was a 'splendid feast', according to a contemporary account, 'in the country house of Mr van Bentinck, Earl of Portland, the faithful companion of William III and his undertakings . . . from his earliest youth'. Bentinck was even compared

with Parmenion, the general of Alexander the Great who contributed to the victories of the Granicus and Issus and was
appointed governor of Media.

Representatives of all the great European powers were present
at Sorgvliet, except for the French ambassador. They included
Count von Berka, the Emperor's envoy; Colonna, the Spanish
ambassador; the Prince of Nassau, governor of Friesland; and
Count van Horn. The King's carriage was accompanied by forty
others, together with his guards and a hundred Switzers; they
constituted a procession more remarkable for its quality than its
numbers. The liveries suited William's liking for simplicity, and
after passing through the Field Gate into The Hague the King was
surrounded by the townspeople. But the state of Europe was too
grave to prolong the celebrations.

At this moment Holland, like England, was at war with France.
In face of this situation the Congress forming the general
assembly of the allies listened in attentive silence to William III's
address, for if he knew how to hold his tongue he was also a
master of the spoken word. The King and Stadtholder knew
what tasks and dangers he now faced: the time for deliberation
was past. The enemy controlled the main fortresses and would
occupy the others if quarrels, indifference and private interest
prevailed. William stated that the general interest alone should be
considered. The foreign invader must be opposed by an immediate union of all the allied forces without delay if the freedom of
Europe, already hard pressed, were not to be lost. William III of
Orange pledged himself to spare nothing to reach a just and
necessary goal with his allies. He would be seen at the head of his
troops in the spring.

At The Hague in 1691 Hans Willem Bentinck found himself
among the foremost diplomats of Europe – English and German,
Spanish and Swedish, Bavarians, Saxons, Hanoverians and
Brandenburgers. William III had chosen his moment to place the
knight from Gelderland, master of the knights of Holland, upon
the European chessboard. Already he had made him Earl of
Portland. Soon he was to dub him Knight of the Garter.

Hans Willem knew how far he had already come in his life and he knew also that the struggle was far from over and that there were still more battles to fight, perhaps at the cost of his life. The peace and liberty of Europe were at stake. Now he must fight to save the United Provinces from invasion by the generals of Louis xiv. The Earl of Portland did not hesitate, but he was concerned about the fate of his children, who had already lost their mother. They had stayed in London to await his return. What if he did not return and what if the King fell too? Before leaving, Hans Willem wrote a note to be given to Queen Mary in the event of their deaths: 'I am going to serve my King as I have always done, and in the event that the good God should dispose of me, and perhaps of the King himself, in such a manner that my children were to lose father and benefactor on the same day. . . . I beg my sister to do with them as the King, or she, shall order. . . .'[5]

Bentinck's thoughts now turned to his sister, the companion of his childhood at Diepenheim. She had taken care of his children after the death of their mother. His letter of 30 March 1691, which contains his note to the Queen, is addressed to Madame van Ittersum of Nyenhuis, in her castle in Overijssel:

My dearest sister, I enclose a letter for the Queen which you will not give into her hand unless I am no longer able to come and take it back; may almighty God who has always guided me and will have mercy upon me keep you in the tenderness and love you have always shown for my beloved children, whom I beg you to consider as your own. You will do with them absolutely as the King and the Queen shall ordain.

After giving instructions for the disposal of his assets, Bentinck continued:

But what comes closest to my heart is what Christian upbringing may inspire in my children; the good Lord has taken their virtuous mother, whom I shall miss to my dying day and whom they will miss after me; in her absence it is to the goodness of the King and Queen and to your care that I must entrust them; take care, sister, to inspire in them the principle of religion and the fear of God at their young age, because these impressions remain most impressed upon their souls, and you know that I have always felt that without these treasures there was nothing worth while in the world.

These lines were written at the moment when Louis xiv was attacking Mons in retaliation against the alliance concluded at The Hague. The town fell on 9 April.

The war lasted a long time. The allies gave Holland too little help for William to be victorious against the standing French armies in Flanders. The fortified towns of the Netherlands that constituted the barrier protecting Holland continued to surrender one by one. When Namur seemed ready to put up a stiff resistance, Louis xiv decided upon a set-piece siege in 1692. In the camp at Gevries he mustered an army of sixty-six battalions and 209 squadrons under Marshal Luxembourg. The King of France himself commanded another force of forty-six battalions and ninety squadrons, aided by the Dauphin, the Duke of Orleans (his brother); the Duke of Bourbon (Prince of Condé, son of the Grand Condé); and Marshal Humières. The famous military architect Vauban, whom Saint-Simon calls 'the soul of all sieges', decided that the town and the castle were to be attacked separately.

The town surrendered after ten days, and in the meantime William iii, at the head of an outnumbered army, tried in vain to intercept the troops attacking under Marshals Boufflers and Luxembourg and Louis xiv. He was prevented because the Meuse was in flood, swollen by torrential rains. By May the French fleet was threatening to invade England. William sent Bentinck back to England, where he ordered three regiments to be ready to embark. The combined fleets of England and Holland gathered at St Helens opposite the Isle of Wight were strong enough to withstand an attack from the French, who had been delayed in mustering their own forces by bad weather both in the Mediterranean and in the Atlantic. Two of their finest ships had been wrecked on the rocks of Ceuta. The English war-weariness, however, combined with William iii's precarious position on the continent to raise the Jacobites' hopes. Louis xiv, speculating on major defections in the English navy, had given Tourville the order to attack when the opportunity arose, and James II was so confident of imminent victory that he had already proclaimed terrible penalties for those Orangists who did not join his troops when they landed.

The Earl of Portland had to use all the diplomacy he could muster to prevent treachery in the navy. He saw at once that James II's threats had been counter-productive and had alienated all those who remembered his previous cruelties, and adopted different tactics, putting trust in the suspected waverers so that they would rally to William III. On his advice Queen Mary sent a dispatch to the officers of the combined fleets on board the *Britannia* at St Helens, including Admiral Russell, Delaval, Ashby, Shovell, Carter and Rooke, and the Dutchman van Almonde. In it she mentioned the rumours about the alleged Jacobite sympathies of the naval officers and dismissed such talk as slander on courageous servants of the state which she was determined not to believe.

The letter was enough to make any sailors who might have speculated on an enemy victory feel that the Queen was putting her trust in them and assure her of the 'alacrity and resolution' with which they would venture their lives for the liberty of England and the Protestant religion. Their message was on its way when the sails of Tourville's fleet were sighted from the cliff-tops.

The allied fleet scored a total victory. The French flagship the *Soleil Royal* was sunk in flames in the port of Cherbourg, and the rest of the fleet which Colbert had built was destroyed in the bay of La Hogue, under the eyes of James II and the troops mustered for the invasion of England. The news of the naval victory was greeted ecstatically in London. William III, who had faced betrayal by one of his first and best supporters, had instructed his faithful colleague Portland not to leave England 'before you see our enemies' design a little more clearly'.[6]

Portland, Sidney and Rochester were immediately sent to Portsmouth to distribute 37,000 pieces of silver to the seamen and gold medals to the officers. The wounded were treated with the utmost care. Fifty surgeons were sent from London, and the hospitals of St Paul and St Bartholomew in London were opened to any casualties at the expense of the state. In recognition of the disabled sailors, William and Mary created the Royal Marine Hospital at Greenwich.

After the battle of La Hogue, Admiral Rooke was appointed Lord of the Admiralty and John Berkeley of Stratton replaced him as commander of the Channel fleet. Berkeley died of pleurisy a year later. His widow was Sir William Temple's niece, later to become Portland's second wife.

In the meantime the siege of Namur was resumed. Now that the town had been taken, the citadel remained to be occupied. Against this background of gleaming swords and muskets, and the sound of drums and bugles, Jean Racine sent up a cry which should still be heard whenever there is any question of war or peace. Before an array of force and power greater than anything in his tragedies, one of the great geniuses of humanity exclaimed: 'I wish with all my heart that all the men I saw were each in their cottage or in their house, with their wives and their children, and me in my rue des Maçons with my family . . . .' He went on: 'Apart from this, I was never so spellbound or so astonished as I was to see so formidable a power.'

On 3 June 1692, just as Bentinck in London was receiving the news of the victory of La Hogue, Racine sent Boileau a description of the sufferings of the defenders of Namur.

. . . All those of our people who have been at these attacks have been astounded by the courage of the besieged. But you will judge of the terrible effect of cannon and bombs when I tell you that our artillery has killed 1200 of their men in two days. Imagine three converging batteries which fire continually upon poor people who are visible from above and from behind and who cannot find a single corner where they are in safety.

They say that the outworks were found full of 163 bodies whose heads had been carried away by the cannon as if they had been cut off by sabres.

The town's defenders belonged to various nationalities, and the citizens did not know for whom they were defending their town, opposing French and Swiss guards giving their lives only out of a sense of duty.

Three days after the victory of La Hogue Portland left by yacht to rejoin the army of Flanders. After the capture of Namur the war continued without any decisive battles. A year later William III had to try to defend Liège and clashed with the French near Landen on 30 July 1693. Bentinck distinguished himself by his bravery and emerged from the battle with several wounds, William himself experiencing one dangerous moment when he escaped death by a miracle. The Count of Solms, lieutenant-general of the Dutch army, was mortally wounded.

These sacrifices made little impression on the House of Commons in London. Its members wanted victories and, forgetting that England too was being defended, turned their resentment against the King's adviser, Portland. They asked William not to listen to any advice but Parliament's.

When a scandal broke in the beginning of 1695 about the use of the secret funds belonging to the East India Company some members of Parliament saw their opportunity to strike at Portland. The real culprits tried to insinuate that Bentinck had received sums of money, in the hope that there would be no investigation for fear of compromising the King's adviser, but a commission of inquiry was appointed, and revealed Bentinck's absolute honesty. He had refused all offers of money. On the other hand Portland did not hesitate to accept legally sanctioned gifts. Some years later, the King offered him a number of fine estates in Wales. A few gentlemen from that region protested to the House of Commons, fearing that they were to be deprived of their revenues, and because Portland did not want to create an incident between Commons and King he voluntarily renounced his acquisitions.

The Flanders campaign was resumed that summer amid difficulties caused by lack of cohesion among the allies and further opposition from the burghers of Amsterdam. During the 1694 campaign the Duke of Württemberg tried to persuade Portland to strike a decisive blow, but he held out against the war party. Perhaps he already had information that France was showing signs of fatigue with a war fought on so many fronts. Louis XIV's refusal to acknowledge William III as king of England still stood in the way of a settlement, but the fighting season came to an end without any serious clash.

The end of the year brought the King a terrible blow which touched Portland deeply. Queen Mary caught the same deadly disease which had almost destroyed William and Hans Willem thirty years before and died of smallpox within a few days. Apart from the King, nobody felt this loss as intensely as Portland. The two letters he wrote to Robert Sutton, the second Lord Lexington, the English minister in Vienna, show his grief and how uneasy he was about the King.[7]

Fortunately, as Bentinck himself pointed out, the death of James II's daughter did not enable William's enemies in England to threaten his own position. It was accepted that he would rule alone from then on.

As the war continued Portland rarely saw his children in London, although he occasionally managed to bring his son to Holland, where they stayed at Het Loo. The Queen's friendship had been a comfort. Now he was left with only the memory of the happy moments that his motherless children owed to Mary.

One night when the King and his adviser were in Whitehall at a ball given by the Queen, Portland had had the pleasure of seeing his daughter, the enchanting Mary Bentinck, still almost a child, dancing and being admired by young cavaliers and their parents. On another occasion he watched his son wearing a sword almost as big as himself, in a Court procession for a religious ceremony. These were brief joys but real ones for the regimental chief who could still expect more battles in the field and more betrayals in political life.

Three years after the capture of Namur by Louis XIV there had been little alteration in the positions of the armies stationed in the southern Netherlands. However in England the economic situation had improved, whereas in France the population was being ruined by crop failures caused by bad weather and lack of manpower, as well as by extortionate war taxation.

William's peace feelers had been rejected, so he decided to try to retake Namur, which was defended by Villeroy and Boufflers, the greatest of the French marshals now that Luxembourg was dead. When William's troops were held up by waterlogged terrain, Boufflers took advantage of the delay to move a force of seasoned defenders into the citadel, while Villeroy was supposed to attack the besieging army outside the town.

Boufflers's little garrison put up a desperate resistance, and Bentinck asked for a parley to beg him to avoid further pointless bloodshed. He refused, and another two thousand young men had to be sacrificed to save his honour. The defences had been rebuilt and improved since the previous siege, and it was the assailants who took the brunt of the losses during the single day's fighting which yielded them the fortress.

After the surrender, on 29 August 1695, the garrison marched past the victors. It still numbered about five thousand men together with their leader and his staff. During the march-past Dyckvelt, who accompanied the allies as the representative of the States General, took a squad of cavalry and arrested Boufflers on the King's orders. It was contrary to the law of capitulation, but the same thing had happened to the Dutch garrison of Dixmude a few weeks earlier, and Boufflers was to remain a prisoner until these men were released.

Portland intervened and ordered that the Marshal be treated with all the honours due to his rank, as a prisoner on parole, with no armed guard. Louis xiv had not approved of the arrest of the Dutchmen, and as soon as he heard of the allies' retaliation he set them free. Marshal Boufflers was then released in turn.[8]

8 ❧ Portland and the Peace of Europe: Ryswick and the Court of Louis XIV

IN SEPTEMBER 1696 William III and Louis XIV finally agreed to call a Congress. The Emperor Leopold of Austria was asked to take part, and his representative Count Auersperg came to Het Loo, William III's favourite residence, formerly a Bentinck property.

William III underlined to Auersperg the importance of seizing this opportunity for rapprochement, especially since the States General and the English Parliament were no longer providing the aid necessary to win the war. Just as Auersperg was leaving without giving way, the King sent Portland after him. Auersperg assured him that the Emperor had every confidence in the policy of William III but argued that events of this magnitude required reflection. Portland then spoke on his own account and maintained that the members of the English Parliament were persuaded that if the King succeeded in convoking a Congress, everybody would rally to it.

In the meantime the English envoys Heemskerk and Lexington had reached Vienna. The Emperor was still hesitating when Auersperg's courier arrived with his recommendation to agree to a meeting. The Emperor yielded.

When the Congress finally met to study the preliminary

arrangements for a peace with France each country was pre-occupied with its own interests and with questions of precedence. The sessions were to take place near The Hague at the Ryswick palace known as the Nieuwberg, built forty years earlier for Frederick Henry of Orange-Nassau, William's grandfather. It was surrounded by moats, and a bridge gave access to the main entrance, which was reserved for Baron Lilienroth, the Swedish envoy, who was presiding over the Congress. To the east and west, footbridges were built over the moats, one for the allies and the other for the French. The allies wanted the French to cross first. The French opted for simultaneous entry.[1]

These formal difficulties, grotesque as they were in view of the interests at stake, could be surmounted, but graver ones subsisted between the Empire, William III and the burghers of Amsterdam. These last were as anxious as ever about their commerce and wanted a policy of concessions towards France. The negotiations were deadlocked.

Portland and William III decided that Portland should ask for an interview with Boufflers, the French commander at Verdun. He at once informed Louis XIV who sent a fast courier from Versailles authorizing the meeting and pointing out how important it was to bear in mind that the request came from Portland. So the duel for peace began, under difficult circumstances for Holland.

On 8 July 1697 the adversaries met in the open air. Bentinck had offered to come two thirds of the way and suggested the little village of Brukom, near Halle, fifteen kilometres south of Brussels. Boufflers had the place inspected to make sure that he would not be arrested again, and they arrived simultaneously, exchanging the usual greetings before dismounting.

The first conference was held in an apple orchard where the two warriors walked up and down talking for two hours. First Portland assured his adversary of the King of England's genuine desire for peace, refuting the rumours spread by the French diplomats in Ryswick according to which William III secretly opposed an end to hostilities and supported the Emperor and the

Spaniards in warlike measures. On the contrary, Portland intended to recommend the acceptance of the preliminary French proposals to the allies. If they refused he would agree to England and Holland concluding a separate peace with France.

Bentinck then developed his sovereign's claims: William III demanded to be acknowledged as King of England, and Louis XIV was to promise not to assist James II directly or indirectly. English law did not permit William III to amnesty the exiled King's supporters, because the decision lay with Parliament. Last of all, Louis XIV's condition – that Huguenots should be barred – for restoring the little state of Orange to William III was contrary to his sovereign rights in the principality. William III was however prepared to give his personal promise not to introduce anybody without the authorization of the King of France.

Concluding this first conference, Portland pointed out that once peace had come and tempers had cooled it might not displease the King of France to have in the person of the King of England an ally as faithful and conscientious in the furtherance of French interests as he had been in resisting them.

Louis XIV's reply from Marly on 12 July bears the stamp of greatness. 'Assure Monsieur de Bentinck', he wrote to Marshal Boufflers, 'that I have learned with pleasure of the expressions with which, through his mediation, the Prince of Orange expresses his keen desire to merit the return of my favour.' Alluding to the last part of Portland's statement to Boufflers he adds, perhaps with a touch of irony: 'It is precisely his stubbornness in alliances against my interest which makes me hope that the contracts I am ready to conclude with him for the good of Europe will be equally durable.'

Louis maintained his refusal to take steps against James II and would only accept a more general clause about the enemies of England. But he did agree to the settlement concerning the principality of Orange, without insisting on written conditions specifying the Huguenots; nor did he insist on a general amnesty in England. The French King ended by advising a return to the normal process of negotiation at Ryswick so as not to arouse speculation about a separate peace.[2]

At the end of July the English ambassadors at Ryswick, Lords Jersey and Shrewsbury, wrote to inform London of Bentinck's meeting with Marshal Boufflers, although they had no certain information. The French, who were always well informed about the actions of the opposite party, shared their perplexity. 'The generals make peace,' Harlay wrote 'while the diplomats make war on each other.' The Emperor seemed unhappy about the arrangements made in the name of William III without consulting him, forgetting that he himself had neutralized part of Italy without consulting anybody.

In a second meeting Portland again drew Boufflers's attention to William's fears about possible invasion attempts by James II. Louis XIV insisted that James was not to be named in the peace treaty and would only promise not to help 'one or several enemies of England'. He had summoned James II each time Boufflers's dispatches mentioned proposals from Bentinck which concerned him.

Portland kept the Austrian representative Auersperg continually informed about the progress of his negotiations, telling him that: 'The salvation of Europe depends upon the good understanding and trust which prevail between King William III and the Emperor.' Auersperg maintained that it was essential for the peace to be lasting and for the first time drew Bentinck's attention to the dangers presented by the question of the Spanish succession. When Charles II of Spain died, France might be led to resume hostilities. This was the first Bentinck had learned of the partition treaties for the Spanish succession. The policies of Leopold and Louis XIV remained dominated by rivalry with one another, and according to Auersperg there must be agreement about the fate of the Spanish possessions once the Spanish King died without issue.

In a conference with Boufflers on 2 August Portland told him that it was impossible to bring the Spaniards into the peace unless they were guaranteed Barcelona. And what would be the equivalent asked for Luxembourg? It also seemed hard to him that the subjects of the Spanish crown in the Netherlands were bearing all the occupation costs occasioned by the French army, and he proposed an armistice. Louis, who was in constant touch with Boufflers, proved reluctant.

In September another meeting had to be arranged between Portland and Boufflers, although William III did not expect many results from it. It took place on 11 September in the parish of Tubize. Louis had given precise instructions to his marshal: 'If Bentinck is as polite as he has been hitherto, you too will conform to your previous instructions. If however he proves arrogant, you will answer him with all the dignity which is my due.'

For this meeting Portland was short of arguments to uphold the cause he was defending. He could not threaten a war which would mobilize the entire armed strength of the allies. The Amsterdam burghers were against it, and the Emperor was non-committal.

At the moment when the peace of Ryswick was at last concluded, and before the end of hostilities, Bentinck wrote to Shrewsbury that while the conditions were not solely to the advantage of France they could have been framed so as to ensure greater future security for the allies. He had been hampered by his obligation to be frank about William's allies' anxiety to settle at all costs.

Once the peace had been signed at Ryswick by France, England and Holland on 10 September and by the Empire a few weeks later, Hans Willem Bentinck returned to London. Before going he had told Auersperg of William's concern about the impending problem of the Spanish succession and stressed the importance of maintaining full unity among the allies.

William III stayed a few weeks longer at Het Loo, hunting and resting. With him was Lord Woodstock, Portland's eldest son, aged fifteen, the age at which his father had left Diepenheim to become a page at the court of The Hague.

Hans Willem wrote from London that the people were eager to see the King, and when William III returned in November he was greeted by an enthusiastic reception. Yet hardly had the peace been officially celebrated than the King ran into more difficulties with Parliament. He felt it necessary to underwrite the treaty's conditions, which meant keeping a standing army. Parliament refused on the grounds of expense, so diplomacy had to take the strain. England needed an ambassador in Paris capable of preventing further European conflicts provoked either by James II's moves against William or by the question of the Spanish succession. The Earl of Portland was appointed to this crucial post.

When Hans Willem Bentinck became the English ambassador in Paris in 1698 he had been a widower for ten years. His son Henry, Lord Woodstock, would be sixteen on 17 March. His eldest daughter Mary, nineteen years old, had just married young Algernon Capell, second Earl of Essex, whose father had been shut in the Tower after the Rye House Plot against Charles II and had died there. Capell had sided with William III and taken part in the campaign in Ireland.

The other four daughters of Hans Willem Bentinck and Anne Villiers were still children: Anne Margaret, who later married the Dutchman Baron Arend Wassenaer; Frances Wilhelmina, later Lady Byron; Eleonora, called after Hans Willem's favourite sister; and nine-year-old Isabella, who became Duchess of Kingston.

Henry Bentinck went straight from Holland, where he was staying with his tutor, to Paris. He arrived first and went to greet his father at Luzarches near Montmorency. In Paris the Earl of Portland found Mary's former private secretary, d'Allonne, and was also joined by the English poet and diplomat Matthew Prior, who had taken part in the Ryswick congress and became Bentinck's ambassadorial counsellor.

Henry Bentinck's tutor was a Protestant born in Castres, Paul de Rapin-Thoyras. The revocation of the Edict of Nantes had forced him to take refuge in England, then in Holland, before returning to England in William's army with the modest rank of ensign; hard times had compelled him to remain in the army as a lieutenant until he was badly wounded at Limerick during the Irish campaign. Hans Willem Bentinck had discovered Rapin's extensive knowledge of ancient languages, modern literature and mathematics and his exceptional gift for music and decided to put his son in his charge. The young Henry Bentinck therefore received a good formal education, as well as travelling widely on the continent.

Now that Bentinck was English ambassador in Paris, perhaps he might at last have more time to spend with his closest advisers, new friends and his son, or to discuss education with Rapin. Till then he had known nothing but revolution, war, tense negotiations and action, always accompanied by restrictions imposed by parliaments or by the burghers of Amsterdam.

Marshal Boufflers sent a carriage drawn by eight horses to meet the Earl of Portland when he landed at Calais. Louis xiv's marshal seems to have been determined to resume good relations with William's ambassador. Hans Willem had brought over a considerable quantity of baggage in order to carry out his mission with proper style. But the splendid Court costumes for the ambassador and his retinue were held up on the frozen rivers, and even before Portland made his official entry into the capital all sorts of difficulties had accumulated, both domestic and political. The former town house of the dukes of Auvergne had been made available for him, but it turned out to be too small and a state dining-room had to be built onto it. The first contacts with the court were clouded by the presence near Versailles of James ii and his courtiers. If Hans Willem went hunting near Meudon with Monsieur, the King's brother, he was liable to run into English noblemen suspected of having plotted against the life of William iii.

One such was the Duke of Berwick, who early in 1696 had been involved in a plot to assassinate William iii and stage a landing in England. Bentinck let slip a hasty remark after meeting him, to the effect that he hoped he was not supposed to get used to seeing his master's murderers at Versailles, and when Louis xiv heard of the incident he sent Marshal Boufflers to placate him. Boufflers insisted that Louis had William's interests at heart, more so than those of any of his other friends!

Nevertheless Bentinck insisted that the verbal agreement to remove James II made in the orchard at Brukom be carried out. When Boufflers was unable to persuade him of his friendly intentions he was succeeded by Marshal Villeroy, who also tried to soften his heart by talking about Louis XIV's esteem and pity for the dethroned King.

Louis and Portland finally met at Versailles, and Portland declared that the King his master 'could not be tranquil in England while James II remained in his realm, within reach of fostering all the cabals that might be raised in his favour in England: ready to receive all malcontents and to give out that he can hope for all sorts of assistance from Louis XIV'.[4] Louis answered that he knew nothing about the part played by the members of the plot, or by Berwick in particular. He would not agree to evict James II from France.

When Portland informed William of this meeting, the King tried to restore his ambassador's mission to its main objective, the Spanish succession, which was infinitely more important for the future of Europe than the issue of James II, since an invasion of England did not seem imminent.

In the meantime Portland's baggage had arrived and he was able to make his formal entry as ambassador of the King of England. On 9 March he passed through Paris accompanied by an unusually large procession. The crowd massed from the Pont-Neuf to the Place du Palais Royal saw a display of uniforms and dress costumes which caught the imagination even in the capital of the Sun King.

At Versailles William III's envoy made a great impression on the courtiers. There was nothing in his manner to justify some of the stories from London that Bentinck was a dullard. Saint-Simon, so often critical of his contemporaries, described him as 'discreet, secret, polite to others, loyal to his master, shrewd in affairs'. He 'served him [William III] very skilfully'. Saint-Simon reported that: 'Portland appeared with amazing personal brilliance, polish, an air of a man of the world and of the court, gallantry and graceful manners; together with much dignity, even hauteur, but with discernment and prompt judgement, nothing wayward. . . .'[5] Twelve gentlemen of the foremost and wealthiest families of England accompanied the new ambassador, each possessed with his own equipage, horses and retinue.[6]

This was one of the peaks of Portland's career. Once again we learn from Saint-Simon of the magnificence of his ambassadorship. 'His suite was numerous and superb and his outlay magnificent on tables, horses, liveries, equipages, furniture, dress, crockery, and all with exquisite refinement and delicacy.'[7]

William's ambassador now found himself confronted by the problem of the Spanish succession. Whichever of the two rivals – France or Austria – failed to win the prize risked annihilation by the other. And how would their lesser neighbours be affected?

The provinces, European possessions and colonies of Spain, though united under a single monarch, were neither geographically, ethnically nor linguistically cohesive. Spain still ruled the southern Netherlands, part of Italy and most of South America. Yet some of the provinces of the Iberian peninsula itself were claiming their freedom. Aragon mourned its independence, the inhabitants of Biscay did not believe themselves related to Valencia, and Catalonia dreamed of the former county of Barcelona. And what about the Flemings and Sicilians who belonged to the same kingdom? A regrouping seemed inevitable once the feeble links maintained by the last representative of the Spanish Habsburgs were snapped.

In this phase of the rivalry between the house of Austria and the Bourbons the attitude of England and the States of Holland might have tipped the scale. Yet William III did not receive any great support from Parliament. England was tired of wars and revolutions; he was not allowed enough funds to maintain the kind of army needed to stand up against forces which could determine the future of Europe.

Portland soon had the opportunity to discuss the object of his mission with two of Louis's greatest ministers and diplomats, Pomponne and his son-in-law Torcy, Colbert's nephew, who came to see Portland less than a week after his dazzling entry into

Versailles. According to them the King wanted nothing more than to achieve a good understanding with William, for the good of Europe and the preservation of peace. But there was reason to fear that war would resume when the Spanish throne fell vacant. If the King of Spain died 'before proper measures had been taken to prevent the troubles that his death would provoke, it would be very hard for peace to be preserved'. They added that the King was glad to raise the matter with Portland rather than anyone else, 'not only because of the trust which the King his master had in him, but also for the satisfaction which his conduct was causing His Majesty'.[8]

To allay the jealousy of the English Louis XIV would prevent Spain and France being united under the same crown. But Portland had to realize that Louis's own jealousy was 'very legitimate and well founded, because of the steps the Emperor of Austria was taking to assure himself of the succession of Spain'. If the lands of the Spanish crown were one day to be joined with those of the Emperor, Europe would see a rebirth of the fearsome imperial power of the reign of Charles V.

Portland foresaw that William III would not be able to decide England's line on his own. Parliament would undoubtedly prefer the inheritance to go to the family of the Emperor, who could not possibly become a maritime rival of England.

Since neither side would yield, Portland brought up a third alternative based on an old will made by Philip IV of Spain. The father of the sickly King Charles II of Spain had named as his son's successor the son of the Prince Elector of Bavaria, whose grandmother was the Infanta Margaret, a sister of Louis XIV's wife. The diplomats' skills clashed. Before Portland had stopped talking about this solution the ministers argued that a will could not 'change the fundamental laws of a realm'. They recalled the last wishes of Henry VIII of England, which had not prevented his son and then his two daughters from succeeding him; similarly, on the death of Isabella of Castile, the crown had gone to her daughter.

France was, however, prepared to commit herself not to touch the Barrier – the belt of strongholds which protected Dutch independence – between the United Provinces and France.

In concluding his report to Louis XIV Torcy stressed that the invalidity of Philip IV's will had been pointed out to Portland and that in any case he had mentioned the will on his own initiative, without instructions from William III.

In a long letter to the Marquis d'Harcourt, the French ambassador in Madrid, on 17 April, the King of France displayed his astonishment: '. . . the Earl of Portland then added that he had no other instructions from his master than to express his desire to contribute to the maintenance of the peace [and] that in his personal opinion it was in the interest of the whole of Europe that the Spanish succession should not be garnered by one of my grandsons.'[9]

Despite all the precautions that might be taken to place this grandson in the hands of the Spaniards, Portland felt that they would never be enough to eradicate his national feelings and the influence of his early upbringing, and that other nations would still fear the unification of the two crowns, which could then lay down the law to the rest of Europe.

Since Portland's arguments in favour of the son of the Prince Elector of Bavaria had made their point, everything now depended for the English on the sincerity of the King of France. In an audience at Versailles, Louis XIV assured the ambassador of his intention to make the peace a lasting one. Why else would he have returned the famous fortresses of the Barrier, 'twenty of the greatest strongholds in Europe'? It was 'strong enough proof to convince the whole world'.[10] If William III would work with him they could 'together make law for the rest of the world'.[11]

Ever since his first audience with Louis XIV Portland had felt certain doubts about his good faith. He expressed his distrust only with the greatest caution, writing to London that if the King's attitude towards him was feigned it was a wonderfully clever performance.[12] The King of France too soon formed his own impression of the diplomatic game played by William's representative. He wrote to Tallard, his minister in London:

'Portland seeks only to discern my thoughts and to hide his master's!'[13]

Yet it was impossible for Portland to know how the King of France hoped to settle the Spanish succession for he did not confide in anybody in his own realm – not even Pomponne or Torcy, nor Harcourt in Madrid, nor Tallard, who had orders to behave in the same way at William III's court in Kensington as Portland was assumed to be doing at Versailles and to try to unearth the intentions of the English.

Portland felt that he had done everything in his power to reconcile the viewpoints of the two realms in the matter of the Spanish succession. On 20 April he attended the King's *levée* at Versailles and was received in audience. As he was talking about the interests of England and Holland, Louis XIV told him 'that he understood that there must be agreement and that treaties must be arranged.' The ambassador struck a note of realism when he replied 'that in addition to treaties it was only prudent to ask for what would give greater assurance to future times than pieces of paper; that there were places in the Indies as well as in the Mediterranean which met the needs of the English and the Dutch, which might serve that purpose.' Louis XIV indicated that since these nations had nothing to offer in exchange they had nothing to claim by right but that he would listen to William III's reply and requests. 'After this overture,' the King concluded, 'we shall see whether the Earl of Portland offers some proposal from the King, his master, and since I am ready to stand by what I have told him it is up to the King of England to explain himself.'[14]

So Hans Willem Bentinck had laid the basis of a rapprochement between France, England and Holland. His proposal was to offer the crown of Spain to the son of the Elector of Bavaria after the death of Charles II of Spain, for he so hoped to bring maritime power for England and peace behind solid borders for Holland. It was now for the French ambassador in London to take things further.

At the end of the audience Portland asked the King's permission to return to England, now that his representative Tallard was with

William III and could advance or conclude what they had begun. Portland's mission to Versailles was practically over. Before he could leave though he had to wait for the appointment and arrival of a permanent ambassador to the French court. William III summoned Edward Villiers, Marquis of Jersey, the brother of Elizabeth Villiers, now Countess of Orkney, and Bentinck's brother-in-law. During these last weeks Louis XIV went out of his way to show his favour to Portland, who had the unusual privilege of being personally shown round some of the King's parks and pavilions. The King even apologized for not being able to turn on the fountains because the cold had frozen the pipes. One night the Earl of Portland was chosen to carry the King's candlestick at his *couchée*, a signal honour.

When the ambassador left France, after taking leave of innumerable noblemen and ministers, Louis XIV arranged his itinerary personally. Several fortified towns on the Atlantic coast were instructed to open their gates to him, and he was received with salutes of guns.

Before leaving the ambassador had sat for the fashionable portraitist Hyacinthe Rigaud. His lively portrait depicts Portland wearing a cuirasse and sash and holding a commander-in-chief's baton, a very different style from Kneller's, which shows him in his most sumptuous ambassadorial finery, dressed from top to toe in silk and ermine. Louis XIV had also presented Portland with his own portrait, which was worth a small fortune, being encrusted with real diamonds.

Portland returned from Paris convinced that Europe could not be saved from war and devastation without a reasonable settlement of the Spanish succession and then only if Louis XIV genuinely accepted a compromise. Lord Somers, the Lord Chancellor, shared his doubts. He wrote to Shrewsbury: 'Bentinck has not been able to bring us proof of the sincerity of Louis XIV.'

In accordance with Louis XIV's suggestion, William III had discussed the plan for the partition treaty with the French ambassador Tallard. He was certainly convinced of William's sincerity but thought that he was too weak to sustain a war.

In August the King of England left for Holland, taking Bentinck with him. In autumn the plan to make the eldest son of the Elector of Bavaria, Joseph Ferdinand, heir to the Spanish crown was passed to Somers, who sealed it and sent it on to Holland. France was to receive Naples, Sicily and Biscay; Holland's integrity would be guaranteed by the Barrier of fortress towns in present-day Belgium; the Empire was to be master of the Milanese. The treaty was signed at Het Loo on 4 September 1698 by the English ambassador at The Hague and by Portland, in the name of William III, by Heinsius and seven commissioners for the United Provinces and by Tallard for France, who needed to revitalize her armies and her finances after the long war that preceded the peace of Ryswick.

9 • *Successions and Treaties*

U NTIL NOW Bentinck's missions over several decades had been crowned with success. He had persuaded the Prince Electors to stand by Holland during the campaigns in England and Ireland; had heralded the arrival of William III of Orange in Whitehall as pretender to the hand of Mary Stuart; and ten years later had discussed with Danby the plans to restore the liberty of the English Parliament.

Portland's resplendent embassy in Paris was not totally successful however. Louis XIV had treated him very graciously, but Madame de Maintenon, whose political influence, although perhaps exaggerated, was considerable, had not received him. Thanks to her, James II and his wife Mary of Modena remained at Versailles with a host of enemies of William III.

Uncertainty continued about the opinion of the King of France on the Spanish succession. Louis XIV had always realized what trouble would ensue if his grandson were to inherit all the territories of the Spanish crown. He had no doubt that the envious princes would have wasted no time in forming 'a new league, even stronger than the last, to oppose my ends'.[1] He concluded the partition treaty so as to mollify the former allies but at the same time instructed his minister in Madrid to 'foster the sentiments of the well intentioned and not to give them grounds for believing in the dismemberment of their monarchy for fear that they should have recourse to the Emperor.'

Portland was extremely apprehensive about the outcome of the drama, although Louis's minister Torcy still believed in the possibility of sharing out the Spanish possessions to keep a balance of power. Fear still prevailed on both sides, and it was a bad counsellor. Portland's position began to suffer when he returned to London, particularly because courtiers more ingratiating than he was had taken advantage of his absence and had begun to sap his personal relationship with the King.

Since his arrival in England on the accession of William and Mary, Hans Willem Bentinck had never submitted to the demands of court life in England, with its refined language and elaborate manners. William III had now found youth, flexibility and an agile mind in the person of Joost van Keppel, who was twenty years his junior and had come to court at the time of the coronation in 1689, at an age when character is still malleable. Keppel's origins were uncertain, in spite of his claims to noble descent, and he lacked the Bentinck stamp.

Van Keppel, whom opportunist courtiers saw as a rising star, excelled in relieving the King of minor worries and in judging when he wanted entertainment or to be left on his own; he never compromised himself. Efforts were made in vain to find some reasonably important diplomatic or administrative post in which Keppel could be of service.

There now arose intrigues to cut Portland off from the court and the King. Elizabeth Orkney, the resentful sister of Anne Villiers Bentinck, who had not forgiven Hans Willem for marrying her younger sister and neglecting herself, was said to have been intimately involved. She could not have adopted a more effective tactic than putting her feminine guile at Keppel's disposal. William III had neglected Princess Mary for Elizabeth, and it is she who is supposed to have encouraged the King to grant Keppel letters patent in February 1696, creating him Baron Ashford, Viscount St Edmondsbury and Earl of Albemarle.

Ever since his childhood Portland had found himself required to sacrifice all his private life to his undeniably valuable work for the Prince of Orange. He showed no jealousy when the Earl of Sunderland or Lord Somers reached those high positions in the realm which his foreign origins prevented him from claiming, and in fact he gave them his support for their usefulness to William III.

On the other hand Portland was not prepared to play second fiddle to a flatterer such as Keppel. His relationship with William III deteriorated; he began to show signs of depression, and considered retiring, realizing that he had lost his close position with William which enabled him to act as the King's link with the outside world. He decided not to become involved in jockeying for William's favour and withdrew from the court making himself available only for the task he had undertaken with the French ambassador Tallard: to help his King to bear the crushing responsibilities that would follow the death of the King of Spain – a burden likely to influence the whole future of Europe.

Just as the continental nations were anxiously awaiting the end of the Spanish dynasty and England seemed indifferent, another death intervened. On the night of 5 February 1699 smallpox struck down the son of the Elector of Bavaria, the boy on whom Portland had pinned his hopes as a claimant to the Spanish crown. Louis XIV did not doubt that the death was natural. Straight away he sent couriers to his ambassadors in Madrid and London, the latter 'to learn from the King of England what measures he judges necessary for a new partition and to assure the tranquillity of Europe upon the death of the King of Spain, settled though it seemed to be by the treaty of The Hague.' Louis added: 'I have reason to believe that he will enter with good faith into all those measures most suitable for the maintenance of peace.'[2]

Faithful to his promise to continue what he had begun, Portland did not abandon William III in this new emergency which had made the partition treaty a dead letter. After the Parliamentary sitting of 1699 the King withdrew to Het Loo to work out a new

E

arrangement, and Bentinck went to The Hague, where he took charge of liaison between Grand Pensionary Heinsius and Louis xiv's envoy Tallard. He also examined with the Emperor's representative the dilemma created by a secret clause of the Grand Alliance of 1689 in which William iii had committed himself to supporting the Empire if France tried to unite the realms of Spain and France under a single crown.

In the meantime the English Parliament had overriden the pleas of William iii and cut the army to 7,000 men, the navy to 10,000 seamen and 3,000 marines sending away William's own Dutch Blue Guards as well. If no agreement were reached with Louis xiv, France would expand her territories and would probably occupy Holland. William iii wanted to avoid this at all costs, hence his concessions, transmitted by Portland, which went so far as to cede the Milanese to the French. Both the King of England and his adviser were placed in a painful position by the wavering of Emperor Leopold and the angry reaction of Parliament when it learned that William had signed the treaty of partition, in the interest of Holland and to the detriment of his own kingdom, as the English thought.

When the new partition settlement was ready, William submitted it to three members of Parliament: Somers, Halifax and Vernon. After some hesitation they agreed to it. Lord Jersey put his signature to it beside that of his brother-in-law Portland.[3] Jersey had been replaced quite quickly as ambassador to Paris by Lord Manchester and was now Secretary of State in London. Tallard and Briord signed for France, one deputy for each of the United Provinces.

The second partition treaty was first signed in London on 21 February 1700 and then at The Hague on 25 March. From then onwards the situation could no longer be altered by William. The Emperor had not signed, but he had reason to hope that the Spanish crown would not fall to France.

What would become now of William's and Portland's efforts for a tolerant, peaceful Europe? Was it possible to create a new policy giving each state the right to live in independence? Could

France be reconciled at last with the House of Austria, as the neighbour of a Spain ruled by the Emperor's younger son? And what about the role of Holland and England? Could Holland remain open to communications among the countries of the far north of old Lotharingia, developing its geographic destiny as it had since the time of the first Bentinck knights, while England's naval power spread its trade to the West and East Indies?

Despite all William's efforts the Emperor delayed signing, although the new treaty gave his second son, Archduke Charles, the whole share previously intended for the unfortunate son of the Prince Elector of Bavaria. In fact Leopold hoped for a will that would give him the whole inheritance, including those Spanish possessions in Italy which according to the treaty were to go to the Dauphin of France. The Dauphin would also receive Biscay and was only to give up the Milanese in return for Lorraine. The solution offered by the treaty was infinitely less dangerous for the peace of Europe than the unification of the crowns of Spain and France or Spain and Austria, which would have constituted the greater part of Europe and Latin America.

Spain was anxious to retain the integrity of all its territories, from the Peninsula to America. To that end the sick King, faithful to the policy of his father Philip IV, opted for his presumptive successor belonging to the Empire. A powerful domestic party preferred the grandson of Louis XIV. A struggle ensued around the bed and within the mind of the dying man.

Portland did not yet foresee the repercussions for himself that would result from royal and Parliamentary decisions and from the lottery of births, marriages, deaths and intrigues on which the fate of nations depended. But there was one family which had remained loyal to him ever since the future of the English Parliament had been discussed on the Bentinck estate at Sorgvliet – that of Sir William and Lady Temple. Temple himself had not accepted any office after William's coronation, although he had been offered the Chief Secretaryship. He had retired first to Sheen, then to Moor Park, about twenty miles north-east of London. There he created a famous garden with the assistance of the

Countess of Bedford's gardener and wrote his *Essay upon the origin
and nature of government*. His view was that power should be based
upon a patriarchal, tolerant principle. Temple had been a widower
since 1695, but his sister Lady Gifford always remained with him,
and it was she who reported on Portland's activities to her niece,
the daughter of John Temple and widow of Baron John Berkeley
of Stratton.

Portland had known Lady Berkeley for many years and had
been a widower for twelve years. In her he was to find a source of
advice and solicitude for the rest of his life and a loving mother for
their children.

The vicar of Mortlake officiated at the wedding at Chiswick
of Hans Willem Bentinck and Jane Martha Temple Berkeley
on 12 May 1700. From then on the couple divided their time
between the house in Whitehall Gardens and Portland's estate
at Bulstrode, near Beaconsfield in Buckinghamshire. Whitehall
Palace had been destroyed by fire in 1691, but the houses in the
gardens were still standing. Hans Willem no longer had a house
at Windsor, and the King spent most of his time in England at
Kensington. Portland had acquired Bulstrode when Judge
Jeffreys left it for the Tower of London, where he died in
1689, still expiating his cruelty towards Monmouth's supporters
and his high-handed behaviour as Lord Chancellor under James II.

The honeymoon at Bulstrode was quickly overshadowed by the
press of events. On 25 July the Duke of Gloucester died suddenly
and unexpectedly at the age of eleven. As William's nephew and
the son of Princess Anne he had been the living guarantee that the
dynasty would continue when his mother died. Anne's sixteen
other children had all died young. The King had been very fond
of Mary's nephew and was heartbroken by his death.[4] Parliament
had grown used to the idea that the Stuart succession would pass
to the young Duke, James II's Protestant grandson. Now these
hopes were dashed, and with them went much of the King's
standing with Parliament – for his dynasty would now die with
him.

The Bill of Rights had been vague about the reciprocal powers and prerogatives of King and Parliament, and this made Parliament all the more anxious to assert its rights, if not always its responsibilities. At this time it was often more concerned with making its voice heard than with the consequences of the decisions involved. Unwilling or unable to attack the King directly, it struck out at his best advisers, of whom Portland was one. Many members of Parliament had always considered him as a foreigner who would not adjust to the laws and customs of the country. Others accused the English members of the King's Privy Council of not respecting them. Strife between King and Parliament was accentuated by the imminent vacancy of the Spanish succession.

At one point the Marquis d'Harcourt, the French representative in Madrid, had seen the partition treaty as offering advantages by removing Spain and its possessions from the House of Austria and adding Naples and Sicily to the crown of France. The combined power of France, England and Holland would be enough to counterbalance the dissatisfaction of Austria and Spain. But there was still a risk that Charles II would draw up a will in favour of Austria. A party headed by Cardinal Portocarrero was already working on behalf of a grandson of Louis XIV.

At the beginning of June King Charles II of Spain had been outraged to learn of the second partition treaty, for which he held the Dutch and English responsible. His annoyance unsettled his previous decision, and he began a new inquiry into the best means of preserving the integrity of the Spanish territories, finally despatching an envoy to the eighty-five-year-old Pope Innocent XII. The Pope's supposed reply in favour of Louis XIV's grandson has now been established as a forgery executed two years after his death.[5]

On the French side Louis XIV was less militant than his ambassador in Madrid, who was now advising him to put pressure on the Queen of Spain to persuade her husband to leave everything to the Duke of Anjou. Knowing Charles II's reverence for his father's memory, Louis XIV confined himself to instructing his ambassador to remain on good terms with the Queen.

It was Portocarrero who took the decisive step. He went to see the dying King on his sickbed and told him that his father Philip IV had made Louis XIV's Spanish wife renounce her rights to the succession as a precaution against the other powers, not because he wanted to infringe on her blood rights. Now there was no reason to prefer the descendant of her sister, Archduke Charles of Austria, as the second treaty of partition provided. On 3 October 1700 the fading monarch appended his signature to the document prepared by Portocarrero, and on 1 November, after a short lull in the course of his illness, the last of the Spanish Habsburgs died.

Two weeks after the death of Charles II, Louis XIV received the Spanish ambassador at Fontainebleau, where the Court was in residence, summoned his grandson the Duke of Anjou, and told the diplomat: 'This is the king whom Spain demands.' Then Torcy, who two years previously had discussed the terms of the partition treaty with Portland, opened the doors. The King told Nicolas de Sainctot, his master of ceremonies, to bring everyone inside, and announced: 'Acknowledge the Duke of Anjou as King of Spain.'[6]

The first official act of the seventeen-year-old King Philip V of Spain was to appoint Portocarrero his prime minister. Harcourt became a duke, his marquisate being elevated into a hereditary duchy, and Louis XIV, who addressed him from then on as 'My cousin', wrote: 'The important services which you have rendered to me deserved the splendid reward which you have just received.'[7]

In his instructions to his grandson when he left to mount the Spanish throne a fortnight later, Louis commended him to: '. . . Live in a great union with France, since there is nothing so good for our two powers as this union, which none will be able to resist. . . . Take care to establish your troops everywhere, and start with Flanders. . . .'

A few days before the death of Charles II Torcy, who had helped to negotiate the partition treaty and was the author of some of its articles, was still so ignorant of Louis XIV's intentions that he spoke to him in favour of partition. He performed an about-turn after the session of the High Council of Madrid on 10 November and became a supporter of the blood rights recognized by Charles II's will. But he felt that he had been duped and wrote to Portland on 7 November: 'What gives me the greatest chagrin [is] that most people here think it more advantageous for the interests of England that France should keep to the will.'[8]

The English Parliament had prevented the King from keeping an army on stand-by for any eventuality. When the spring session finally assembled in 1701, William III was obliged to justify his foreign policy before a Parliament which included various new Tory ministers strongly opposed to the royal prerogatives and eager to extend their powers at the monarchy's expense. The two Houses had hitherto tended to follow the Crown's directives, though the King had to show that the goals he pursued were in harmony with British interests. Nothing could be taken for granted, and the King had to earn, not to command, the thanks of the two Houses for his speech from the throne.

To illuminate his foreign policy the King displayed various documents and treaties. When Parliament saw the signatures of Portland and Jersey at the bottom of the partition treaty they paid no attention to the signature of Louis XIV's envoy Tallard, which ought to have made them ask themselves which side had broken its commitments. They thought that the treaty had only served to arouse the anger of Spain, which was now in a position to harm British commerce. By concentrating on the names of Portland and his brother-in-law Jersey they were striking at the King's authority in foreign policy. They immediately began impeachment proceedings against Bentinck, who was accused of not having submitted the project even to the Privy Council and held Portland responsible for all the misfortunes which already threatened Europe and which he had done his best to avert. Portland never gave a thought to defending himself by shifting the blame onto the failure of Louis XIV and his ministers to stand by their promises.

The King recognized the gravity of the situation, and without replying to either party he tried to recall the Commons to their patriotic duty. Two weeks later he declared that to remain without security and dependent solely upon the good will of France would be the worst of all evils:

You have deemed the partition treaty hurtful to Europe because it gives so much territory to Spain and France, yet you yourselves do not care that that power may take all. You leave the Dutch defenceless while the French are already on their threshold, until it should be too late to come to their aid. Thus you act contrary to the treaties, inimically to the Allies, contrary to the honour of the English, without regard either for the security of the country or for the Protestant religion.

After that speech it seemed unlikely that Portland and the accused Lords would be condemned. Yet the Tory party tried to delay the verdict until the dissolution of Parliament. Nothing would quench the quarrel – neither the necessity for rapid action to reinforce the alliance with the Empire, nor the need to maintain the peace of England and the liberty of Europe and so to reduce the exorbitant power of France. The Whig majority in the House of Lords assembled before the dissolution despite Tory protestations and acquitted Somers, Orford, Halifax and Vernon. They forgot Portland, who was therefore never formally acquitted or condemned. Readers may judge him for themselves.

When Louis XIV heard that Portland had been put on trial for signing the partition treaty he felt sure that he ran no risk from the English Parliament, without whose authorization William III could not make war. By the same token he thought that he was immune to attack from the Emperor, who though deprived of the Spanish realms for his descendants could not attack on his own. In the autumn Bentinck stayed with William in Holland for the last time – they had been drawn together again by their common dilemma. The King was already suffering from the illness which eventually killed him. They had heard that Louis XIV's generals were occupying the so-called Barrier towns which should have been protecting Holland. Furthermore, on the death of James II in 1701, Louis XIV had recognized the Pretender, the dubious son of the last of the Stuart kings, as King of England.

In the next spring, in March 1702, three successive couriers brought news of the King to Bentinck in his retirement at

Bulstrode, where he was redesigning his estate. The third messenger persuaded him to go straight to Kensington. When he arrived William could no longer speak, but he placed his friend's hand on his heart, which had never ceased beating for the cause of truth and liberty.

What now remained of the achievement of Hans Willem Bentinck? Two historic statements sum up his career. The first Bentinck made after landing in England in 1688: 'Everything will have to be examined by a Parliament.' The second was made by Louis XIV: 'The Earl of Portland then added that in his personal opinion it was in the interest of the whole of Europe that the Spanish succession should not be garnered by a grandson of mine.' Bentinck's wisdom was justified by the terrible war of the Spanish Succession that broke out in 1702, the year of William's death. Louis XIV was faced with a coalition of England, Holland and the Empire.

A twelve-year holocaust exhausted France and the Netherlands, the theatre of the war. The consequences for France were disastrous. By the peace treaty signed at Utrecht, England received possessions and commercial privileges in the Mediterranean and overseas far in excess of anything envisaged by Portland during his embassy to Louis XIV at Versailles: Gibraltar, the gateway to the Mediterranean, and Minorca remained with the British, and they also gained Newfoundland and Acadia, the entrance to the St Lawrence and to Canada. The port of Dunkirk, a thorn in the side of the Dutch and English, was closed. Spain lost Sicily to the Duke of Savoy and had to cede the kingdom of Naples, the Milanese, Sardinia and the Belgian Netherlands.

During the reign of William III's successor, Queen Anne, Hans Willem no longer held advisory or administrative posts under the crown. In any case it is hardly likely that these would have been available to him, since Marlborough was placing his closest supporters in the seats of power. He even lost his position as superintendent of the royal gardens to a supporter of Marlborough.

Yet William's intimate adviser did undertake several more

diplomatic missions. In July 1704 he went to The Hague to discuss Portuguese affairs with the States General. Just as he had earlier involved himself in the fate of the Protestants in Orange, Portland also negotiated with the States General about assistance to be given to the inhabitants of those regions, known as the Camisards, who had been persecuted for their religion since the revocation of the Edict of Nantes.

After his return to England Portland was gladdened by the birth of a son, Willem, on 6 November 1704 at Whitehall. His only surviving son by his first marriage to Anne Villiers was Henry, Viscount Woodstock, who was to inherit all his titles and estates in England. Portland now had an heir for his estates in Holland, in particular Sorgvliet and the seigneury of Rhoon and Pendrecht, near Delft. Jane Martha inscribed the names of Willem Bentinck's godparents in the family Bible; they were her brother Temple, Baron Torck von Rosendael and her aunt Gifford, William Temple's sister.

The last of the children born at Whitehall was Harriet, on 12 December 1705. The two youngest were born at Bulstrode – Charles John in 1708 and Barbara in 1709, who was hardly a month old when her father died. In the year of Charles John's birth the Portlands were delighted to receive a visit from Queen Anne at Bulstrode.

The names of the godfathers and godmothers reveal the close relations Hans Willem and Jane Martha maintained with their families in both Holland and England. The godmother of Martha Jane's first child was Hans Willem's beloved sister Eleonora, who left Nijhuisen not to her god-daughter Sophia Bentinck, who remained in England, but to her nephew Charles John Bentinck. Charles John's godfather was an elder brother of Hans Willem, the lord of the old Bentinck estate of Schoonheten, now the home of Baron Rolf Bentinck, one of his very distinguished descendants. Harriet's godmother was one of Hans Willem's younger sisters, Agnes Bentinck, canoness of Almelo. Martha Jane's Bible also contains the names of a Baroness Borre van Amerongen, lady of Sandenburg, the godmother of Elizabeth Bentinck, in addition to the Countess's brother- and sister-in-law, Berkeley of Stratton, her father John Temple and his sister Lady Gifford, widow of Sir Thomas Gifford, and his other sister Lady Dixwell. Harriet Bentinck was the god-daughter of Lord Scarborough; Charles John the godson of Lady Cullum.

One topic of conversation between the Earl and Countess of Portland and their friends the Cullums was the upkeep and improvement of gardens. Garden design had always fascinated Hans Willem, whether at Sorgvliet, at Windsor and Kensington, where he was in charge of the royal gardens, at Versailles, where Louis XIV had acted as his personal guide, or at Bulstrode. The Countess's nephew Sir Dudley Cullum cultivated orange-trees and exotic plants in his vast greenhouses at Hawsted. At Bulstrode Portland tried to break up the monotony by introducing curved lines, and at the end of the tree-lined avenue he dug a long pond known as the Long Water in the form of a canal, to remind himself of Holland. These alterations made the grounds more comfortable and less solemn; they were carried out with the help of Henry Wise, who had previously worked under him on the royal gardens.

Portland also did a great deal of good in the area around Bulstrode. Gerards Cross received its first school thanks to his donations, and when it opened it provided education for twenty boys and sixteen girls, who were also clothed at his own expense. He paid £20 a year each to the schoolmaster and mistress.[9]

To the end of his life, Portland continued to pay regular visits to Holland, where he maintained friendly relations with the States General. He always stayed faithful to the idea of the Grand Alliance of England, Holland and the Empire and became an ardent supporter of the Hanoverian succession to the English throne of the family of Hanover after the death of Queen Anne.

In October 1708 the Earl of Portland returned from Holland with plenipotentiaries from Denmark and the Republic of Genoa. The Duke of Marlborough consulted him about Dutch affairs. In 1709 he crossed the Channel with Marlborough for the last time. Hans Willem's strong constitution had finally been undermined by the years of exertion in the service of his Prince and King on behalf of Europe, the independence of his native land and the liberty of his adopted country. The days were gone when he could bear up to a stormy Channel crossing and dangerous ice floes to ride beneath the triumphal arches from Sorgvliet to The Hague.

In mid-November Hans Willem was surprised by the cold in the draughty halls of Bulstrode and took to his bed. He died on 23 November of pleurisy, at the age of sixty. A modest ceremony at Whitehall was attended by all the family, and his remains were laid to rest at Westminster.

10 ✦ Willem Bentinck's Plan Makes the Stadtholderate Hereditary

⁘

THE COUNTESS OF PORTLAND remained at Whitehall Gardens with two of the daughters of Hans Willem's first marriage and the six children of her own, four of the children of her husband's first marriage having already married. In 1701 Anne Margaret had married a Dutch baron, Arend Wassenaer, lord of Duivenvoorde. He came to London in 1714 as envoy extraordinary of the States General to the English Court and remained accredited to George I until 1716. Mary's husband was Algernon Capell, second Earl of Essex. He belonged to a family long dogged by misfortune, since his grandfather Arthur Capell had been executed as a royalist in 1649 and his father, who became first Earl of Essex on the Restoration, died in the Tower after the Rye House Plot, although innocent of any involvement. After Algernon's death Mary, Hans Willem's favourite daughter, married Sir Conyers d'Arcy, a member of Parliament and officer of the Horseguards under Queen Anne and then George I.

Frances Wilhelmina, the third daughter of Hans Willem Bentinck's first marriage, had married William, the fourth Lord Byron, late in 1706. They had three sons and a daughter, all of whom died single. Frances died in 1712 at the age of twenty-eight. Lord Byron was a gentleman of the wardrobe to Prince George of

Denmark, the consort of Queen Anne of England. His third wife was a half-sister of Frances Bentinck, the daughter of Jane Martha. Their son William, the fifth Lord Byron, killed Lord Chatsworth in an obscure quarrel in a gentlemen's club in Nottingham and lived in seclusion at Newstead Abbey, where he beat his wife. He left his title and fortune to his grand-nephew, the poet Byron, the grandson of his brother Vice-Admiral John Byron.[1]

Isabella Bentinck, born at The Hague not long before her mother's fatal illness, married Evelyn Pierrepont, one of the commissioners for the union of Scotland and England, in 1706. George I appointed Pierrepont to the Privy Council in the same year and raised him to the title of Duke of Kingston-upon-Hull the year after. His political principles were very much in line with those of the Bentinck family, and in a memorable speech to Parliament in 1716 he asserted that it was the role of that assembly 'to rectify old laws as well as to make new ones'.

Constantine Netscher painted charming portraits of the daughters of Hans Willem Bentinck. Lady Mary, Countess of Essex, is seen against a background of great masses of majestic trees in a park, with a vista across a little bay overlooked by a hill. She has the air of a distant princess, with dreaming eyes under a high forehead. Isabella is portrayed with her hair in artful curls, one lock falling to her neck, holding a few flowers at the low-cut neckline of her silk dress; she has a clever face and a malicious mouth.

Henry Bentinck, Lord Woodstock, second Earl of Portland, the ancestor of all the dukes of Portland and Cavendish-Bentincks down to the present day was raised by George I to the title of Duke of Portland and Marquis of Titchfield in 1716, partly in recognition of Hans Willem's support for his succession. While his father was still alive he married Lady Elizabeth Noel, daughter of the second Earl of Gainsborough and Catherine Greville. In 1722 he was appointed Governor of Jamaica. The new governor's wife did not find Jamaica as pleasant a place to live as London, and both of them cast envious eyes on the lush Barbados, though she found 'the beef & mutton as good as in sweet dear England, & I think their poultry is much better. . . .' In a letter to her mother-in-law, Jane Martha, dated 26 December 1722, the Duchess wrote that the great heat had made her forget that it was Christmas and wished her many more New Years, with all the satisfactions the world could offer. She also wished 'that you may never be obliged to leave your own country'.

In Jamaica the Duke of Portland applied himself to taxation and the organization of labour, chiefly for the sugar, indigo and cocoa crops, which were the main resources of the island. In 1725 he corresponded with Parliament about the Deficiency Bill.[2] Noting that certain privileges had been re-established, whereas the previous system had suppressed the legislative assembly and imposed swingeing taxes, he obtained a compromise whereby Jamaica paid a fixed revenue to the Crown while any further taxation had to be submitted to the local legislative assembly. The law was passed in 1728, after the Duke's death. In his leisure moments he made notes on the natural history of Jamaica.[3]

Portland never saw his beloved England again nor his children. He died in 1726 at the age of forty-four, a victim of the tropical climate, leaving his titles and the estate at Bulstrode to his son William. His younger son George became a colonel of foot, two of his daughters married in England, and the third married a Baron Wassenaer, as her aunt had done.

When Duke Henry died his son William was seventeen and George ten. They had stayed behind in London with their grandmother, Jane Martha, who still had her own daughters living with her. Her two sons had been in Holland for four years with their tutor and teachers. The vigorous dowager now applied her remarkable mind to bringing up her daughters and grandchildren and maintained a ceaseless flow of correspondence with her sons in Holland and other European countries. All this was in addition to her activities as governess of the four daughters of the Prince of Wales, the future George II, a post she had received in 1718. This position was by no means merely nominal. She played a most effective part in their moral and intellectual education for many years and laid down a fixed daily timetable for them.

The painter Philipp has left us a picture of royal domesticity. At a tea party in the Countess of Portland's drawing-room, Jane Martha sits in the middle, with Handel, the court composer, seated at the harpsichord – a charming scene which looks forward to the grace of the eighteenth century.

On the Prince of Wales' accession to the throne in 1720, his daughters continued to keep in touch with the Countess of Portland and other members of the Bentinck family. Thus in that same year Amelia, the eldest of the princesses, wrote to the Countess expressing her pleasure at renewing her acquaintance with one of her younger daughters, Henrietta Bentinck, who had recently married James Hamilton, Viscount Limerick, Earl of Clanbrassil: '. . . She will have seen by her reception the sincerity of my friendship for her. She was presented to papa & mama this morning where I assure you she made a great show.'⁴ In her letters she also mentions hunting, a meeting with the Duchess of Kingston, and especially music. On 11 October 1729 Amelia wrote to the Countess that the previous day she had twice heard the new singer, Strada, whose voice was better than all her predecessors, and 'mighty good & easie'.

In 1724 the Countess called in a Swiss tutor, John Achard, for her two grandsons, William and George, the sons of Henry, Duke of Portland, then aged fifteen and nine respectively. On 21 December 1724 the Duchess of Portland had written to Achard from Jamaica, informing him that they had learned of his appointment from 'My Lady Portland' and that they were very pleased with her account of him. The Duchess expected him to do everything in his power to convince them of his reputation, by preparing her sons to become a solace to them and an honour to himself.⁵

In spite of all the titles he inherited and the decorations bestowed upon him, William Bentinck, who became second Duke of Portland on his father's death in 1726, never became a figure of the first rank, though his wife played an important part in cultural and artistic life. She was born Margaret Cavendish Harley, only daughter of Edward Harley, second Earl of Oxford, and of Lady Henrietta Cavendish Holles, herself the daughter and heiress of the Duke of Newcastle. William took a great interest in the politics of the Netherlands, and we shall encounter him again alongside Willem Bentinck in the mid-eighteenth century. George Bentinck, the younger of John Achard's pupils, became a colonel of foot in England and died young, in 1759, without issue.

Hans Willem Bentinck left all his English property, with the exception of Terrington, to the sons of his first marriage and his Dutch seigneuries to Willem, the elder son of his second, his younger son Charles inheriting the estate of his aunt Eleonora van Ittersum. Jane Martha bravely cut herself off from her sons Willem and Charles when they were old enough to be entrusted to a tutor, Count Johan Hendrik van Wassenaer-Obdam, at The Hague, and to a guardian, Willem Carries. When they left their mother in June 1719, Willem was fourteen and Charles only eleven. The separation was hard, and Willem Bentinck missed his native country for a long time. As late as 1727 he wrote to his mother: 'The thought of passing the rest of my life in Holland, upon any condition whatsoever, always makes me melancholy and presents itself to me in a disagreeable view. Whereas the false and deluding hopes of returning to England always please and divert me.'[6] He would prefer a situation in England to a better one in Holland.

Willem Bentinck never failed in his devotion to his mother or his work as a student. When Lady Portland reproached him for not writing, he hastened to reassure her. Even if he were sometimes unable to hide how much he missed her, he never gave her grounds for complaining of his actions.[7] Willem lived on the fine estate at Sorgvliet where his father used to receive the Prince of Orange and where the preparations for the march on London had been discussed. Though the comings and goings to The Hague seemed to him desperately dull his studies at Leyden soon filled the void in his adolescent existence.

Boerhaave was still teaching anatomy at Leyden when Willem Bentinck came to Holland. The school had been famous for philosophy, with students such as Guez de Balzac, Théophile de Viau and René Descartes. Behind the university, near the canal, the Frenchman de Lecluse had founded a botanical garden intended for the study of medicinal plants. Later on, greenhouses were built for exotic plants. An observatory in the complex of university buildings dates from 1632.[8] The famous physicist s'Gravesande became Willem Bentinck's teacher, and he made rapid progress in algebra, a discipline which stopped seeming disagreeable as soon as his teacher showed him its uses. Once a week s'Gravesande visited the Bentincks, and once a week his pupil came to Leyden. Between his courses he also did a great deal of private work and could never be accused of being idle.[9] Although he was interested in the natural sciences, Willem did not neglect history and literature. He wrote to his mother that he had read Humphrey Prideaux, the author of an excellent book on the antique marbles in the Arundel collection at Oxford, with great and unexpected pleasure.

As well as his studies, Willem gradually came to take a real interest in the Sorgvliet estate, the beauty of which was growing every day. Willem was already thinking how delighted his mother would be when she discovered how much the grounds had been improved.

Early in 1724 Carrier, a pedantic tutor who spent hours nagging his pupils about trifles, was replaced by Bernège, who was more to the taste of the elder Bentinck. He responded at once to the great good sense, judgement and penetration of his new teacher, and Bernège himself was agreeably surprised at the effects of the change, writing to Willem's mother: '. . . His humour and manners have softened, his way of life is steadier, his expenditure more regulated, and Monsieur de Wassenaer has congratulated him upon it. His valet Hubert who sees him close up, and at all hours, instead of the complaints he used to make, came to tell me very naturally that he found his master alto-gether better. . . .'[10]

Willem and his younger brother had now been given permission to pay a visit to England. Willem was so overjoyed that he lay awake all night. 'Everything presents itself to me now under such an agreeable prospect,' he wrote to his mother on 29 May 1724, 'that I almost don't know myself again, nor the persons nor the places I see every day.'[11]

Willem's young brother Charles was thought to have a less open character than Willem. Fatherless, removed from his mother's affection too young, and less well off, he withdrew into himself and did not present himself to his best advantage. Those who knew him later appreciated his scientific abilities, deepseated honesty, loyalty to friends and absolute trustworthiness.[12]

On his return from England Willem Bentinck led a more eventful social life, visiting the council pensionary Simon van Slingenandt and the treasurer general Adriaan van der Hoop and dining with the French ambassador, the Marquis Salignac de Fénelon, who was trying to establish good relations between Holland and France.[13] Bernège would have liked his pupil to be even more popular and more communicative though his musical ability on the harpsichord and sometimes the viol helped him to make easy contact with those political figures who delighted in artistic pleasures. During the winter of 1725–6, which was very cold, everybody was sleigh-riding and skating on the canals. One evening there was moonlight driving until 10 o'clock, then supper and dancing at the house of a Mr van Twickle. Willem spent the whole evening dancing with the Countess of Albemarle's daughter. Fortunately he never gave a thought to marrying into the family of his father's former rival, and Bernège wrote: 'Nobody ever paid less heed to marriage. He talks about it like a confirmed bachelor.'

Seeing that the English visit had done her sons so much good, the Countess of Portland realized that it was time to introduce them to other parts of Europe and to give them a chance to improve their languages. She therefore sent Charles to stay in Geneva with a tutor called Montagny, and the following year Willem started on his continental travels.

Charles was seventeen when he arrived in Geneva late in 1725 to stay with Charles-Frederick Necker, a professor at the Geneva Academy. Necker came from Kustrin, in Brandenburg, and had received the freedom of Geneva in 1726. Charles's tutor in history, Greek and Latin was Pierre Crommelin, born in Picardy, like Calvin, but more liberal-minded than his compatriot. He had gone to Lausanne at the time of the revocation of the Edict of Nantes and had moved to Geneva in 1700. His wife belonged to the Croppet family of Huguenot pastors who gave their name to the district of Geneva known as 'les Cropettes'.

As well as being introduced to the great families of the Protestant town, Charles Bentinck was also received by Armand-Louis de Saint Georges, Count of Marsay, owner of the chateau of Changins, near Nyon, on the banks of Lake Geneva. Marsay later became the English minister in Geneva. His sister made up her mind to do something about Charles's laziness, which she tried to correct by constant teasing. Charles also frequented the beautiful chateau of Aubonne, halfway between Geneva and Lausanne, which belonged to the Marquise Du Quesne, daughter-in-law of the famous Norman seaman. As a Huguenot refugee, Du Quesne had restored the chateau and designed the courtyard in the shape of the ship on which his father had won great victories for Louis XIV before being disowned for embracing the Reformed church.

The French monarchy maintained a representative in Geneva, M. Pierre de La Closure, who had held the post with great distinction for nearly thirty years. During the Geneva revolutions of 1707 and 1734 he mediated between the aristocratic party and the defenders of popular rights; later on he was in touch with Jean-Jacques Rousseau. We know from a passage in one of Montagny's letters that Charles was invited to dinner with La Closure.

Although Charles Bentinck then seemed indifferent to public life, his later activities were stimulated by the new ideas he had acquired in a Geneva more eclectic and tolerant than in Calvin's time. His tutor Montagny also had extraordinarily enlightened educational principles for those days. In a letter to the Countess of Portland in 1726 his ideas were like those Jean-Jacques Rousseau was later to take up. Proceeding from the notion that Providence has granted all men a certain basic goodness of heart, he concludes: that the first duty of any man entrusted with the education of another human being is to study the character of his pupil; that it is his duty to apply himself principally to strengthening and perfecting a pupil's natural qualities; and that in inculcating the necessary qualities in the pupil it is a good thing to use his natural qualities so as to induce new talents by slow degrees.[14]

Charles Bentinck and his teacher naturally took a very special interest in a feast day called by the Republic of Geneva in honour of King George I's birthday. Charles's father had taken a hand in having George invited to take the throne, and his mother, the Countess of Portland, had taught the King's grand-children. Montagny described the festive occasion:

On the 12th of this month [June 1726] we celebrated the King's birthday. The whole Council had been invited, but only half of them were there. The French Resident came to compliment these Gentlemen. . . . It was very gay, and we drank the health of King George, the Prince and Princess of Wales, the royal family, the prosperity of the British nation in Church and State, and of the Syndic and Council of Geneva and the Town and Republic of Geneva, to the sound of a discharge of ten to fifteen cannon which were placed along a promenade close to the Town Hall, where we ate. . . . There was an infinity of people . . . they were attentive and seemed interested in our celebration. The good Monsieur Bonnet[15] had taken Monsieur Bentinck under his protection in case an accident should happen. But what had not been anticipated was that Monsieur Bentinck was cautious about the wine and did not drink too much, but his protector, wishing to display his joy and zeal for the British nation, soon found himself over the globe and into the clouds. . . .

I am very glad that Monsieur Bentinck was present at this feast, on a day which is of interest not only to all good Protestants but also to England and all the lands of Europe.

This gives me the occasion, dear Madame, to inform you that I am very hopeful that you will see a great change in him, in both manners and conversation.[16]

While Charles was continuing his education and getting to know various people in Geneva, Willem was preparing to leave The Hague and set out on his 'Grand Tour' of Europe. He started in April 1726, with his tutor Bernège and two servants, travelling through the southern lands then governed on behalf of the Empire by a Regent from Lorraine and visiting the fortifications of Namur, where his father had been victorious over Marshal Boufflers at the time of the second siege. He was well received by those who remembered the Earl of Portland.

The journey took them through Luneville, the residence of the Duke of Lorraine, Leopold Joseph, who gave Willem Bentinck a princely welcome. The Duchess talked about the Earl of Portland and about Lord Woodstock, Willem's half-brother, then Governor of Jamaica, whom she believed to be her visitor's father. Willem spent several weeks at the Court of Luneville, where he frequented M. de Pigerolle's Academy and attended plays and balls. The Prince of Elbeuf, who had known his father well when he was ambassador in Paris, invited Willem to stay with him in his chateau, and he also dined with the Prince of Craon, the Duke of Lorraine's prime minister and favourite. When he went hunting with the Duke, they killed three boars and lunched in the heart of the forest, in the Duke's tents.

In September Bentinck and Bernège continued their journey by way of Strasbourg, stopping at Hesse, where they were the guests of the young Prince. After visiting several German principalities where his father's name was fondly remembered from the days of his diplomatic missions there, Bentinck reached Berlin. He took close note of the parade before King Frederick William, the toast to the success of the Treaty of Hanover, and the questions which the King asked him at table while he smoked his long pipe. The young heir-apparent, the future Frederick the Great, made a deep impression on Willem, and he wrote to his mother: 'The Prince is mightily handsome, genteel, well made, extremely polite and very tall for his age, and has the character of being very merry, mightily generous and good natured and having a great deal of wit and sense. I have heard particulars of him, which prove that character to be true. . . .'[17]

As for the Princess of Prussia, Willem Bentinck found her beautiful, whereas Bernège disagreed and thought her very sickly looking. The young man also took the trouble to inquire about her character and heard nothing but praise, which he was very happy to pass on to others. Why this brief investigation? He was too well brought up to venture to be in love, but he could not have been unaware that there had been discussions about a double marriage between Princess Amelia, the Countess of Portland's correspondent, and the heir apparent of Prussia, and between Princess Frederika and the Prince of Wales. The split in the alliance between Prussia and France and England put an end to the project but Willem Bentinck liked to form his own judgements wherever he went.

From Berlin the two travellers went southward to Dresden, but they did not stay long because Augustus the Strong, King of Poland and Elector of Saxony, was then visiting his Polish lands. In Dresden Willem had the opportunity to play a harpsichord made available by Count von Wackerbarth and spent New Year's Day with him. Wackerbarth was a brilliant engineer, officer and diplomat who had toured Greece to draw plans of the Venetian fortifications there and had fought in the Netherlands during the war of the Spanish succession. Augustus had appointed him commanding general of all his armies in Saxony. He was married to the beautiful Catrina Paolina Balbiano, who had been the secret wife of the Margrave Karl Philip of Brandenburg, of the Schwedter branch. The Margrave had died in the year of their marriage, which was never recognized by the Court of Prussia.

In Dresden Bentinck had also discussed the Netherlands with Count Heinrich Friedrich von Friesen, who was born there during the war of the Spanish succession, when his father fought against Tallart. Friesen had fought in Russia and taken part in the battle of Poltava.

The next stage of their journey, through the mountains of the

Erzgebirge and Bohemia to Prague, was rough travelling. Their postchaise developed a faulty wheel, and since the precipitous route overlooking the Elbe was unsafe they had to follow the coach on foot. At halts they slept on smelly mouldy straw, crawling with bugs, fleas and other vermin. Instead of complaining, Bentinck found it good training and wrote: 'This is the best country in the world to use one's self to hardness.' At last they reached the Moldau and saw the sights of Prague.

In Vienna, which they visited after Prague, Bentinck was irritated at first by the protocol-ridden court of the Emperor, which affected diplomats and the Austrian nobility alike. The Dutch representative, van Burmania, lived there as if he were in his own house at The Hague. When he took Bentinck close to the Emperor as he dined with the Empress, the young man left without presenting himself to the Imperial couple because he would not submit to the custom of kissing hands. 'All this court is nothing but ceremonies and vain display, as disagreeable for the Emperor as for his subjects,' he wrote at the time. In Vienna he found the Duke of Lorraine's son François, who had been brought to Court by the Emperor Charles VI. François was to marry the Emperor's daughter and heir to the throne, Maria Theresa.

He also made the acquaintance of a former envoy of the King of England, François-Louis de Pesmes de Saint-Saphorin, who at first seemed to him 'a very curious kind of man, who sees very little of the world save those who go to see him'. M. de Saint-Saphorin came from Switzerland, where he held the seigneury and splendid chateau of Vuillerens, near Lake Geneva. During his chequered and distinguished career he had served in a Swiss regiment fighting for Holland and commanded the Danube fleet as an officer of the Empire. It was Saint-Saphorin who signed the defensive alliance between the Bernese and the United Provinces at The Hague in 1712, before he finally entered the service of Great Britain and became George I's minister in Vienna.

Willem Bentinck soon realized that his judgement of Saint-Saphorin had been too hasty and that he was in fact a man of considerable wit and intelligence, whose great experience in negotiations made his conversation as instructive as it was enjoyable. Consequently he spent whole afternoons closeted with his new friend without noticing the passage of time and learned more in a few days than he might from others in as many months. Bentinck was to return to Vienna in very different circumstances in later years, but he left for Venice in February 1727.

In the early eighteenth century it was the custom for visiting princes to call at the workshop of the painter Rosalba Carriera, near the Palazzo Venier on the Grand Canal. She painted the most beautiful of the Venetian women of her day, their great dark velvet eyes contrasting with the dazzling white of their pearls. Bentinck had previously admired her portraits of King Augustus in Dresden. Carriera's pastel of the young traveller in Venice has not survived, so the best-known portrait still in existence is by another famous pastellist, Jean-Etienne Liotard. Willem sat for it in Holland, where the Genevese artist had made his home.

We shall not pursue Willem Bentinck and Bernège into every little town on their Italian journey towards Rome, where they arrived at Easter 1727.

The peace of Utrecht might have put an end to the war of the Spanish succession but it had not settled every national and territorial problem or the long-standing rivalries between Europeans both on the Continent and for territory overseas. All the same it had achieved a détente among the signatory countries – France, Spain, England, the Netherlands and Austria – and among the various European religions. Political rapprochement encouraged artistic and philosophical exchanges, literary correspondence, music, painting, the collection of antiquities and *objets d'art* and natural history.

The fanaticism of the wars of religion had now given way to tolerance and sometimes mutual understanding. A French cardinal, Melchior de Polignac, who had been Louis XIV's envoy to the Congress of Utrecht and French ambassador to the Vatican for the previous two years, gave an immediate and generous reception to the son of the man who had fought a bitter struggle against Louis XIV for the independence of the Netherlands. Both in Rome and in his country house at Frascati, near the breathtaking Aldobrandini, Torlonia and Mondragone villas, the Cardinal was only too ready to provide Willem Bentinck with introductions.

At Frascati it was Cardinal Colonna who gave Bentinck hospitality and accompanied him on the violin when he played the harpsichord. At Tivoli, Bentinck toured the Villa d'Este gardens. He visited the convent of St Cecilia and talked to the daughter of the late King Jan Sobieski of Poland, who lived apart from her husband the Elector of Bavaria and was bored in Rome.

Bentinck had been put in touch with Philipp von Stosch, the archaeologist and great collector of gems and medals. He had known Fagel, the Secretary of the States General in Holland, for both were numismatists. The British government was paying Stosch to keep an eye on the activities of the Old Pretender, James Stuart, son of James II and Mary of Modena, but it was antiquities that he explored with Willem Bentinck on their excursions around Rome. They visited Cardinal Alessandro Albani, whose Roman villa at Albano was a noted museum of antiquities. The Cardinal maintained close relations with the English, and had sided against the Pretender, contrary to the wishes of his uncle Pope Clement XI.

In a brief escape from this intoxicating atmosphere of Roman intrigue and natural and artistic beauty, Willem Bentinck went to Naples with Bernège. There they made an excursion to the foot of Vesuvius, then in full eruption. Bentinck walked in the ashes, withstood the baking heat, kept a respectable distance from the crater and never stood still for fear of scorching his soles on the cinders spat out by the volcano. In Naples he admired the natural setting of the town but complained of the pride and arrogance of its hordes of dukes and princes and found the common people lazy and treacherous.

Back in Rome, Bentinck spent the remainder of 1727 learning to draw and to speak Italian. Although he was a doer, not a dreamer, his affections ran deeper than he showed, and eventually he longed to return to Holland or, better still, to England, his mother and his boyhood friends. His appointment as a knight of Holland and counsellor of the dikes during his absence obliged him to acknowledge these honours and take the road to The Hague, passing through Florence and Milan, where he was sidetracked to the Borromean islands on Lake Maggiore by the wife of Prince Borromeo, to whom they belonged. At Turin, the capital of the Kingdom of Sardinia, he was received by King Victor-Amadeus II of Savoy. A few days later Willem and his kindly tutor took the scenic road from Turin to Lausanne, where Willem was reunited with his brother and obtained permission to take him to Paris.

The visit to Versailles was brief. Louis XV was eighteen years old. He received the son of Louis XIV's old antagonist with dignity, but nothing memorable seems to have been said. It was particularly moving for Willem to talk to a few ageing courtiers who remembered the Earl of Portland, although the young dandies of his brother Charles's age seemed shallow to him. He was more impressed with older men of character and experience.

The Bentinck brothers were in Paris at the moment when the European plenipotentiaries had just arrived to take part in the Congress of Soissons, called to settle the Gibraltar question as well as that of the Ostend Company which the Emperor had set up to trade between the Austrian Netherlands and the East Indies. The gathering at Soissons promised to be a stormy one, and Bentinck, who always advocated peaceful settlement of disputes, took great interest in observing the diplomats and their preoccupations.

The rest of the Paris visit was mainly sightseeing, without any contacts with the thinkers and scholars who were to become Bentinck's correspondents when he was appointed curator of the University of Leyden.

Back in the Netherlands, Willem Bentinck divided his time between Sorgvliet and the Voorhout house at The Hague, near the palace where his father had spent his youth with William III of Orange. This magnificent private residence is situated in an avenue parallel to the Mauritshuis. As a knight of Holland,

Willem could put himself forward for important posts which only
a few other knights could share. He was twenty-five years old,
with a gravity that belied his age, with no known vices and not
short of seigneuries and estates. All he lacked was a wife.

Willem had been fatherless since childhood and separated from
his mother by circumstances at an early age. He does not seem to
have gone out of his way to make himself agreeable to women.
His former tutor, Count Wassenaer, decided to help. He inquired
into the most likely matches and resolved to make contact with a
German nobleman and big landowner in the former states of the
dukes of Oldenburg – Anton II, Count von Aldenburg. His
daughter by Wilhelmina Maria von Hesse Homburg was
Charlotte-Sophia von Aldenburg, heiress to a considerable
fortune which her father had himself received from Anton-
Gunther, Count von Oldenburg, the last male representative of
the cadet branch of the house of Holstein-Oldenburg.

Charlotte-Sophia was young, noble and the heir to very large
estates, at Varel and Kniphausen in Friesland and in Gelderland; her
marriage therefore depended on conditions which it was hard to
fulfil. Willem had to spend the summer of 1732 in Varel to address his requests to the King of Denmark, who had to authorize
the wedding and guarantee the lordship of Varel and Kniphausen
to Count von Aldenburg and his descendants whether in the male
or the female line. At the same time it was only fitting for
Willem Bentinck to hold the same title as his future wife; this he
could only obtain through the Emperor in Vienna. It cost him no
less than eight thousand Dutch guilders.[18]

On his side, Count von Aldenburg was very pleased with the
prospect of seeing his estates at Doorwerth in Gelderland fall
within the sphere of interest of a Dutch nobleman who would take
good care of them. His letters to the King of Denmark show his
awareness of his future son-in-law's abilities. The Countess of
Portland was more anxious on her son's behalf. She had heard that
the girl was pretty and lively but capricious and flirtatious.
Charlotte-Sophia's mother had her doubts too and would rather
have seen her marry a German prince.

Willem was soon entangled, caring about little else but his fiancée, her friendship and her conversation. He wanted only happiness for Charlotte-Sophia and himself, swearing that he was totally dependent upon her and that there was no one in the world, without exception, who wished her so much good as he or so desired true happiness for her.

Willem Bentinck could not win the heart of Charlotte-Sophia, whose grandmother and great-grandmother had given theirs to the men they loved in the teeth of all opposition. Nevertheless the marriage did take place, and they soon had two healthy and precociously intelligent sons. The household only stayed together as long as Count von Aldenburg lived. After his death in April 1738 Charlotte-Sophia spent the winter and then the summer of 1739 in Varel. The little county near Bremen and Hanover cultivated the arts and literature, and Charlotte was fond of the theatre, particularly Marivaux's comedies.

Since life is not a comedy, theirs might have turned to tragedy if Bentinck had not borne the separation with such remarkable self-control. When the Aldenburg family adviser, who subsequently remained attached to Count Bentinck, came to The Hague in September to inform him that his wife would never return, he was overcome; a few months later he was back on his feet. In a moving letter to his mother he wrote that he had done nothing to be treated in such a manner and that he had 'business enough' not to think about it: 'As long as I can preserve the esteem of the public, my own approbation and my health, I defy all the wives in the world to make me miserable. I have the happiness of having the children by me and the hopes of bringing them up well. In short, I am a great deal better so than if my wife had staid here.'[19]

'Business enough' and the upbringing of his children were the aims which Willem Bentinck pursued throughout his noble life.

There was no shortage of work for Hans Willem Bentinck's son. He had decided at an early age to uphold his country's independence, strengthen the links between the provinces and maintain the traditional alliances abroad. By now he was a deputy to the States General, not just to the States of the province of

Holland, as earlier. Before taking an active part in this assembly he spent some time gaining experience of the life and politics of the United Provinces as a whole.

When the war of the Austrian succession broke out in 1741, Bentinck expressed his own individual and pertinent judgements of the sovereigns involved and argued confidently on behalf of Dutch neutrality. He advocated the alliance with England, fearing a French invasion of the Netherlands, and took due account of the rising power of Frederick II of Prussia. But although Holland should stay neutral, he believed, it should also attach more importance to the army. Bentinck was uneasy because the army was undermanned and poorly officered and was also critical of the navy's upkeep of its ships. Though new ships were being built, the existing fleet also needed improvements and repairs.

Willem Bentinck had made a number of visits to Prince William IV and the Princess of Orange at Het Loo. William IV's wife, Princess Anne, was the daughter of King George II of England and had been taught by Bentinck's mother. Willem was perturbed about the inadequate powers accorded to the Prince of Orange. He stressed to the States of Holland how important it was for Dutch and European stability to re-establish the position of a Stadtholder who would rule the whole of the United Provinces. He also attached great importance to the defence of the Barrier towns on the frontier of the southern Netherlands, now in Austrian hands, as the bulwark of the United Provinces. This was the same argument that his father had advocated to Louis XIV during his embassy in Paris.

In 1748, at the end of the war of the Austrian succession, Willem Bentinck insisted that the United Provinces should appoint a leader capable of uniting all the people behind a struggle for independence. He should be empowered to defend the entire country. Sensing that William IV of Orange, Stadtholder of Friesland, needed encouragement, Willem Bentinck sent him an address urging the need to organize a central power under his command when the belligerent powers laid down their arms and decided the future of the European nations. He argued that it was no longer a simple question of the attitude of the Prince of Orange to the problems of the state of Friesland, the treasury reserves or similar local issues. He argued in his address that:

We would still be under the yoke of Spain, or of France, if we had debated in 1572 as we do at present – at the moment when the northern provinces came together as the Republic of the United Provinces to resist the atrocities of Philip II of Spain;

in 1672 – when William III took charge of the army to defend the Republic against the attacks of Louis XIV, who was already occupying part of the United Provinces;

in 1688 – when William III, aided by Hans Willem Bentinck, replied to the appeal of the English Parliament and received the crown of England with Mary;

in 1702 – when Louis XIV had occupied the Barrier towns and thus provoked the war of the Spanish succession.

I will go further, My Lord! The public, I say the whole public, expects these feelings of you. You owe them to yourself and to the name you bear, and it would be the most unpopular thing in the world not to proclaim them. . . . You would be wronging not only yourself but the cause of all honest men who honour you and who would be lost for ever if your zeal for religion and liberty were to be doubted for a moment. You would also lose the affection of the people, which is a very essential point at present. . . .[20]

In April 1747 William IV of Orange, who had been Stadtholder of Friesland since 1711, of Groningen since 1718 and of Gelderland since 1722, was elected as Stadtholder of all the United Provinces and appointed Captain-General and Admiral-General of the Union. Some days after his appointment William toured several provinces and met with a triumphal reception from the overwhelming majority of the population. He was accompanied by Willem Bentinck, who had worked hard to bring this event about, and by Count Maurice of Nassau and Mr van Grovestin. All four travelled to Rotterdam in the same carriage and went on by boat.

At Delft, although the Prince was in a hurry to catch the tide for Zeeland, he could not refuse to visit the Burgomaster, van

Berkel, passing through a double line of burghers armed with a variety of muskets, half-pikes, drawn sabres and bucklers, all shouting: '*Vivat* Orange, onward Orange!'

All the way from The Hague to Rotterdam they were surrounded by rejoicing crowds. Willem Bentinck wrote an account of the welcome given to the man who now succeeded to the highest position in the United Provinces, which had been vacant for so long. At Ryswick and Overschie he noted the swelling crowds as the Prince passed under leafy archways. On the outskirts of Rotterdam the horses could go no faster than walking pace, and countless spectators in the streets shouted with delight. Every window on every floor was open and jammed with people. Some had climbed onto the rooftops and were applauding the 'liberator of the country'.

Bentinck walked between two rows of halberdiers on his way to the Prince's yacht, where the gangplank was covered with carpeting for the occasion. The ships in harbour swarmed with sailors up to the mastheads. On his way out of the roadstead the Prince received a triple salute of guns from the town and all the ships at anchor in the Meuse.

William IV was now in charge of relations between the United Provinces and their allies, and in 1747 he sent Willem Bentinck to London, to investigate the steps to be taken in the event of attack by the French troops under Maurice de Saxe. King George II described it as a dangerous situation and proposed to accept any offer of negotiation. Bentinck dropped a few remarks on the risk of the King being disavowed by William IV if the peace measures were taken in too much haste. The King finally came round to Bentinck's way of thinking, and 'concluded with saying, he was determined that the negotiation, wherever it was carried on, should be managed by me'.[22]

Bentinck had already written to the Duke of Newcastle: 'I confess that I would be in despair to lose the fruit of so much work at a single stroke . . . here we are busy making ready to repulse the enemy. . . . In the name of God, My Lord, do not suffer all to be marred by too much haste.'

A Landscape with a Stream by Meindert Hobbema (1638–1709). It was in country-side like this, flat and dotted with water- and windmills, that the Bentincks had their roots.

A watercolour of the chateau at Middachten before 1672, by Jan de Beyer (1703–68). This home passed into the hands of the Bentincks through their marriage alliances with the van Reedes.

LEFT A portrait of Hans Willem Bentinck, by Rigaud. Hans Willem was devoted in his service to his master William of Orange both before and after the latter took over the English throne.

BELOW The great hall at Middachten as it is today: on the right there is a portrait of Hans Willem by Simon du Bois.

RIGHT William of Orange: a portrait of him in his youth by an unknown artist. Hans Willem was to accompany him to England in 1688, when the Dutch Stadtholder became William III of England in the 'Glorious Protestant Revolution'.

BELOW Part of Westminster, showing Parliament House, Westminster Hall and the Abbey: an etching by Wenceslaus Hollar, dated 1647.

Civitatis Westmonasteriensis pars

nt House   the Hall   the Abby

Weller fecit, 1647

ARLYAMENT IS ILLEGALL ... THAT E
PARLYAMENT OVGHT TO BE FREE - THE F

LES LORDS ET LES COMMVNES PRESENTENT A GVILLA
ET A MARIE LA DECLARATION DES DROITS DES ANG

A relief on the Monument of the Reformation at Geneva, showing the presentation of the Bill of Rights to William and Mary by the Lords and Commons in 1688. Hans Willem is shown (fourth from left).

William III visits Holland for the first time after his coronation as King of England. He is seen passing through the gateway between Sorgvliet and The Hague, built in his honour by Romeyn de Hooghe, after dining with Hans Willem at Sorgvliet. The engraving is by Romeyn de Hooghe and appeared in Nicolas Chevakier's *Histoire de Guillaume III*, Published in Amsterdam in 1692.

Sorgvliet, shown on the title-page of *Ouderdom, buyten-leven, en Hof-gedachten, op Sorg-Vliet* by the Dutch national poet Jacob Cats, published in Amsterdam in 1656. The book was a collection of 'Thoughts of the olden days, of life in the open and of the garden' at Sorgvliet, an estate which had belonged to Cats but was given to Hans Willem by William of Orange in 1674.

ABOVE Jane Martha Temple, Hans Willem's second wife: a portrait by Simon du Bois. The painting now hangs at Middachten.

LEFT The Portland vase, formerly in the collection of the Portlands, and now in the British Museum. This side shows (*left to right*) Poseidon, the head of Pan and Hermes. The vase dates back to the first century AD.

The Tea Party at the Countess of Portland's by Philips. Handel is playing the harpsichord (*left*), and the children in the painting are those of George II.

Frederick, Prince of Wales, and his Sisters: a Music Party, painted by Philip Mercier in 1733.

Bulstrode Park, which belonged to the notorious Judge Jeffreys until his imprisonment in the Tower. After this Hans Willem acquired it and it became the home of the Portlands.

A view of Jamaica engraved by J. Mérigot from a painting by Louis Belangé. Henry Bentinck, first Duke of Portland, became Governor of the island in 1722.

RIGHT Willem, son of Hans Willem and Jane Martha: a portrait by J. E. Liotard, painted in 1755. His particular interest was in the natural sciences, though he was politically and culturally active, too.

BELOW Charlotte-Sophia van Aldenburg as a child: a portrait by an unknown artist. Her marriage to Willem, contracted for reasons of expedience, unlike the love-matches of her grandmother and great-grandmother, was shortlived.

A. TREMBLEY
né a Geneve le 3 Septr 1710

CHARLES BONNET F.R.S.
Author of the Contemplation of Nature

The CHAIN of NATURE

J. Prins del. ad viv. 1744.   J. v. Schley sculp.

MÉMOIRES
POUR L'HISTOIRE
DES POLYPES.

LEFT Margaret Cavendish Harley, Duchess of Portland: a portrait by Michael Dahl. Rousseau thought very highly of her talents as a naturalist and wrote: 'I know one animal which would be delighted to live in your menagerie, awaiting the honour of being preserved in your cabinet one day. . . .'

RIGHT Mary Delany, friend of the Duchess of Portland: a portrait by John Opie.

OPPOSITE, ABOVE LEFT Abraham Trembley, the naturalist from Geneva whose researches Willem encouraged: an engraving by J. F. Clemens.

OPPOSITE, ABOVE RIGHT Charles Bonnet, philosopher and physiologist, and cousin of Trembley: an engraving after a portrait by Jens Juel. He was the author of *The Contemplation of Nature*.

OPPOSITE, BELOW A page from Trembley's *Mémoires pour l'histoire des polypes*, with one of the illustrations engraved by Schley after Pronck's paintings of Sorgvliet.

WILHELMI BENTINCK

ORATIO

DE

CONSTANTIA ROMANORUM

Publice recitata Trajecti ad Rhenum.

A.D. IV NON. MARTII. MDCXCVI.

TRAJECTI AD RHENUM,

Ex Officina FRANCISCI HALMA, Academiæ Typographi.
cIↃ Iↄc xcvI.

LEFT The title-page of *The Constancy of the Romans by* Willem Bentinck, nephew of Hans Willem.

BELOW Schoonheten, one of the oldest homes of the Bentincks, where Willem lived. It now belongs to Baron R. Bentinck.

BOTTOM Diepenheim, where Hans Willem was born. His nephew united the Schoonheten and Diepenheim branches of the Bentinck family when he married Mechtild Anna Bentinck.

William, third Duke of Portland: engraved by John Murphy after a portrait by Sir Joshua Reynolds. His political career in England included two periods as Prime Minister, in 1783 and again from 1807 to 1809.

The third Duke of Portland with his brother Lord Edward Bentinck: an engraving by Smith after Benjamin West.

Lord William Cavendish Bentinck, son of the third Duke of Portland: an engraving after a portrait by Sir Thomas Lawrence. As commander of the British troops in Sicily, he was instrumental in securing a freer constitution for the island. He later distinguished himself as Governor-General of India.

Lord William in later life: a portrait by Joseph D. Court. The artist was painter to Louis Philippe at Versailles and was a friend of Lord William both in Sicily and afterwards in Paris.

Lord George Bentinck, whose major interest was the reform of some of the more dubious practices of the Turf. This contemporary caricature is now in the British Museum.

Lord George: a marble bust by T. Campbell.

LEFT The chateau of Amerongen, near Arnhem, which, like Middachten, the Bentincks acquired through their marriage alliances with the van Reede family.

ABOVE Sorgvliet today: it now belongs to the state and is the official residence of the Prime Minister of Holland.

LEFT The late Baron Adolphe Bentinck, Dutch Ambassador to England and Assistant Secretary-General of NATO.

But the allies found it impossible to achieve a separate peace with the King of Spain, and there had been uprisings in the provinces of Holland and Zeeland, which Bentinck had helped to quell but which might yet break out again. Both these considerations forced the conclusion of an early peace.

Before leaving for England, Bentinck had drafted a bill to make the Orange family the hereditary holders of the Stadtholderate. His initiative guaranteed continuity of the executive power by settling the succession and provided for a Regency in case of the death of the Stadtholder while his children were still minors. He had sent his text to the Prince and Princess, the Secretary of the States General and his brother. By the time he returned his plan had been accepted by the Grand Pensionary, and the burghers of Amsterdam had withdrawn their opposition. On 16 November 1747 the States of Holland declared the Stadtholderate hereditary in the male and female line, thus paving the way for what has become one of the most stable and best loved dynasties in Europe. The Bentincks' learned tutor announced the news to the Countess of Portland, and added: 'Messrs Bentinck are more and more loved by the public. . . .'[23]

By the end of the war of the Austrian succession, the United Provinces had gained stable government. Willem Bentinck was appointed plenipotentiary to the Congress of Aix-la-Chapelle, and although Holland could make no extensive claims he applied all his skills to reconciling the former belligerents. When the preliminaries began to falter, Bentinck was one of a small group of plenipotentiaries which 'set to work without delay, and everything went quite quickly from then on'.[24]

As Lord Sandwich remarked, Bentinck had made himself indispensable to the progress of the negotiations.[25] He had lost some illusions during the conference, but since it was impossible to win a war, he wrote to Fagel: 'if peace is to be made, it must be made, and if not as we would, then as we may'. For him, the crucial need was to maintain his country's alliances, with Austria and of course with England.

F

11 ❧ Willem Bentinck at the Court of the Empress Maria Theresa

D URING THE WAR of the Austrian succession the United Provinces had been unable to defend the so-called Barrier towns in the Austrian Netherlands. The Empress Maria Theresa could barely bring herself to forgive them, and she withdrew the subsidies which had enabled the Dutch to keep a garrison there. In August 1749 Willem Bentinck went to Brussels to talk over these difficulties with the Regent of the Austrian Netherlands, Charles of Lorraine, Duke of Vaudemont, Maria Theresa's brother-in-law. However no permanent settlement could be reached without the consent of the Court of Vienna.

The attempt to settle the Barrier question gave Willem Bentinck a third reason for visiting the Imperial capital. The other two were political and personal. He was uneasy about Holland's future in the event of the death of William IV of Orange, and wanted to know whether the Duke of Brunswick-Wolfenbüttel would be willing to enter the service of Holland, where his great military abilities would be of immediate use and where he would be available to help Princess Anne in the event of a regency. Personally, he wanted to settle the situation over the Varel and Kniphausen lands which had belonged to his father-in-law, and this was a matter for the Aulic Court in Vienna.

So Willem Bentinck went back to Vienna in late summer 1749, twenty-two years after his Grand Tour of the Continent, as envoy of the Stadtholder William IV. Francis of Lorraine was now the Empress's husband, after succeeding his father as Duke regnant of Lorraine, then as Grand Duke of Tuscany after Lorraine had been exchanged for Tuscany. When Willem Bentinck reached Vienna after the peace of Aix-la-Chapelle the ownership of lands in Europe was still at the mercy of successions, alliances and wars, to the point where nobody could be certain of immunity. Bentinck and his wife, separated as of 15 April 1740 by an Act recognized by the Imperial Court, were themselves threatened with these political reshufflings.

The free seigneury of Varel and Kniphausen was the smallest of the German states (having an area of twenty-four square kilometres), an enclave within the duchy of Oldenburg belonging to Charlotte-Sophia Bentinck's mother, Countess von Aldenburg. Charlotte-Sophia had spent much of her time there since separating from her husband. The King of Denmark did not want to lose the little independent seigneury so close to his own realm, and Countess Bentinck had gone to Berlin to persuade the King of Prussia to intervene. Disputes between noblemen of the Empire were the province of the Aulic Court, and the effect of the decision on Willem's children was in itself enough to justify the Vienna visit.

Count Bentinck's departure from The Hague for Vienna did not escape the notice of the French, who were still as active in diplomacy as in the days of Hans Willem's missions on behalf of William III the previous century. The Marquis of Hautefort therefore received precise instructions from Louis XV's foreign minister

... to unravel the main objective of Count Bentinck's mission to Vienna. The official answer is that the Dutch minister was dealing only with personal business as regards the so-called Barrier strongholds of the Netherlands, but many people are claiming that he had to negotiate some far more essential points, and that it is not impossible that these had to do with long-term measures to be taken against the King of Prussia....[1]

In pressing for the application of the Barrier Treaty of 1713, by which Holland reserved the right to maintain garrisons in several towns in the Spanish Low Countries, the Stadtholder based his case on the maritime powers' assistance to their allies during the war of the Spanish succession. Austria reproached them for their neutrality in the war of the Austrian succession. This treaty also settled the tariffs and rights between Holland and the Empire. The Austrian Netherlands based their case on economic hardships which compelled them to apply new tariffs introduced by the French. There were further disagreements concerning the tax on salt. The occupation of the Barrier strongholds by Louis XIV had sparked off the war of the Spanish succession, and it was important to settle any differences between the Empire and the United Provinces so as to avoid a possible attack.

Willem Bentinck entered Vienna on 20 September and was met by the Dutch ambassador, van Burmania, who invited him to dine. That evening they both joined the Austrian foreign minister, von Ulfeld, in his box at the Opera. They dined with him next day, a Sunday, and on Monday they went hunting with Count Jörgen at Schönau.

An audience had been arranged with the Emperor for 23 September. At the time appointed, Bentinck and Burmania entered the courtyard of Schönbrunn, driving between two obelisks surmounted by the Imperial eagle, and approached the monumental façade of the Palace. All summer long the castle had been the focus of an intense literary and artistic life and a centre for the discussion of Imperial policy. The Empress had impressed all Europe with her forceful pursuit of the war of the Austrian succession.

The Emperor's Grand Chamberlain, Count von Kevenhüller, was waiting for the two Dutchmen in the antechamber, and announced Count Bentinck first. He paid the customary homage to the standing Emperor before disclosing the object of his journey and commending himself to the monarch's protection. Francis had had a high regard for Bentinck ever since they had discussed the relations between the Empire and the maritime powers at the Court of Charles VI, when Francis had been a young officer who aspired to the hand of Maria Theresa. He advised Bentinck to talk to Count von Kaunitz about his personal business. Kaunitz had considered himself Bentinck's friend since the treaty of Aix-la-Chapelle.

Now Bentinck could raise the subject of his political mission, and he presented a letter from the Prince of Orange which he had previously avoided mentioning in order to escape the notice of foreign observers. Bentinck asked on behalf of William IV for Louis von Brunswick-Wolfenbüttel, then in the service of Austria, to be authorized to take command of the department of the army in the Republic of the United Provinces. As he explained his reasons to the Emperor, His Majesty interrupted to point out that, while he was very ready to give proof of his friendship for the Prince of Orange, the matter required further reflection. He advised Bentinck to take it up with the Empress.

Shortly afterwards, Count von Kevenhüller conducted Bentinck to the Empress's apartments. Half an hour elapsed, then Count Palfi, grandson of the Palatine of Hungary and chamberlain of the day, opened the doors of the Empress's room.

It would be wrong to deduce from the previous encounter that Francis I had no part to play in Maria Theresa's policy or that he deferred to her or her ministers. Bentinck's conversation with the Empress shows that the Emperor had used the interval to talk to her about their guest.

Bentinck repeated his message that Austria would be rendering the greatest possible service to the Prince of Orange, the Republic and the common cause by releasing the Prince of Wolfenbüttel to the United Provinces. The Empress spoke of the sacrifice this would mean for herself, since she was very fond of Prince Louis and did not have many men capable of leading an army. As Bentinck replied that the Empress would gain more from Wolfenbüttel's presence in Holland than if he were to stay in Vienna, since the Republic could certainly do nothing without her, still less against her, Maria Theresa laughed and exclaimed: 'Provided you will make war when I do! For this is what you have not done, although I will not reproach you for it, or bring up unpleasant subjects in a first conversation. . . .'

Willem Bentinck wanted to make it possible for Holland's pledges to its allies to be kept and needed Wolfenbüttel's help. In particular, if anything happened to the Prince of Orange, Wolfenbüttel would be there to back the government. This argument seemed to have had an effect on the Empress, who knew how sad it was to need help and be unable to get it because of a change of monarch. Still she asked to think it over and added that military questions must not obscure financial ones.

William IV's envoy deferred seeking a further audience for a while, realizing that there were many eyes upon him. On 10 October the Empress invited him to a play given at Schönbrunn by the archdukes and archduchesses. Bentinck took the opportunity to ask for an interview with the Emperor, and four days later he was with Francis I in Marshal Bathyany's room at Schönbrunn, while the Emperor lounged against a window and smiled: 'Well, here I am. What have you got to say?'

Bentinck stated that he hoped to be put in a position to give the Prince of Orange the information necessary for running the affairs of the Republic in a manner which would support Her Majesty's views. The Emperor advised caution. What more could be done, he asked, than the alliances already concluded?

Another week passed before the Empress received Bentinck in her turn and complied with his request for information about her talks with Wolfenbüttel. Although she regretted losing him, Maria Theresa had suggested that he accept the Prince of Orange's offer. Wolfenbüttel himself was holding out; he wanted to keep his regiment and remain an infantry general. According to the Empress he was trying to retain the option of returning to Austria.

In her talks with Bentinck, Maria Theresa seemed preoccupied with current rumours that she intended to recover Silesia by force. Far from wishing to fight the King of Prussia she was afraid of being attacked by him, especially if France and Turkey aligned themselves with him. Only Russia could help her then, and she said that England would confirm her view.

During Bentinck's talks at Schönbrunn the Empress also discussed what help might be expected from Russia and pointed out that it would be to England's advantage to subsidize the empire of the Tsars. There was no question at the time of an alliance with France. Maria Theresa made only passing mention of the possibility of the King of Prussia taking advantage of a Turkish attack to invade her territory, in which case she would be 'obliged to fall in with the wishes of France'. Willem Bentinck made note of this fact.[2]

During Bentinck's prolonged visit to Vienna he drew favourable notice at Court and established amicable relations there. He went hunting with the Emperor and visited Maria Theresa's mother, the Empress Dowager, who remained inconsolable after Charles vi's death. He found her seated in a black armchair, under a black canopy, before a table covered in black, in a room covered, like the rest of her apartments, in black velvet. She received Bentinck simply and kindly, recalling that she knew of him through Prince Charles. She asked after the health of the Prince of Orange and praised the young Princess for feeding her children herself, for few ladies in her position would have done so.

The Emperor and Empress also took a personal hand in helping Bentinck with his family affairs in Kniphausen. Couriers were sent to the King of Denmark, and the tiny state was not swallowed up inside his kingdom. Thanks to the Aulic Court a solution was found some years later, and Count Willem Bentinck's eldest son received the seigneury.

Bentinck made more than one attempt to elicit a firm answer on the Barrier question, and each time the Emperor enjoined patience. He had written to his brother, the Regent of the Austrian Netherlands, but the reply was still pending. Maria Theresa had annotated a memorandum from Bentinck to her minister Uhlfeld on the subject: 'I have admired in him the good citizen and friend, and his courage. I have found truths here which are good for me. I read them out to the Emperor a second time, and that augmented the esteem he already felt for him [Bentinck]. I will be charmed to be of service to him. I hope that

the matter of Prince Louis will also succeed. . . .' The matter of
the Prince (Wolfenbüttel) was in fact satisfactorily settled.

Before he left, Bentinck wanted a full and exact briefing on the
plans and intentions of the Court of Vienna. It was essential for
him to have a solid basis of information for the talks which were
to be arranged on the affairs of the Netherlands. He was in favour
of negotiations in which England played a part.

Willem Bentinck's stay in Vienna had not gone unnoticed,
even as far away as Rome. Old Cardinal Alessandro Gonsalvi
wrote to recall 'the friendship of which Bentinck had long granted
him the honour', referring to his visit to Rome with his tutor as a
young man.

On 27 July 1750 Count Bentinck spent the evening at Schönbrunn. The Empress joined him in the garden and assured him
that she too wanted to reach a final settlement with the maritime
powers and to live in friendship and understanding with them.
Bentinck had told her that the people of the Austrian Netherlands
had seemed to him as loyal to Maria Theresa as subjects could
be, and he praised the administration of Prince Charles of
Lorraine. As for the Empress, she felt that things had reached a
point at which any failure to settle their differences would be
owing to some unlucky star of the Netherlands, since both sides
were favourably disposed. William IV's envoy was unable to
learn any more and failed to receive any promises about the
question of the Barrier towns.

Count Bentinck's last visit to Maria Theresa was enhanced by
a musical occasion unique of its kind. When he asked permission
to take his leave, the grand chamberlain summoned him to
Schönbrunn on 2 August. He found the Empress standing by a
harpsichord on which she was accompanied by the virtuoso
composer Wagenseil, the organist of the Empress Dowager
Elizabeth Christina, whose operas anticipate Glück.

'I really must be a friend of yours to do what I'm doing,' the
Empress apologized, more intimidated by performing a drawing-
room song than by ruling an Empire. She sat down and sang an
air, then a second, which went much better, and a third, which

went better still. She wanted to stop, but the Emperor was so insistent that she sang two more. Bentinck remarked that she resembled one of those fairy-tale princesses who have magically been granted every accomplishment. Maria Theresa laughed, and replied: 'But there's always some wicked fairy who comes and spoils everything!'

It was the last remark by the Empress to be noted by Bentinck. Previously she had hinted that he might like to mention the recital to the Princess of Orange, in view of their mutual love for music. Anne of Orange, the daughter of King George II of England, had learned to love music in the Whitehall salon where Handel had played for Willem Bentinck's mother.

By the beginning of September Count Bentinck had reached Hanover, the German court of George II, who was Elector of Hanover as well as King of England. There he met the Duke of Newcastle again.

During Bentinck's year-long absence in Vienna, his foreign policy had been under attack at The Hague, but on his return he resumed his duties as adviser to William IV and set about devising an improved governmental organization based on the Stadt-holderate. In October 1751 the Prince of Orange called the council on foreign affairs which Bentinck had suggested setting up.

The sudden death of William IV in October 1751 brutally interrupted Willem Bentinck's revision of the constitution of the United Provinces. He at once strongly recommended that the regency should be given to Princess Anne straight away, until the three-year-old William V was old enough to take his place as Stadtholder.

At the start of the regency Bentinck's voice was influential. He held to the traditional alliance between the maritime powers of England and the Netherlands and Austria. In 1753 he visited Brussels again and then London, still with the aim of ensuring the defence of the Barrier, but nothing positive resulted.

After the reversal of alliances in 1755 and 1756, when Kaunitz secured the alliance of France and Austria, who had for so long been enemies, Bentinck saw that the United Provinces could no longer rely on outside help against possible aggression and advised the States General to buy more arms and muster more troops. The Seven Years' War was imminent, and he envisaged a sort of armed neutrality for the United Provinces. On the death of s'Gravenmoer, doyen of the knights of Holland, Willem had taken his place, thus becoming president of the councils of the southern quarters.

When Princess Anne died in 1759, William v was only eleven, still too young to rule. The States General therefore constituted themselves regents. The United Provinces remained neutral during the Seven Years' War, but, with the notorious thankless-ness of republics, nobody was grateful to Bentinck for a policy which had helped to keep the country prosperous while the storm raged over Europe. Jan van Back, who had been William iv's private secretary and held high office during the Regency, had been working against the traditional alliances ever since 1750. Bertram Philipp van Gronsfeld, who had received his knighthood and his membership of the council for foreign affairs through Bentinck, worked directly against his benefactor. The Prince of Brunswick-Wolfenbüttel, who owed his very presence in Holland to Bentinck's mission to the court of Maria Theresa, monopolized the positions of power and squeezed his sponsor out of public life.

Willem Bentinck maintained an aloof dignity. His tastes and lively mind drew him towards the sciences, letters and music, and in these respects he was a true representative of the century of the Enlightenment.

12 ✺ Willem Bentinck, the Leyden Jar and Fresh-Water Polyps

A T LEYDEN UNIVERSITY Willem Bentinck had studied under s'Gravesande, who was mathematician, astronomer, physicist and professor of philosophy. Later on, as curator of the University, he met the most learned pupils of the famous anatomist Boerhaave. In the laboratories and botanical garden he also noticed a young naturalist from Geneva, Abraham Trembley – a descendant of a Calvanist refugee who went to Geneva from Lyons at the time of the Reformation, who had started as a student of theology. Trembley had come to Holland to tutor Count Wassenaer's children, a post he held for three years.

Bentinck recognized Trembley's abilities, especially his precision and exceptional gifts of observation, and when Wassenaer no longer needed his services he asked him to tutor his own children, John and Anthony. Since they were still too young to benefit from the naturalist's teaching, Bentinck introduced him in the meantime to his former brother-in-law, the Count of Hesse-Homburg, in Varel, where Trembley spent two years. In October 1739 he returned to The Hague and was soon practically one of the family in Count Bentinck's town house and at Sorgvliet. Abraham devoted all his attention to learning and teaching. He concentrated on the problems of life, starting with the most simple forms, plants and insects. His extraordinary discoveries during his eight-year residence at Sorgvliet were greatly facilitated by Willem Bentinck's interest in them. The ponds on the estate provided material for observation, and the rooms put at Trembley's disposal were transformed into real laboratories as well as study rooms for the children.

As well as their intrinsic value, Trembley's experiments had two further implications. First they drew Willem Bentinck's attention to the possibility and usefulness of teaching children to observe and develop their talents through reasoning, rather than just subjecting them to rote learning. Second, he realized that knowledge and scientific research knew no national boundaries and existed within a world community where people did not meet one another solely across ramparts or on battlefields. If barriers were still necessary, it was to guarantee neutrality and peace, or so Willem Bentinck hoped at the time of his missions to Aix-la-Chapelle and Vienna.

The abundant duckweed in the ponds at Sorgvliet made a good habitat for all sorts of insects and plants, and Trembley took samples in jars for observation by himself and the Bentinck children. He then noticed that some green straws which looked like plants would wriggle if the jar were shaken and spread out their fronds, which turned out to be more like feet. When these little creatures spread their tiny feelers again, Trembley examined cuttings from them and realized to his astonishment that each part reconstituted a whole new living creature. He communicated this discovery to his cousin, the philosopher and physiologist Charles Bonnet, in Geneva.

Sensing the importance of Trembley's discovery at Sorgvliet, Bonnet at once passed on the data to Réaumur, the inventor of the thermometric scale which bears his name and a member of the Paris Academy of Sciences. A physicist of considerable influence, he was then completing the sixth volume of his *Mémoires pour servir à l'histoire naturelle des insectes*. Soon Trembley and Réaumur were corresponding directly, an exchange which stopped only on the death of the French scholar. Most of Trembley's letters have a Sorgvliet heading, and Count Bentinck is often mentioned.[1]

Réaumur's curiosity was so aroused that he asked Trembley to send him some of these odd little animals in a bottle. Although the 'little organized bodies' arrived after sunset he examined them by candlelight and wrote to Trembley: 'They are certainly animals.' He added: 'You do not need urging to follow up the observations you have taken so far already and which will put you in a position to produce a piece of natural history which is more singular than anything I know.'[2]

Trembley's reply on 6 April 1741 shows the scope of the deductions arising out of his Sorgvliet observations concerning the origin of species: 'It took a verdict like yours to remove my doubts. I confess that I could not see the polyps' movements without thinking that they were animals. So they are, then, but they teach us that there are even more connections between animals and plants than had been believed hitherto. . . .' The discovery of an animal which reproduced itself just as plants propagate from cuttings caused a considerable stir in European scientific circles. Réaumur had read out the Sorgvliet letters to the Academy, and its members were unanimous in their praise for Trembley's meticulous observations. Buffon, the superintendent of the King's gardens, appropriated Trembley's findings and sent them to the Royal Society in London, but it received a letter from Charles Bentinck at the same time and attributed the discovery to his nephews' tutor.

Finally, on 15 January 1743, Willem Bentinck, now a member of the Royal Society, sent its president Martin Folkes an extract from Trembley's journal of his experiments, with a covering letter in which he attested the truth of the noted facts and pointed out: 'These experiments are not unique, but have been repeated more than 20 times.' He expressed his hope that other researchers would be tempted to carry out the same experiments and convince themselves with their own eyes. The insects could almost certainly be found in England, and if not it would be easy to send them.

Soon the Sorgvliet experiments were being tested elsewhere. In Geneva Charles Bonnet investigated a slender water-worm; Lyonnet, well known for his work on caterpillars, who had come to at The Hague from Lorraine, observed a larger one; Réaumur took the gifted botanist Jussieu and the mineralogist Guettard to the coasts of Poitou and Normandy, where they set about plotting the limits of the vegetable kingdom.

In Geneva, Charles Bonnet wrote to his colleague Professor Gabriel Cramer: 'Oh I do ask you, Monsieur, what is this? An animal which can be multiplied by cuttings, an animal whose little ones emerge from the body as a branch emerges from a tree. . . . These are the marvels, the prodigies, which we owe to Monsieur Trembley.'[3]

Oliver Goldsmith and Rousseau scoffed at the surge of interest in the reproduction of these little creatures, but in vain. The way was open to what Bonnet called the ladder of living beings. A contemporary engraving depicts him surrounded by 'a chain of nature' going from the mineral to the human, by way of plants, insects, shellfish, snakes, flying fish, birds, bats, lions and monkeys. Between the palm tree and the beetle lies the polyp or hydra recognized at Sorgvliet as an intermediary species of animal possessing plant characteristics.

Réaumur hastened to insert an important passage about the facts recognized for the first time by 'M. Trembley, a gentleman of Geneva, now resident in Holland', in the preface to the sixth volume of his massive work on insects. The Royal Society had obtained and published the manuscript of this preface, with Réaumur's permission, before the volume was published.

Meanwhile the Duke of Richmond, Charles II's grandson through his *maîtresse-en-titre* Louise de Kéroualle, had been Count Bentinck's guest at Sorgvliet in 1743. As a major-general in the British army, Richmond took part in the defeat of the French under Marshal de Noailles by English, Austrian and Hanoverian troops at the battle of Dettingen in Bavaria in 1743. The Duke was a Fellow of the Royal Society and had been present when the letters about the Sorgvliet experiments were read. He was the brother-in-law of Charles Bentinck, who had inherited the Nijhuisen estate of his aunt van Ittersum, Hans Willem's sister. The elder and younger sisters of the Duke of Cadogan, Sarah and Margaret, had married the Duke of Richmond and Charles Bentinck respectively.

The Duke of Richmond came to Sorgvliet to verify Trembley's observations on the spot and took note of the prodigious and rapid increase in the numbers of polyps and their strange transformations. On 15 January 1743 he wrote a long letter from Utrecht corroborating the Sorgvliet findings.[4]

Aware of the progress which had been made in the life sciences, Willem Bentinck did everything in his power to enable the author of the discovery to make known the phenomena of the evolution from plant to animal. He brought an artist to Sorgvliet to record the setting of the experiments and to depict the master and his pupils, his own sons Anthony and John.

Cornelis Pronck, an author and designer, painted portraits of Trembley and his pupils leaning over a pond and fishing up the famous polyps, with the big semicircular greenhouses of Sorgvliet in the background. In another painting the Bentinck children, accompanied by their dog, are using a cap to fish insects out of a tree-lined ditch which resembles the canal dug by the Earl of Portland on his Bulstrode estate. A third picture shows the same figures in Trembley's study, examining the creatures in jars. Engravings were also made after the paintings to illustrate Abraham Trembley's *Memoirs pour servir à l'histoire des polypes.* Trembley kept a close eye on the preparation of the subjects to be reproduced in the illustration of his experiments. On 2 May 1743 he wrote to the publisher Prosper Marchand giving his precise instructions on engraving the plates:

You will find here, Monsieur, the letter I received yesterday from M. Allamand. I replied to him that M. Lyonet had not the faintest idea about engraving my plates; that I did not want the engraver Spijl; that I knew van der Schley through you, and personally, that I had every reason to think that he would work well and diligently, and that I was absolutely determined on him. . . . Since you are writing to van der Schley you can tell him to come and ask him to give me as much advance warning as possible about the day of his arrival, so that I may prepare the objects he is to study. . . .[5]

At Sorgvliet, Willem Bentinck had fostered and helped to publicize research which assumed an unexpected importance. His position as curator of Leyden University placed him at the centre of another great discovery, the electrical condenser known as the 'Leyden jar'. Two professors of Leyden University made the discoveries: Pieter van Musschenbroek and Jean-Nicolas Allamand, the son of a professor at the Academy of Lausanne, who came to Holland to tutor s'Gravesand's children and later succeeded him in the faculty of science and philosophy.

On 4 February 1745 the Bentinck children's tutor wrote from The Hague to the president of the Royal Society, Martin Folkes, informing him that he had seen Allamand put a little mercury in a tube, cork it tightly and shake it, whereupon light was produced. Trembley continued his letter with a description of the famous experiment:

There is an experiment that Mr l'Allamand has tried; he electrify'd a tin tube by means of a glass globe; he then took in his left hand a glass full of water, in which was dipped the end of a wire; the other end touch'd the electrified tin tube: he then touch'd, with a finger of his right hand, the electrified tube and drew a spark from it, when at the same instant he felt a most violent shock all over his body. . . . Mr Musschenbroek the Professor has repeated his experiment . . . and he says he experienced a most terrible pain. . . .[6]

The team of scientists associated with William Bentinck had made a great discovery. Many later developments in television, transistors and electronics depend upon it. In 1750 the surgeon in chief of the Royal Hospital at Rouen, Le Cat, told the Royal Academy: 'Two main discoveries will make our century memorable in centuries to come: Electricity and fresh-water Polyps.'

Anthony and John Bentinck were soon too old to need a private tutor, and the Duke of Richmond, impressed by Trembley's methods at Sorgvliet, brought him to London to look after his son. To begin with, Trembley lived in Whitehall, in an apartment belonging to Willem Bentinck's mother, the old Countess of Portland, and was able to tell her about her grandsons' progress.

Count Bentinck saw Trembley again at the Congress of Aix-la-Chapelle, which he attended as the representative of the Duke of Richmond, now a prominent member of King George II's government. On 16 November 1748 Trembley wrote from London to tell Prosper Marchand that the Duke of Richmond was taking him to Paris, where he had been appointed ambassador. This opportunity to explore France did not materialize, however, and it was from London that Trembley made several more visits to Count Bentinck and his former pupils.

Back in Geneva Trembley married and wrote an underrated book on education based on his own experience with his family and Count Bentinck's. Bentinck played a further part in Genevan learning when Allamand submitted the manuscript of Charles Bonnet's *Méditations sur l'Univers* to him, redrafted under the title of *La Contemplation de la nature*. Allamand wrote to the author about this work:[7] '. . . It is so proper to bring truly philosophical reflections to birth in readers' minds that it would have been a real loss for the public had it been deprived of them. Thus I shall not hesitate to send it to press. Count Bentinck the elder has already read part of it at my house, and shares my opinion of the contents. . . .' The *Contemplation de la nature* appeared in Amsterdam next year under the imprint of M. M. Rey, the famous publisher of the works of Jean-Jacques Rousseau, and enjoyed a considerable success.

13 • Jean-Jacques Rousseau, Godfather to Sophie Bentinck

I N HIS CORRESPONDENCE with Charles Bonnet, Trembley's cousin in Geneva, Count Willem Bentinck was principally concerned with the problems of natural history that he had studied with Allamand and Trembley himself. It was to Willem that Bonnet addressed his *Essai sur l'âme*, together with a letter casting light on his methods. His experiments had moved on from zoology to psychology. He wrote to Willem:

I have undertaken to apply the methods of observers to examining the operations of our soul. I came to believe that to arrive at a little knowledge of how man is made it was necessary to study him as the physicists study all the productions of nature. I have therefore brought my attention to bear on the facts. I have compared, contrasted and combined them, and sought to discover the consequences that followed most immediately. . . .

The principles I have applied are interlinked with one another, and this is a natural effect of the analysis. Therefore I had only to let myself be led by the thread I held in my hand. . . .[1]

It was also to Charles Bonnet that Willem Bentinck's brother Charles defended the ideas of Jean-Jacques Rousseau from the first, while Willem tried to apply those which had to do with education. Since his return from Lausanne with Willem at the end of his Grand Tour, Charles had pursued an honourable military career, reaching the rank of lieutenant-colonel. Like his brother he was an ardent supporter of the Orangist cause and became a member of William IV's privy council. Before the Congress of Aix-la-Chapelle in 1748 he was sent to London at almost the same time as his brother to draw the British ministers' attention to his country's lack of financial resources.

Charles Bentinck must have felt a special pleasure in following the family tradition when he was appointed bailiff of the Twenthe, a region dear to his ancestors, some of whom had held the same post. After the Dutch domestic crises of 1754 Charles took little further part in politics, although he held the post of Master of the Mint until his death.

Of the two brothers, it was Charles Bentinck who felt more attracted to theoretical philosophy. While denying that he was 'a judge in matters so abstract', he sincerely admired Bonnet's *Essai analytique sur les facultés de l'âme* and remarked: 'If necessary, M. Trembley will tell you that I am no flatterer....'

It was not long before Charles Bentinck became acquainted with the work of another philosopher from Geneva. Rey's publication in Amsterdam of the philosophical and social writings of Jean-Jacques Rousseau caused a sensation: he was held to have attacked Christian doctrine. Charles Bentinck had time at Nijhuisen to read and reflect, and he imparted his astonishment to Charles Bonnet. In his opinion, Rousseau had not attempted to argue with the true teachings of Jesus and would have been wrong had he done so. What he had attacked was the attitude of bigots and fanatics who saw the ways of the profane as crimes – who believed that dancing, for instance, was an invention of the devil and that a young girl should have no other amusement but work and prayer.

Bentinck disagreed with Rousseau's concept of the 'noble savage', living by himself in the woods outside society, but argued that such a man was not as far removed from his true destiny as those who lived in society. As Bentinck saw it, all Rousseau had in mind was the re-establishment of law in the Republic of Geneva.

Bonnet's correspondent was among the first to understand that Rousseau had had no idea of the way his theories would be used. 'I write to you on this subject', Bentinck wrote, 'as a man aware enough that he is above humanity to hold power in his hands and not abuse it, and who has felt its effects for having wished to oppose the progress of despotism; and who had rather sacrifice everything than give way to it and seek his own advantage.'

On 7 June 1768 Charles Bentinck informed his friend in Geneva about the blow which had fallen on his brother Willem, whose eldest son, Anthony, had just died at the age of thirty-three. He left a widow, Catherine, born van Tuyll-Serooskeren. Anthony's mother, Charlotte-Sophia von Aldenburg, had left him the seigneuries of Varel and Kniphausen for which his father had pleaded at the Court of Vienna. Part of the inheritance now went to the Count's younger son, John Albert Bentinck, a captain in the British navy and owner of the estate of Terrington, in Norfolk, which had belonged to his grandfather the Earl of Portland.

Anthony's son, Wilhelm, continued the line of the imperial Bentinck counts and married a Baroness van Reede, daughter of the Netherlands ambassador to the Court of Prussia, who had become first Baron, then Earl of Athlone. Through their connections with the van Reedes the counts Bentinck became lords of the chateaux of Middachten and Amerongen, the former near Arnhem, the latter halfway between Arnhem and Utrecht.

The unexpected death of his nephew Anthony, coinciding with the accidental death of the syndic of the Republic of Geneva when he fell from his horse, made Charles Bentinck ponder about the problem of death. Both he and Bonnet were sick men, one suffering from pains all over his body, 'that machine to which your fine soul is so closely wedded', the other from defects in 'the most delicate and precious organ, the organ of sight'.

Bentinck wrote: 'When we too have reached harbour, a permanent happiness will absorb the storms of this little sea. . . . Is not the man who is always prepared happier to be dispatched promptly than to languish for months? Many ordeals are spared him; departure is certain for us all.'

Charles Bentinck did not defend Rousseau's new ideas only in his correspondence with Charles Bonnet. He and his brother Willem were ahead of their time in taking up Rousseau's book on education, *Emile*, at a moment when its heterodox notions were under attack from all sides and when opposition to the oligarchic and monarchic philosophies then prevalent were considered so revolutionary that *Le Contrat social* had almost cost its author his freedom.

Since Willem Bentinck had openly defended Rousseau's works in Holland, the attitude of the two brothers soon became known in Paris, where Rousseau still had a few supporters. Among these was Comtesse Marie-Charlotte de Boufflers,[2] who had been the first to hear some of the passages in *Emile* while the book was still in manuscript (Rousseau had read them aloud to her one evening at the Three Flags inn, in Saint-Denis). She was an educated woman, fluent enough in Latin to have published a translation of the 'Letter from Brutus to Cicero', which later saved her from the attentions of the revolutionaries during the French Revolution. The Countess was a friend of the Prince de Conti, Louis xv's cousin, and was hostess to the many distinguished guests who came to discuss art and literature in his salon in the Temple, formerly a fortified Templar lodge. She was the first to send the Prince a message at Montmorency, where Rousseau had taken refuge, warning him that a warrant was out for Rousseau's arrest. It arrived in time for the philosopher to escape to Switzerland.

From his retreat at Môtiers, in the Swiss Jura, Rousseau kept up a correspondence with his publisher Marc-Michel Rey in Amsterdam. Since Rey had also published Trembley's book on fresh-water polyps, at Willem Bentinck's request, Willem was among the first in Holland to read *Emile*, which was published in 1762 at the same time as *Le Contrat social*, and it was through Rey that he expressed his admiration of the author's educational method. On 1 November 1763 Rey wrote to Rousseau: '. . . In case I forget, I must tell you that Count Bentinck, lord of Rhoon, one of our chief magistrates, whom I saw a fortnight ago, has asked me to present his compliments and to tell you that if he had read your *Emile* thirty years ago he would have had his children brought up in your way. . . . .'[3] Rousseau was deeply moved and replied on 10 December: 'I beg you to visit Count Bentinck on my behalf and tell him that the approval of men who think as he does is a consolation for a great many hardships. . . .'

Rousseau was not the only eminent figure to be introduced to Bentinck by Rey. When Diderot was on his way to St Petersburg in 1773 to meet the Empress Catherine, he stayed with Prince Galitzin at The Hague and saw Rey on business. When Bentinck was informed that the principal author of the *Encyclopédie* was at The Hague he sent his carriage and brought him to Sorgvliet.

In 1763 the Comtesse de Boufflers heard that the curator of Leyden University was passionately interested in the problems posed by *Emile*, and therefore decided to send her son Édouard to study there. The relations between him and Count Bentinck were very different from those which had prevailed between the great Marshal of France and the Earl of Portland.

Willem Bentinck had taken an active part in his sons' upbringing, keeping abreast of the latest ideas, as in John Locke's essay, *Some Thoughts Concerning Education*. As early as March 1743 he wrote to his mother, the Countess of Portland: 'Certainly forming the character is the great point in education. After all nobody can answer for the event, but everybody must act for the best.'[4]

After her son had been at Leyden for some time, the Comtesse de Boufflers herself went to Holland in company with the Duke and Duchess of Holderness. The Duke had been British minister to The Hague and a member of the Pelham government. In his retirement he liked to visit the town where he had represented his country.

After the end of the Seven Years' War in 1763 with the Treaty of Paris, a fruitful cultural network developed in Europe. In the spring of 1764 the Comtesse de Boufflers was dining at the French embassy in The Hague when William Bentinck, one of the guests, voiced his admiration for the author of *Emile* at a time when the town magistrates were burning his new book, as were those of his native town. She was delighted to be able to write to Rousseau:

One day I was dining at the French embassy when Count Bentinck, first nobleman of the Republic and a man of truly worthy character, who was next to me at table, said to me, though your name had not been mentioned:

'Madame, permit me to drink the health of a person whom I infinitely respect and whom I know you love very much – I mean Jean-Jacques Rousseau.'

I answered that he could do me no greater pleasure. . . . His brother, Count Charles Bentinck, the most noble, most virtuous republican there has ever been, is also your admirer and your friend. They had no part in the condemnation of your book. . . .[5]

The authorities of Rousseau's adoptive country made no great fuss of him, and he greatly appreciated the attitude of the leader of the knights of Holland and his brother: 'I am moved by what you tell me about the Counts Bentinck. Judge, Madame, how the good will of worthy men is precious to me, when I am always overcome even by that of men whom I do not esteem! I do not know how fondling might have affected me. . . . I was born weak; harsh treatment has strengthened me. . . .'[6] This came at a moment when Rousseau's taxing and thankless work was under general attack. In three years at Montmorency, from 1761 to 1763, he had finished *La Nouvelle Héloïse* and written all of *Emile* and *Le Contrat social*. The perceptive, tolerant Bentinck spirit was bound to be drawn to the solitary herald of a freer society.

On her return to France the Comtesse de Boufflers helped Rousseau to travel to England, where we shall encounter him in the company of the Duchess of Portland. Once she was back in circles which were often hostile to new ideas, the Countess's letters to Willem Bentinck reveal a certain uneasiness about Rousseau's educational methods as they were applied to her son, who was by no means a gifted boy. Bentinck's personality melted her fears like a morning mist, and, besides, Bentinck's native land had impressed her with its 'simplicity, sincerity, and republican morals and virtues'. Her son could not be in better hands.

The fond mother expressed her gratitude to the eminent curator and diplomat with the utmost grace and charm. She also enclosed a copy of a letter she had received from Rousseau but asks Bentinck to burn it: 'It is so full of praises far beyond my deserts that it would become a satire against myself were it to be published.' Her discretion consequently deprived literary history of a page of Rousseau. On 6 July 1764, Willem Bentinck replied from Sorgvliet:

I am obliged to you, Madame, for the copy of Jean-Jacques's letter. I was touched by his condition. For I am his firm friend, and very attached to him for his principles. The accordance of his taste and judgement concerning yourself with my own attaches me all the more strongly to him. The letter shall be burned, and will not be seen by anyone outside my household.[7]

Édouard de Boufflers spent two years in the Netherlands. He returned in spring 1766 and found his mother at Montmorency, with the Maréchale de Luxembourg, widow of the nephew of the formidable Marshal whose advance had been checked by the flooding of Holland in the days of Hans Willem Bentinck and William III of Orange. She lived in the chateau where Rousseau composed the fifth book of *Emile*, in 'the enchantment of concerts of birds and the smell of the orange flower'. The room above the kitchen, decorated in blue and white, remained empty and silent. Thanks to Marie-Charlotte de Boufflers, Rousseau was Grenville's guest in England by then.

The Countess was soon back in Paris, and Allamand described life in the Prince de Conti's household to Willem Bentinck between two sittings of the Academy of Sciences in a letter dated 19 August 1766:

The Prince de Conti was good enough to ask me to stay with him, and I find around the Comtesse de Boufflers all the most distinguished people in Paris, both for their birth and their way of thinking, by which I mean the purest good sense, with no admixture of modish wit. What I am seeing here proves to me concretely how easy it is for a prince to alter the behaviour and character of those about him. The Prince de Conti in the middle of Paris is what your brother is at Nijhuisen, or yourself at Doorwerth;[8] there are the same leanings towards hunting in moderation, simple conversation, and also towards the fine arts, the sciences, good books. . . . He will be sending a gardener to Sorgvliet, to learn from your own man how to look after the plants kept in cool greenhouses, without heating.[9]

It was an altogether different kind of problem with which Rousseau was presented by Count Willem's second son, John Albert Bentinck, in the year when the Comtesse de Boufflers was visiting The Hague. Since the content of his letter has to do with feelings, morality and naval defence, one wonders whether it is to the author of *Emile* or of *La Nouvelle Héloïse* that Bentinck is addressing himself.

It was a long time since John Albert and his brother Anthony had studied the natural sciences with Trembley at Sorgvliet. At the age of fifteen John had gone to Plymouth and enlisted on board a ship, where he went through the hard apprenticeship of the sea without assistance from his father, who considered the experience character-forming. 'He's suffering a little at present,' Willem wrote, 'but everybody goes through that. The more you learn when young, the better it is. . . .'[10] Fortunately John Bentinck came of hardy stock, and by 1758 he had attained the rank of captain. After serving in various ships, accompanying a convoy to Newfoundland and taking part in engagements against the enemy, he began to make use of the technical knowledge acquired at Leyden and perfected the chain pump then used on ships to the point of being considered its inventor.

After the Treaty of Paris he married the charming Renira van Tuyll, the daughter of Johan van Tuyll-Serooskerken, lord of Heese and of Leende, in northern Brabant. Renira's mother, Christina van Reede, was the grand-daughter of Godard van Reede, first Earl of Athlone, Hans Willem Bentinck's companion in arms at the battle of the Boyne and the siege of Athlone. Five years previously Renira's elder sister had married Willem's elder son, continuing the line of the Bentincks of Varel and Kniphausen. Renira was painted by several great portraitists, including George Romney.

In 1764 John Albert was staying with his father at The Hague.

His young wife remained in London with their son, another William Bentinck, the future Vice-Admiral, who was then less than a year old. It must have been after hearing Willem talk about Rousseau, who was still in retreat at Môtiers, that John wrote the letter in which he asks for advice on his most pressing cause for concern: each time he set sail on the high seas, his wife was racked with anguish at the thought of losing him. What made it easier for John to write to Rousseau was that Renira had read *Emile* and sincerely admired Sophie, the model pupil idealized in the book. The letter is dated 28 December 1764:

Perhaps, Sir, you will be surprised to receive a letter from an unknown; perhaps you will be even more surprised to see its subject. I have read your writings . . . but since I know that you dislike compliments, I shall make none.

Let me tell you therefore that I serve in the fleet of His Britannic Majesty; I am 27 years old and have never conducted myself in such a manner as to prevent my friends from advancement to the rank of post-captain, a position I have had the honour to hold for more than 6 years. . . . I mention my age only to bring you to read this letter with patience, apart from it being necessary for you to know my general history, so that I may make you understand what I desire from you.

After the war I married, and I wish to make complaint to you concerning my wife; you can be of service to us both, and I cannot believe that you will refuse me. Here then is my story and my grievance; they may be unusual, but they are true.

My wife is 21 years old, quite tall, not at all ugly, well made, and for conjugal society sweet, gay, tender, wise and virtuous – in a word, full-grown; she is talented in music, drawing, and in other accomplishments. . . . She has a son whom she loves as women of that age do love their children. . . .

John Albert now lists his wife's peculiarities – actually 'merits', as Rousseau later described them:

First I can never convince her that what she does, she does well; she always thinks that another does it better, which causes her to do it awkwardly, and less well than she really can.

Second, she has so excessive a fondness for me that she bears even the shortest separation very ill. She knows that I love the service . . . so that the idea of a war is unbearable for her. Mention it and all's lost! When she wishes, she thinks with a wonderful breadth of mind on all topics, but not this one. I do not dare to broach it. . . .

By now you must see my drift, Sir; you have given many a good lesson to those unable to be good, but have said nothing yet for the happiness and comfort of those who are too good. There are so few, you will say, that it had never entered my head; that may be; but once there are any at all, their fewness in number only renders the task more worthy of you. . . .[11]

John Bentinck concluded by saying that he and Renira would like Rousseau to become the godfather of their next child.

No one could guess from Rousseau's reply, dated 27 January 1765, that it was written at a time when he had trials and dangers of his own to contend with:

I am moved, Sir, by the expressions of esteem and confidence with which you honour me, but as you very rightly say, let us leave aside the compliments and proceed, if we can, to what is useful. . . .

The truth is, Sir, that I am enchnated with you and your worthy wife. How amiable and tender must a husband be, who paints his wife with such charming touches! She may love you too much for your own comfort but never too much for your merit, nor you enough for hers. I know nothing more absorbing than the portrait of your union traced by yourself. . . .

Rousseau enclosed another letter addressed to Renira Bentinck: 'I learn, Madame, that you are a virtuous and amiable wife, that you have as much affection for your husband as he for you, which therefore means as much as is possible.'

He expressed the intention of corresponding with her when the approaching happy event made him their child's godfather. As for the duties which would sometimes remove her husband from her, Rousseau congratulated her on a merit which placed her above fear and a husband who was so aware of it. He continued:

During those interludes you will pass your time sweetly thinking about him and his precious pledges of affection, talking about them to him in your letters and talking to those who have a share in your union. Shall I dare, Madame, to include myself in their number? My sentiments give me that right; try whether I hear your own, whether I sense your anxiety, whether I may sometimes allay it. I do not presume to alleviate your woes, but it is something to share them, and I shall do that with all my heart.

On 21 June 1765 Renira van Reede Bentinck gave birth to her second child, Rousseau's god-daughter, Sophie-Henriette. Her grandmother, Charlotte-Sophia Aldenburg Bentinck, Count Willem Bentinck's estranged wife, would never call her Sophie except ironically, when she talked to her about her 'famous god-father' whose achievement had, in her view, been to lead intelligent people astray and to bring about the loss of morality, the destruction of religion, law and order, and even the total neglect of mankind.[12]

Sophie-Henriette was only ten years old when her father died; he had commanded the *Centaur* until two years before his death. She herself married a British naval officer, James Hawkins, who became an admiral. We do not know if Renira Bentinck had brought up her daughter on Rousseau's principles, but it can be said that John Albert and Renira had taken note of his advice, so that Sophie's mother could pay this magnificent tribute: 'Since I have had the good fortune to belong to the Bentinck family, we have lived in the utmost harmony.'

Nor did she ever forget her father-in-law, the owner of Sorgvliet and curator of Leyden University, Willem Bentinck: 'I miss, and shall respect throughout my life the memory of, my late father-in-law, who always showed me marks of his sincere affection, as did my brother-in-law, who always lived in the greatest intimacy with my husband.'

14 ✒ *Margaret Cavendish Bentinck, Duchess of Portland*

WILLEM BENTINCK felt a close personal and political affinity with England throughout his life. It was his mother's native country, his father had been ennobled there, he himself had been born there and had made friends among the most influential Members of Parliament.

Among these was Thomas Holles Pelham, Duke of Newcastle, his companion at the Conference of Aix-la-Chapelle, in London and at the Court of King George at Hanover, after his visit to Vienna. The two families were bound by even closer ties than friendship. The eldest son of Henry Bentinck, Duke of Portland, was William Bentinck, who inherited the title when his father died in Jamaica. In 1734 William married Margaret, only daughter of Edward Harley, Earl of Oxford, and Lady Henrietta Cavendish Holles, who was the daughter of John Holles, Duke of Newcastle. His huge fortune was shared at his death between his daughter and his nephew, Willem Bentinck's friend Thomas Pelham, the heir to the title.

Margaret Cavendish Harley had been brought up partly at Welbeck, and after her marriage to the Duke of Portland this became the favourite residence of the Bentinck dukes of Portland down to the present day, although after William's death Margaret lived mainly at Bulstrode, where her husband's grandfather had spent his final years. An ancestor of Margaret, Duchess of Portland, had built the long, nine-gabled façade of Welbeck which faces a small lake, terraces, broad lawns and pools, and beyond them the forest. In October 1695 Margaret's grandfather had received William III there when he returned victorious from Flanders, at the zenith of his glory. Among the eminent northern dignitaries who gathered to welcome him were the Lord Mayor of York with his chief magistrates and the Archbishop of York and several fellow clerics.[1]

The Duchess of Portland's mother, Margaret Cavendish, Duchess of Newcastle, was a gifted writer, and John Milton had admired her poetry, especially her 'Dialogue between Mirth and Melancholy'. Her father, Edward Harley, Earl of Oxford, had assembled a remarkable collection of paintings, illuminated manuscripts and *objets d'art* which their daugher had admired since childhood. Harley's old librarian noted in his diary that 'the young Lady Margaret', who was then eleven years old, often came to see the illuminated books. One day 'our dear young Lady came and I showed her a book ornamented with beautiful pictures'.[2]

Margaret Cavendish Bentinck also collected *objets d'art* herself, as well as shells, rare plants and minerals, spars, fossils, corals, fish and English and exotic insects, many of them from New York. She once spent a whole evening with the poet Horace Walpole discussing how to obtain the sort of red spider described by Admiral Boscawen.[3]

Long after the death of Edward Harley part of his collection of books and manuscripts was presented to the British Museum, where they form the basis of the famous Harleian Library. Some of these documents had remained with the dukes of Portland, at Welbeck. The second gift to the British Museum in 1950 included the splendid Beaulieu Cartulary, the manuscript of the travels of Thomas Baskerville, various eighteenth-century documents concerning the building of St Paul's, Greenwich Church and Blenheim Palace, and a plan for a new Royal Palace.

As the wife of William Bentinck, Duke of Portland, Margaret lived with him on their estates at Bulstrode and Welbeck and at Whitehall. She had made the acquaintance of his uncle, Count Willem Aldenburg Bentinck, when he came to England as the envoy of William IV of Orange, and their correspondence revolves around their collections. On 20 May 1757 the Duchess of Portland wrote from Bulstrode to Count Bentinck, whom she addresses as 'Sir and dearest uncle', to inform him that she had finally found somebody to send a painting, probably a portrait, and the frame. She hoped that the moulding of the frame would not be damaged in transit and then assured him that nothing could give her greater pleasure than his esteem for herself and her daughters. A few weeks later Willem Bentinck sent her an ornamental box full of shells, which were far more beautiful than she had expected.[4]

The Duchess had talked to Willem Bentinck about Matthew Prior, the poet who was secretary to the British embassy in Paris when Hans Willem Bentinck was there on behalf of William III. As a child she had often seen him with her parents; at their home he was loved by everyone in the household – master, child, servant, even the animals.[5] Another visitor had been Mary Wortley-Montagu, author of the well-known *Letters*, some of them written while she was with her husband on his mission to Turkey.[6]

One of the Duchess's favourite occupations was the cultivation of rare plants for her herbariums and growing flowers in the grounds at Bulstrode, where she had imported Daniel Solander, a Swedish botanist and former pupil of Linnaeus, to supervise the design and care of the gardens.

In the early summer of 1766 we learn through a letter from Mrs Mary Delany, later a member of the Queen's entourage, that the Duchess of Portland visited her friends Bernard Granville (Mary Delany's brother) his niece Miss Dewess and Mrs Delany herself. She had admired the lush flora of the Granvilles' estate at Calwich in Staffordshire.

The Duke of Portland had arranged for the botanist and churchman John Lightfoot to be appointed Rector of Gotham, near

Welbeck. He was also the Duchess's chaplain. His work on the flora of Scotland, illustrated by Moses Griffith, is dedicated 'To her Grace the most noble Margaret Cavendish, Duchess Dowager of Portland, the great and intelligent admirer and patroness of natural history'.[7] According to the naturalist Thomas Pennant, Lightfoot's conversation on the subjects of conchology and especially botany was very illuminating. He helped the Duchess to classify her magnificent collection of shells and rare plants.[8]

The Duchess's friendship with the Granvilles of Calwich was long-standing, and she loved visiting the converted abbey and examining the profusion of heathers and mosses in the locality. As early as August 1737 she wrote to Mrs Ann Granville to thank her for some bee-orchid roots which she meant to tend and plant out.

Almost thirty years passed after these early visits to Calwich when Mrs Mary Delany wrote to Lady Andover:

The Duchess of Portland has written to tell me that she would be very glad to meet you at Calwich. . . . My brother too desires and impatiently awaits that honour, and is afraid only of not being capable of treating you as you ought to be, but he will offer you the spectacle of seeing Mister Rousseau, who is in the neighbourhood. . . .[9]

We had left Jean-Jacques Rousseau persecuted on the Continent, hesitating about accepting an invitation to Holland from Charles Bentinck and finally accepting an invitation from the philosopher David Hume to come to England. When Hume did not find him the country house he wanted, Rousseau chose the house offered by a wealthy admirer of his books, Richard Davenport, who usually lived on another of his estates, at Davenport Hall in Cheshire, as a gentleman-farmer. The house he lent to Rousseau was at Wootton, at the foot of the Weaver Hills, only two miles from Calwich Abbey. Bernard Granville lost no time in visiting him there.

On the arrival of the Duchess of Portland at Calwich, she and Rousseau began a series of botanical excursions, looking for flowers for her herbarium. They were plentiful along the valleys of the River Dove, on the edge of the forests and along the local footpaths, as well as beneath the giant beeches which surrounded the former abbey. A few weeks after their meeting the Duchess wrote to Granville that she had sent Mr Rousseau a few plants. Later she recommended to Rousseau a book by the pharmacist and botanist Petiver, with engravings of English plants by Ray.

The Duchess returned to Calwich at the end of August 1767 with Countess Cowper. 'Who else but the Duchess of Portland could arrive at 8 o'clock?' asked Granville's niece, Miss Dewess, whom Rousseau had met on the Calwich–Wootton road dressed as a shepherdess and tending her flock. 'She had come from Kedlestone this morning and seemed very glad to find us.'

In September, the Duchess received a delightful letter from Rousseau,[10] who also mentions her in his letters to Bernard Granville:

Once I had a passion for liberty and equality. . . . Now my tastes have changed, and it is not so much liberty as peace that I love; I sigh after it incessantly, I prefer it above everything now; I want it at all costs with my friends, and even with my enemies, if possible. . . . When you see Milady the Duchess of Portland, give her my respects, I beg you. . . .[11]

Rousseau's ideas on liberty and equality were making their own way in the world. He no longer had to nurse them. In the new flurry which arose about him, in part as a result of his tendency to see attacks on his works as plots against himself, it was Margaret Cavendish Bentinck who helped to bring him to his senses and restore 'that precious serenity of mind given by contemplation of the wonders which surround us'. He wrote to the Duchess: 'If I never had the honour of knowing I would at least have the pleasure of learning, and learning from yourself, and whether or not I become a better botanist I would surely become wiser and happier.'[12] When he wrote to thank her for sending him various botanical works, he added:

Happy is he who can appreciate these absorbing writings enough to need nothing else, and who, distrusting the teachings of men, who are

G

liars, attaches himself to those of nature, which does not lie. You study it with as much pleasure as success, you follow it into all its preserves: none of its products is foreign to you. You can classify minerals, shells and fossils, grow plants, tame birds. . . . I know one slightly wild animal which would be delighted to live in your menagerie, awaiting the honour of being preserved in your cabinet some day. . . .[13]

Jean-Jacques Rousseau's botanical letters to the Duchess of Portland are worth further consideration because she inspired some of the finest pages ever written about the natural world. Writing from Wootton on 12 February 1767 he tells her what a shame it is that the plates in James Petiver's book *Museum Petiverianum,* are in black and white and regrets that Linnaeus made known the class and order of a plant but not whether it is large or small, or whether the flower is blue or red! 'In the mean time . . . I sometimes need art to maintain myself in this precious calm in the midst of the disturbances that trouble my life.'[14] Rousseau lacks nothing but sad memories disturbing his peace and solitude: 'I want to forget men and their injustices; I wish to be moved each day by the wonders of him who made them to be good, and whose work they have so unworthily degraded: the plant life in our woods and mountains is still just as it originally left his hands, and it is there that I love to study nature.'[15] The correspondence on botany continued. From Wootton he writes to inquire about a fern; he sends her a little Adiantum, which is not uncommon in the rocks around Wootton, to be planted along the walls of Bulstrode.

Less than three months later, early in 1767, Rousseau was in flight once again, scoffed at by Horace Walpole, quarrelling with David Hume and angry with his benefactor Davenport. In France again, he lived incognito in the Prince of Conti's chateau of Trye, in Normany. From there he wrote to Bulstrode asking to become the Duchess's official herbalist: 'The herbalist of Milady the Duchess of Portland will console himself for the death of Jean-Jacques Rousseau without difficulty if he thereby ceases to bear the name under which he has been so unhappy.'[16]

The Bulstrode botanist John Lightfoot joined in the game with

good grace. In any case the author of *La Nouvelle Héloïse* had
added that he would try not to make the title purely honorary,
and he kept his word. On 17 September he sent the Duchess of
Portland an *Anthemis nobilis*[17] and a *Sagina procumbens*, on another
occasion a centaury. In a letter to his friend Du Peyrou he com-
plains that the study of plants is still regarded as a branch of
pharmacy:

This superb carpet that covers the earth is nothing but plasters and
enemas to their eyes, and they believe that I spend my time making
purgatives. What a shock for them if they had seen Milady the Duchess
of Portland, whose herbalist I have the honour to be, climbing on rocks
where I could barely follow, in search of the Chamaedrys frutescens
and the Saxifraga alpina![18]

From Trye, Rousseau moved on to Dauphiné, where after
June 1768 he divided his time between the Fontaine d'Or inn
at Bourgoin, halfway between Lyons and Grenoble, and a farm
at Monquin belonging to a M. de Césarges. He was writing
his *Confessions*, but still did not forget that he was the Duchess of
Portland's herbalist. In order to make up a herbarium for her, he
organized an expedition to the slopes of Mont Pilat, the source of
the River Gier, a tributary of the Rhône. Although the flora were
less plentiful than in spring he brought back a fine haul and sent a
list to the Duchess, with an asterisk against the names of those of
which he had been able to collect seed. The list included various
foxgloves, arnica, aconite, bilberries, Alpine roses, melissas,
daphnes, and many others with less familiar Latin names.

So that the plants would reach Bulstrode in good condition,
Rousseau asked Madame Delessert, née Boy de la Tour, for a
quantity of strong blue and red paper, 'for wrapping the plants I
have brought from Pilat for sending to Milady the Duchess of
Portland'.[19]

A local scholar, M. de la Tourette, visited Mont Pilat the
following year and described the frozen source of the Gier and
the meadows near La Grange where Rousseau had collected his
specimens. He concluded his account by noting: 'I have had

occasion to make use of the excellent notes on some late-flowering plants of Mont Pilat provided by a famous man who, after plumbing the depths of the human heart with a philosopher's gaze, has not felt it beneath him to turn his eyes upon plants and mosses.'[20]

During his last years Rousseau kept in touch with the Duchess of Portland and his friends at Calwich, Bernard Granville and his niece 'the Shepherdess', who grazed her sheep along the footpath from Wootton. In one letter, dated 14 September 1774, Mrs Delany informed him that the young Duchess of Portland, née Cavendish, the daughter-in-law of Margaret Harley Cavendish Bentinck, Dowager Duchess of Portland, had been 'brought to bed of a fine stout boy'.[21] The words were well chosen, for this child displayed his exceptional vigour as British representative in Sicily during the Napoleonic wars, afterwards as Governor-General of the East Indies.

Margaret, Duchess of Portland, had lived at Bulstrode ever since her husband's death in 1762, leaving Welbeck and its impressive gallery of ancestral portraits to her eldest son. At Bulstrode she retained her enamels and miniatures and the paintings that she had bought from the collection of the Swiss-born diplomat Sir Lucas Schaub. The Duchess was famous for her collection of blue and white porcelains from Japan and China, with their scenes of storks flying above river landscapes, fishermen in small boats, a servant holding a parasol over his master's head, a tiger behind a bamboo thicket, and in the background a lady standing with her servant by a waterfall. When she died these precious objects made up only a tenth of a collection, which was chiefly devoted to the natural sciences.

Towards the end of her life the Duchess bought two world-famous pieces from Lord Hamilton, who had acquired them in Rome from Prince Barberini, through the offices of James Byres, his guide to the ruins of the Eternal City. The antique deep blue and white glass vase with mythological figures in cameo relief is now known as the 'Portland Vase' and is one of the wonders of the British Museum. The other piece is a head of Jupiter Serapis carved in green basalt, of Egyptian origin. It was bought by Horace Walpole when part of the Duchess's collections was sold after her death on behalf of her younger son Edward Cavendish Bentinck and his sisters. Walpole wrote of the bust: 'The countenance is highly expressive of sublimity & dignity tempered with sweetness and grace.' His well-known collections at Strawberry Hill owed a great deal to those of the Duchess of Portland.

A number of historical mementoes preserved by the Duchess came from her husband's grandfather, Hans Willem Bentinck, first Earl of Portland, and most of them testify to his friendship with William III of Orange and his wife Mary, daughter and grand-daughter of the Stuart kings. They include a pearl worn by Charles I at the moment of his execution and his communion chalice. A model of William III's armed yacht dates from 1665, three years before his coronation; on the masts float the words 'Royal Standard' and a flag with the crosses of St Andrew and St George. With this model are wooden sculptures dating from 1690, bearing the royal arms and the initials W.M.R.

The most moving memento is undoubtedly the silver-handled pink crystal seal bearing the Bentinck arms, which have not changed since the Middle Ages. The moline cross is surmounted by a helmet and a shield with the repeated initials W and P, William and Portland, beneath an earl's coronet.

The simplicity of the old Bentinck arms was altered as the family added the quarterings of other noble families with which it became allied. In 1801 William Henry, son of William and Margaret, Duke and Duchess of Portland, who had married the only daughter of a Cavendish – William, fourth Duke of Devonshire – received the King's authority to add the Cavendish name and arms to his own. The Bentincks of the English branch now became the Cavendish–Bentincks. The line of Lord Edward Charles Bentinck, who was the second son of Margaret, became extinct in the next generation with the death in 1862 of the Canon and Archdeacon of Westminster, William Harry Edward Bentinck and of his brother Cavendish Charles Bentinck who was drowned in the Mediterranean during the Napoleonic wars, in 1809.

William Henry, third Duke of Portland, held a number of the highest positions in the realm. He was only twenty-seven years old when he entered Lord Rockingham's first Cabinet in 1765. In the following year he married Dorothy Cavendish, only daughter of the fourth Duke of Devonshire. Rockingham gave way to the Duke of Grafton in the same year, and Portland remained in opposition for a long time. In 1783 he spent a brief period as Prime Minister in coalition with Charles James Fox and Lord North. For some time he opposed the policies of William Pitt but eventually came over to him, becoming Home Secretary in 1794, a difficult job which he carried out wisely and conscientiously.

Pitt had great respect for the Duke of Portland, and when he resigned as Prime Minister wrote to Lord Sidmouth: 'The Duke of Portland agrees to remain in the Cabinet, without portfolio. Nothing could be kinder or handsomer than his whole conduct.'

The rivalry between George Canning and Lord Castlereagh obliged the old Duke to go back into harness as Prime Minister in 1807 as a mediating force. Portland's eldest son had become a brother-in-law of Canning when he married his wife's sister.

Thus the Duke of Portland was in power at the height of Napoleon's success. England failed in the attempt to land at Walcheren in Holland while the Emperor was engaged at Wagram in July 1809 and Portland died at Bulstrode three months later.

15 • Vice-Admirals Wolter and William Bentinck, their Ancestry and Descendants

BEFORE LOOKING at the career of Lord William Cavendish-Bentinck, son of the third Duke of Portland, who gave a constitution to Sicily and then fought for greater justice in India, we must return to the Dutch branch of the descendants of Eusebius Bentinck, Hans Willem's brother, to pay tribute to the hero of an unhappy, pointless war between the rival maritime powers.

Eusebius Bentinck's descendants remained lords of Schoonheten in Overijssel. Hendrik, the elder brother of Eusebius and Hans Willem, had no sons, and one of his daughters married her second cousin Willem Bentinck of Schoonheten, author of the remarkable essay on *The Constancy of the Romans*. The seigneuries of Schoonheten and Diepenheim were thus united in his hands and then to those of his son Berend Bentinck, knight of Overijssel and coadjutor of the Teutonic Order, who married the daughter of Ambrosius du Tertre.

Two of Berend's sons died young. A third, Wolter Jan Gerrit Bentinck, distinguished himself in the war between Holland and England after the American War of Independence and the Dutch decision to cling to the principle of armed neutrality.

When the war broke out on 20 December 1780 the Dutch

were outnumbered in men-of-war. The principal battle was
fought off the Dogger Bank in the North Sea. Wolter Bentinck,
who took part in it, had left his parents to join the navy as a mid-
shipman at the age of thirteen. Without boasting of his ancestors
who had fought under the dukes of Gelderland against those of
Burgundy, and against the kings of France and Spain, but aware
of their courage, he acted like a brother towards the ordinary
seamen from the outset. When he became a captain at twenty-
nine, he cared more for them than for himself.

In the battle of the Dogger Bank, Wolter Bentinck occupied
the most exposed position as commander of the 54-gun *Batavier*,
in Rear-Admiral Zoutman's squadron. He was hit and badly
wounded in the shoulder by a ball from the 60-gun *Buffalo*, relin-
quishing command to his first officer. His only hope was to break
off the action and return to harbour for medical treatment. Instead he gave the order to stay and fight.

The attacking British ships were the *Fortitude*, the *Amelia*, the
Preston and the ironically named *Benevolent*. At the end of the day
the *Batavier* was a floating wreck, but the English ships had suffered heavy damage and broke off the engagement. The courage
of the *Batavier*'s captain had avoided defeat. Wolter Bentinck
battled against death for eighteen days, finally dying on the night
of 23 August. Before his death the Prince of Orange had appointed
him his adjutant and Vice-Admiral.

At the funeral a vast crowd of mourners crammed into small
boats on the canals around the Nieuwe Kerk in Amsterdam.[1]
Four of Wolter's brothers represented the family: Volkier Rudolf
Bentinck, lord of Schoonheten, adjutant to the Prince of Orange
and commander of Utrecht; Dietrich Bentinck, lord of Diepenheim and knight of Overijssel; Carel Bentinck, a lieutenant-
general of infantry; and Bernard Hendrik Bentinck, lord of
Buckhorst and Salk, stadtholder of Overijssel and commander of
a cavalry regiment. They were accompanied by Vice-Admirals
Zoutman and Kinsberg and by numerous officers, burgomasters,
Admiralty and other officials. The events were the subject of a
number of contemporary prints, and the medals struck for the

occasion have been piously preserved in numerous Dutch families. It is particularly moving to find them, together with a portrait of Wolter in his red officer's uniform, in the family of a direct descendant of his brother at Schoonheten, Baron Rudolf Floris Carel Bentinck. He and his wife and daughters live in the fortified manor where the hero of the Dogger Bank was born, among the proud souvenirs of several centuries. Wolter's tomb is in the Bentinck chapel at Rhoon. The ambassador Adolphe Bentinck, to whom we shall refer later, is another direct descendant of Wolter's brother.

Hans Willem's son from his second marriage, Willem, died in 1774. His two sons were already dead, and all his titles therefore passed to his twelve-year-old grandson Willem Gustav Friedrich.

Fifteen years later the French revolutionary government announced its intention of restoring the 'natural frontiers' of its country. When General Pichegru entered Holland, the authority of the Stadtholder William v had been undermined and he did not have enough troops to defend his country. It was Willem Gustav Friedrich Bentinck who helped him to escape into exile in England in 1795, when his life was threatened.

W.G.F. Bentinck's Orangist loyalties compromised him with the new occupying power, and he was made prisoner at The Hague and placed under guard at the Ten Bosch Palace, near Sorgvliet. William v's wife was Wilhelmina of Prussia, and when two years later her brother the King helped the stadtholder to return to Holland, W.G.F. Bentinck was appointed first colonel, then major-general. From then on he fought against Napoleon's domination.

After the defeat of the allies in Holland and the treaty of Alkmaar in 1799, Bentinck withdrew to his estates of Varel and Kniphausen, in the former duchy of Oldenburg. There he ruled over a miniature sovereign state. He even struck his own coinage, and there are still silver half-thalers in existence today, dated 1807. The gold thalers minted at St. Petersburg never went into circulation.[2]

In 1807 Napoleon learned from his new foreign minister J.B. Nompère de Champigny, Talleyrand's successor, that Bentinck was still operating an independent mail. Thus English products might slip through the meshes of the continental blockade decreed by Napoleon the year before. On 14 September 1807 Napoleon replied to his minister from Rambouillet: 'I don't know who this M. Benting is who has a mail service; presumably he will be included in your report on the small ports to be closed to England.'[3]

In 1813 Count Bentinck was captured in Bremen by the French and taken to Paris. He was released in 1814 and pleaded successfully at the Congress of Aix-la-Chapelle for the restoration of the rights over Varel and Kniphausen for which his grandfather had petitioned in Vienna.

W.G.F. Bentinck and his brother Jan Carel had married respectively Baroness Ottolina Friederike Luisa van Reede in 1791 and Jacoba Helena, Countess van Reede, the daughter of the lord of Amerongen and Middachten, in 1785. The former had only one son, who died at the age of thirteen, and two daughters. One of them became the daughter-in-law of Baron van Neukirchen, a knight of Nijmegen, the husband of Friederike Christina Henrietta Bentinck. She was thus matched with the last descendant of Alexander Bentinck, of the Aller branch, who had been one of the founders of the United Provinces in 1579. The other daughter married Baron van Nagell, the King's chamberlain.

Jan Carel had three sons who carried on the line of the Counts Bentinck. The oldest, Willem Friedrich Christian, inherited the chateau of Middachten, which he shared with his brother. Willem's only daughter married Magnus van Solms, thus linking the Bentinck family to that of William III of Orange, whose grandmother belonged to the van Solms family.

Jan Carel's second son, Carel Anton Ferdinand, rose to the rank of lieutenant-general in the British army under Wellington. He fought in Spain, where he was wounded in the battle of Borossa in 1811, and at Waterloo. Afterwards, when Europe was at peace and Holland free, he lived at Middachten with his wife Caroline Mechtild, daughter of the reigning Count of Waldeck-Pyrmont. She published the correspondence of William III's wife Queen Mary.

Carel Anton and his brother fought an interminable legal battle for Varel and Kniphausen, but to no avail. They lost them for ever in 1854.

The third son, Count Hendrik Jan Wilhelm, made a brilliant military career in Great Britain and commanded an infantry regiment during the Crimean War, taking part in the battle of the Alma and the siege of Sevastopol. He married his distant cousin Renira Antoinette, daughter of Admiral James Hawkins Whitshed, one of the heroes of the battle of St Vincent, and Sophie-Henriette Bentinck, the god-daughter of Jean-Jacques Rousseau.[4]

William Bentinck, the son of Captain John Albert, also reached high rank in the British navy and as a diplomat. Outside occupied Europe the city of St Petersburg had become the capital of the opposition and in July 1812 Vice-Admiral William Bentinck was one of the representatives of various allied countries at the Court of Tsar Alexander I. They included Swedes, Germans, Englishmen and even anti-Bonapartist Frenchmen. General Bernadotte, who had won great victories for Napoleon before being adopted as crown prince of Sweden by King Charles XIII, had broken with the Emperor when it became obvious that the French intended to invade Sweden. He decided to throw in his lot with Russia, and Vice-Admiral Bentinck reached an understanding with the Tsar to arrange a conference between him and Bernadotte at Abo. Bentinck returned from Sweden from his successful mission on 15 August, two days before the arrival of Madame de Staël. It was agreed at Abo that Bernadotte would fight on the side of Russia and that Norway was to become part of a kingdom governed by Bonaparte's former general.

Together with Baron von Stein, Bentinck was one of the few foreigners to be received at the Tsar's table. On 1 September he was the guest of Madame de Staël, who had also invited the official English representative, Lord Tyrconnel, two more

Englishmen, Wilson and Cathcart, Baron von Stein and Joseph de Maistre.[5]

Elsewhere she describes her reception by the Tsar's foreign minister Romanzov, admiring his manners if not his delay in withdrawing from the Napoleonic system. Other visitors to Romanzov were:

... Lord Tyrconnel and Admiral Bentinck, both remarkable-looking men; they were the first Englishmen to reappear on the Continent from which they had been banished by one man's tyranny. After ten years of so terrible a struggle, ten years during which success and defeat had always found the English faithful to the lodestone of their policy, conscience, they were finally returning to the country which had been the first to throw off the universal monarchy. Their accent, their simplicity and their pride aroused in one's mind that sense of thoroughgoing truth which Napoleon had discovered the art of obscuring in the eyes of those who read nothing but his gazettes and listened to none but his agents. . . .[6]

Whether at sea, in the palace of the Tsars or with the general staff of General Suvarov in Italy, as we shall see, the Bentincks opposed a dominant autocracy in Europe just as their ancestor Hans Willem had fought against the unification of Spain and France under Louis xiv and his grandson.

The Vice-Admiral kept up his correspondence with Madame de Staël until his premature death at St Petersburg in February 1813.[7] As she left the banks of the Neva in September 1812, she had had a foreboding that she would not see all her new friends again, much as she had been drawn to them, including 'the witty Admiral Bentinck', by their common beliefs. Leaving a few days after the battle of Moscow, she wrote: 'Never had the fate of the world known greater danger. As I said farewell to those worthy knights of the human race, I did not know which of them I would meet again.'

16 ❧ Lord William Bentinck: the Struggle for a Free Parliament in Sicily, and the Vision of Italian Unity

IN THE ERA when Wilhelm Gustav Friedrich, Count Bentinck, great-grandson of Hans Willem Bentinck, first Earl of Portland, was fighting for the independence of Holland and also trying to retain his lands of Varel and Kniphausen, the second son of another of Hans Willem's great-grandsons, the son of the third Duke of Portland, William Cavendish-Bentinck, distinguished himself in the military and diplomatic service of His Britannic Majesty. He was then known by the name of Lord William Bentinck.

At the age of seventeen William was an ensign in the Coldstream Guards, and a year later he was promoted to a captaincy in the light dragoons. In 1794 we find him on the Duke of York's staff during the ill-fated campaign in Flanders, where he met his cousin Wilhelm. On his return to England he was elected to Parliament several times, often as member for Nottinghamshire, which contained the family estate of Welbeck.

In May 1799 William Bentinck was attached to the headquarters of the Russian General Suvarov,[1] whom at Vienna's request the Tsar had just released from his cruel exile in northern Russia to take command of the Austrian army in Italy. Ousted from the army, despite outstanding military successes, by the jealousy of Potemkin and then persecuted by the courtiers of Paul I, Suvarov had only agreed to take up arms again when the Tsar begged him to 'take the situation of Europe into consideration'.

William Bentinck took part in Suvarov's victory over the armies of the Directoire at Cassano, the Trebbia and Novi and followed the Russian general when he crossed into Switzerland over the St Gotthard Pass and the terrifying Pont-du-Diable, though they arrived too late to defeat Masséna. In the forest cantons of central Switzerland they found nothing but orphans and destruction, despite the heroic resistance of the Schwyzois de Reding.

Suvarov had to retreat by way of the Vorarlberg and Austria. He had momentarily freed Italy from foreign occupation and was convinced of the Italian states' right to freedom, an opinion he shared with Bentinck. At table, where he kept in personal touch with the men under his command, Suvarov would say grace himself, then speak to each guest in his own language. Once he embraced an Italian poet who came to read a work on 'The Liberation of Italy'. Another night he addressed the whole table in Bentinck's presence, and declared: 'I love the land where the Dukes of Portland and the Lords Bentinck were born.'[2]

In 1800 William Bentinck was with the Austrian army at the battle of Marengo when it was defeated by the French generals Kellermann and Desaix. They were assisted by General Suchet, whom Lord William was to encounter again in Catalonia. Suvarov had been disowned for contravening a petty regulation; in spite of all his brilliant campaigns he was exiled once more and died a month before Marengo.

After the peace of Amiens William Bentinck joined the staff of General Ralph Abercromby and was sent to Egypt, fighting victoriously in the battle of Canopus, near Aboukir. During the brief period of peace that followed his return to England he married in 1803 Mary Acheson, daughter of the Earl of Gosford, a woman of distinction who later contributed a great deal to her husband's diplomatic successes. In the same year, he was appointed governor of Fort St George in Madras by the British East India Company. Eight months after reaching India he already knew enough about the country to be picked to draft an address to his superior, the Governor-General of Bengal. In it he described India as ravaged by internal strife among unprincipled native leaders whose sole object often amounted to robbery and pillage. He advocated the extension of a uniform mutual obligation and tolerance throughout the sub-continent. It would be a noble achievement to base British greatness on the happiness of the peoples of India.[3]

Unhappily the application of these principles came up against all kinds of difficulties. Despite the 'truly British spirit, sound judgement and hereditary integrity and honour' which the Governor-General recognized from the outset, William Bentinck was unable to fulfil all that was expected of him. Bonaparte had been planning an expedition to India from Egypt, and the French defeat there did not completely rule out the threat of a landing on the western coast. In the interior, there was talk of the territories recently captured by the British being entrusted, in the form of vast estates, to a kind of native revenue-farmer known as zemindars. Bentinck opposed these measures and defended the free peasant small-holders. He was on the point of leaving on an inspection tour of these lands when he was turned back by dangerous uprisings in the army, which was composed mainly of Indians.

Some young officers from the British capital had drafted a set of regulations which imposed uniform dress on the soldiery, a foreign hair style and a ban on beards. These rules were contrary to local religious customs and provoked refusals to serve. In two instances the rebels were sentenced to severe corporal punishment. William Bentinck had had nothing to do with the regulations about uniforms, or with the verdict, and had immediately rescinded the regulation forbidding the sepoys to wear their former insignia. Nevertheless he believed that once the sentence was passed it would be a mistake to show weakness by interfering with the punishment of the mutineers. It is still hard to judge whether the ensuing bloody uprising in Vellore was caused by whippings or by a broader movement because of the presence in the fort at Madras of the Tipu family, which may have aimed at restoring Muslim rule in Mysore and the south of India.

In its uncertainty, the Company court of directors in London held Bentinck partly responsible, and while recognizing his hard work in their service they objected to various unspecified measures taken by him and withdrew their support. Since he himself felt that he had restored order and confidence and preserved the sepoys' native character, Bentinck returned to England, repudiated but with his conscience clear, in 1807. He had been promoted to major-general during his absence and rejoined the army as a member of the forces protecting the Essex coast. In 1808 he joined the staff of Sir Harry Burrard, who commanded the landing in Portugal. From there he embarked on a special mission to Madrid for talks with the Spanish government in anticipation of Napoleon's arrival in Spain.

After the battle of Corunna, where he commanded a brigade, Bentinck was promoted to lieutenant-general and served directly under Arthur Wellesley, the future Duke of Wellington. A short time afterwards – for events moved fast in the time of the Napoleonic wars – he was sent to Germany, where he managed to raise a force during Napoleon's occupation of central Europe.

This success, and the training he had gained, first in Italy with Suvarov and Archduke Charles and then in Spain and Germany, singled Bentinck out for an important post in the Mediterranean. In Sicily a small army made up for the most part of Neapolitans and French deserters, and assisted by a larger English garrison, remained, while the British navy cruised off the coast. Bentinck was appointed minister plenipotentiary in Palermo and commander of the English garrison in the hope that he would make for Spain with the Sicilian troops and help Wellesley in his struggle for the Iberian peninsula by creating a diversion on the eastern coast.

When he reached Sicily on 21 July 1811, William Bentinck

found a very tense situation. For centuries the ancient feudal liberty of the lesser nobility had been subject to foreign domination. After the war of the Spanish succession the treaty of Utrecht had temporarily put an end to the Spanish hegemony in favour of Savoy, which had then ceded the island to the Spaniards. Then at the peace of The Hague in 1720 Sicily had passed to Austria, and four years later it became attached to the Bourbons of Naples.

In 1759 Ferdinand, son of King Charles III of Spain, had mounted the throne of Naples and Sicily at the age of nine. After being driven out of Naples by Napoleon, who placed first his brother Joseph then his brother-in-law Murat on the throne, Ferdinand and his wife Queen Marie Caroline were ruling in Palermo with virtually absolute power when Bentinck arrived.

Two days before the new ambassador landed, five of the best known and most capable noblemen on the island were arrested and thrown into common prisons for presenting a petition against various new taxes and sales of land; they considered that the Sicilian Parliament should have been consulted about these. There was general commotion among the Sicilians, who were asking for a constitution along the lines of the English model, for their Parliament consisted of three chambers, representing the landowning nobility, the military and the Church. The people were not represented at all, nor were ancient feudal rights respected.

The fear was that if discontent degenerated into rioting the French might be encouraged to intervene. Lord Amherst, who preceded Bentinck and had withdrawn at the same time as the English military governor of the island, recommended military action. Bentinck lost no time in writing to Ferdinand's government. He expressed his surprise at the new tax on all cash payments, the sale of land from the royal domain and the sale by lottery of goods belonging to the Church and the order of Malta. He also protested at the arrest of the five members of the chamber of noblemen and the excessive influence of the Neapolitans introduced into the government and administration by the Queen.

Although England maintained an army of 15,000 men in Sicily and paid an annual subsidy which has been estimated at as much as £400,000,[4] Bentinck received a negative answer at the Queen's instigation; the King devoted his time to hunting and tunny fishing. The Parliament referred to by Bentinck really existed only to present petitions, not to give advice; it possessed no sovereign rights, and its deliberations carried no weight unless they were sanctioned by the monarchy.

Bentinck tried in vain to remind the tempestuous Queen of the services rendered by the English and had no better return when he reproached her for corresponding with a Napoleonic agent. He was indignantly informed that the Queen was the mistress of the realm and that he was a common sergeant sent to bow and scrape at the behest of the Prince Regent of England.[5]

The hostile attitude of a reactionary, anti-constitutional Queen who was no friend of England, taken in conjunction with the discontent resulting from the high cost of living and above all the necessity to defend the internal and external security of the island, convinced Bentinck that his powers were insufficient. Less than six weeks after arriving in Sicily he left for England where he reported on the situation. He returned in full command of all the troops in Sicily and of the Mediterranean fleet and with authority to stop the funds which maintained the army from being paid direct to the Court.

In 1812 the pace of events quickened. On 16 January King Ferdinand decided to withdraw to the country, claiming ill health. Without abdicating, he appointed Crown Prince Francesco 'vicar-general'. The noblemen were released, as Bentinck had been asking for some time. At the same time two of their number, the Princes of Belmonte and Castelnuovo, were entrusted with drafting a constitution, a task they passed to the Abbé Balsamo, a professor of political and agricultural science.[6] The learned professor drew his inspiration from the English constitution, taking additional elements from the former law of Aragon and the fundamental French and Italian laws.

Balsamo's plans reduced the three chambers to two – a high

chamber combining Church and nobility and a chamber of commons. One article provided for the abolition of feudal rights, and other privileges of the barons disappeared, in particular their plurality of votes according to the number of their domains. Finally judicial power became distinct from executive and legislative powers, and the individual rights of all Sicilians were recognized: no one could be arrested, exiled, punished or molested in the possession or enjoyment of his rights and property except by virtue of specific laws.[7]

On 18 July the Sicilian Parliament was opened by the Vicar-General and adopted the constitution. The King did not sanction it until 10 August, on the grounds that it was too different from the British constitution! On 4 November Parliament met to dissolve itself in favour of a new assembly.[8]

So it was not Bentinck who imposed the model of the British constitution but the King, who was afraid that articles more in tune with the times would remove more of his powers, although these were expressly reserved: 'The executive power will reside in the person of the king. The person of the king shall be sacred and inviolable.' But thanks to Bentinck the fundamental law had been made and established by a free Parliament.

When the constitution had been adopted and the new Parliament set up, Bentinck saw that the time had come to carry out that part of his mission which consisted of ferrying troops from Sicily to the Iberian peninsula and creating a tactical diversion there. First, though, he managed to have Queen Marie Caroline removed from Sicily to Vienna. She travelled by sea by way of Turkey, escorted by two British men-of-war, the *Edinburgh* and the *Leander*.[9] A few weeks after reaching Vienna she died peacefully at Hetzendorf castle. Less than two months later King Ferdinand married the Princess of Partanna.[10]

In May 1813 William Bentinck sailed for Catalonia, where he had dispatched Sir Frederick Adam with a contingent of troops. There he came up against Marshal Suchet again and found him still a formidable enemy. Since Marengo he had shone in all Napoleon's campaigns, including Austerlitz and Jena; now he

was occupying Lerida and had recaptured Tarragona. He defeated the advance guard under Adam at Ordal pass, a few miles
from Barcelona, despite the fact that he was attacking a superior
position. Suchet's superior local knowledge enabled him to make a
flanking attack along roads leading to Villafranca.[11] But Bentinck's
arrival had shown the determination and bravery of the Spaniards
who sided with the English. It also kept Suchet in Catalonia, which
took some pressure off the English positions on the Atlantic side.

News from Sicily soon led Bentinck to ask permission to
return to Palermo. The Sicilian government had changed, and the
new Parliament had split. Although Wellington did not consider
the island in danger and would have preferred to keep him,
Bentinck sailed for Palermo on 22 September and arrived at
daybreak on 3 October. He now faced the task of trying to get a
new Parliament called and reconciling the hostile parties and
embarked on an electoral tour. The dilemma was that the
Sicilians had refused to be unified with Naples – which had never
been a viable arrangement – but that left to themselves Bentinck
thought them likely to fall prey to the ideas of the French Revolution. He despaired of a practical solution and was left to dream of
some sort of protective power, perhaps even England, which
might stand by Sicily when the war was over. He communicated
these hopes to Crown Prince Francesco.[12]

Although he was only talking speculatively his suggestion
pleased neither King Ferdinand's son nor the British government.
The English Prime Minister realized that Napoleon's day would
soon be over. He was more concerned to defend the interests of
the monarchies of the Holy Alliance than the aspirations of the
people of a small island.

This withdrawal was to reduce Sicily to the condition in which
Bentinck had found it and as Nelson had described it – no corn,
no army worth the name, the people oppressed and the middle
classes restless for change. According to Nelson, Sicily would
have preferred the English to the French, but preferred the French
to no change at all. Their frigates had already been sighted off
Messina.[13]

In a short time Bentinck had organized the expeditionary force, taken measures against the high cost of living and granted a sizeable loan to the administration for the most pressing requirements. He had allowed the Sicilian Parliament a free vote on the constitution which had been drafted by the island's representatives, not imposed by him, as Lord Castlereagh was later to claim. Yet it was impossible to reform the country by waving a magic wand and to change deep-rooted habits and abuses at a stroke. All over Europe the fall of Napoleon had restored authoritarian governments to power, and the King of Naples, supported by the Holy Alliance, destroyed the entire achievement of the friends of the constitution.

Bentinck advocated the liberation of nations on a broad scale and felt that a liberated Italy would constitute a formidable barrier against France and Austria.[14] A free Parliament, a constitution, a barrier protecting independence: the full weight of the Bentinck tradition lies behind his vision at the beginning of 1814. But his inspiration did not stop at the repetition of a hard and glorious past. As long as they were liberating influences, not just a pretext for wars of conquest, the evolution and revolutions of the late eighteenth century were in harmony with English liberal ideas. The Austrian General Nugent and Maria Theresa's grandson Francis d'Este, Archduke of Austria, were both thinking about independence for Italy. The Archduke saw Metternich and Murat as scoundrels eager to carve up Napoleon's remains.

Bentinck's vision was of a union between England and a unified Italy, minus the south and the Vatican states, which would not be based upon the old Europe of partitions and successions. It was in that spirit that he landed at Livorno in March 1814 with a contingent of Sicilian and English troops and issued a proclamation:

Will the Italians alone remain beneath the yoke? Will only Italians fight Italians, to a tyrant's gain and for a country's servitude?

Warriors of Italy, we do not ask you to come to us, we ask you to enforce your own rights, and to be free.

Call upon us and we will make haste and our united forces will make Italy become what Italy was in its finest hours, and what Spain is. . . .[15]

The operation continued on the beaches of La Spezia, Rapallo, Sestri, Chiavari and Lerici, where five English vessels and a Sicilian corvette landed troops. On 7 April they were in Nervi, in the neighbourhood of Genoa. Further support arrived from Toulon in the shape of Admiral Pellew, who six years before had provided Bentinck with a ship for his return from Madras. On the 19th Genoa surrendered, the ancient banner of the city floated above the harbour and the constitution of 1797 was in force once again. The outlook for the march from Genoa to Milan seemed promising. The enterprise had been encouraged among others by the King of Naples' son-in-law, the future King Louis-Philippe, then Duke of Orleans.

Whereas Bentinck was working for an independent Italy and had written to Lord Castlereagh that it would help to buttress the peace of nations, the British Prime Minister would not look beyond the interests of Metternich and the Tsar, who were both afraid of any movement towards liberation. Besides, Wellington wanted to use the full weight of the British forces in the Mediterranean to expel the French from Spain. Castlereagh also supported Metternich's vision of an Austrian-dominated Italy which could be thrown into the balance against the growing power of Russia after the battle of Moscow. In a letter dated 3 April 1814, Lord Castlereagh wrote to Bentinck from Dijon with orders: '. . . To furnish no plausible occasion, no pretext, which might give umbrage to those with whom we are acting but with whom our relations are not such as to engender confidence. . . . It is not an insurrection we need now, no more in Italy than elsewhere. We need disciplined forces, dependent upon sovereigns whom we can trust.'[16]

The military campaign had been well prepared, with real enthusiasm and lofty aims. As the Duke of Vicenza had written to Napoleon on 27 November 1813, the issue was the creation of a kingdom of Italy, 'the idea of the *risorgimento* of liberty, images which brought a gleam to the eyes of a people with a burning imagination'. A month later the Duke wrote: 'Lord Bentinck was the first to make an open display of intentions and aims which were bound, he knew, to captivate the Italians and encourage a movement of emancipation. . . .'[17]

Although his government disowned him, Bentinck did not dream of continuing the conquest of Italy by surrounding himself with rebels, thereby betraying his trust. He remained loyal, and when he was recalled he withdrew into private life, first in Florence, then England. He remained convinced that the presence of a superior Austrian army under the command of the allied powers might put a brake on events but would not stop them and that it would have been better to permit the triumph of the Milanese patriots than to chance a general war.

Events bore him out, but only over a much longer time-scale. In Sicily too the people relapsed under the absolute monarchy of the Bourbons of Naples. Lord William Bentinck made a last intervention in the Sicilian question in a motion he put down in the House of Commons on 21 June 1821. By then the revolts of the liberals in Naples and Piedmont had been followed by ruthless repression. At the Congress of Laibach the allies had expressed their determination not to accept any constitution which had not been legally established.

Bentinck argued that the liberty demanded by the Sicilians rested upon a sacred authority, legally established. When he left Sicily it had been solemnly stipulated that the rights and privileges of the people were not to be infringed by any change of adminis-tration. How had these solemn provisions been observed? 'Far from receiving the slightest observance, I know on the most reliable authority that never was there a more thorough annihila-tion of all rights, all privileges . . . never did a greater accumula-tion of injustice, oppression and cruelty tarnish the annals of a country.'

As the representative of conservative opinion, and in defence of his own policy, Castlereagh replied that if England had played a part in Sicily it was not on behalf of the welfare of Sicilians but out of consideration for the condition of Europe and to throw up a barrier to French expansion. He dismissed Bentinck's arguments as mere oratory and claimed that the court of King Ferdinand had received no complaints from Sicilians about alleged injustices on the part of the Neapolitan authorities. Besides, Lord Bentinck's motion had come too late.

Castlereagh had received information about events in Sicily from Court, Bentinck's successor as British representative there. In 1816 Castlereagh had written: 'England has the inarguable right to require that no individual should be molested in his person or property for the part he may have taken in the establishment and support of the constitution, and the security of every individual is to be viewed as the sine qua non of the protection of the alliance with England.'[18] Now he flouted his own commitment to the Sicilian people and instructed Court to adhere to the principle of non-intervention, boasting to the Commons that he was not prepared to take responsibility for a fabricated constitution. He had in fact received no such request, only a recommendation to offer His Majesty respectful representations concerning the steps taken by the government to reduce the rights and privileges of Sicilians. Castlereagh was however quite prepared to accept the replacement of the Sicilian Parliament by a chancellory of the realm, of Austrian fabrication.

After Castlereagh, Sir James Mackintosh rose to speak in favour of Lord Bentinck's proposal, rejecting Castlereagh's sneers about the Sicilian constitution of 1812 and reminding him that a British minister ought to have held altogether different sentiments about a people's struggle for liberty. Mackintosh had been stirred in his youth by the ideas of the French Revolution, only to be repelled by its subsequent excesses.

As the author of a study of the revolution of 1688, Mackintosh was able to judge contemporary events in Sicily with a historian's impartiality. 'In 1814,' he reminded the House, 'the government had not yet taken as its motto the horror for anything resembling popular rights and the fear of public liberty. . . .' Castlereagh claimed that the constitution of 1812 had proved impracticable; Mackintosh observed ironically that whereas 'the experience, personal observation and diligent inspection conducted by the noble lord [Bentinck] in situ deserve no respect, the speculative sagacity of the noble marquess is to be believed without the slightest proof.'

A new constitution could not be expected to be as strong or as stable as a constitution sanctioned by time. Was this any reason not to grant the Sicilians, as Castlereagh had put it in his dispatch to William Court on 6 September 1816, 'the happiness and liberty they formerly enjoyed'? Why not present a humble address to His Majesty to this effect, as Lord Bentinck proposed? Mackintosh was scathing about a passage in the decree of May 1821 granting the Sicilians 'as much independence as is good for them'. In 1821 the Whigs were too weak to enforce the adoption by the conservative majority of a member state of the Holy Alliance of a few improvements in the lot of a small defenceless people. William Bentinck was not too late, as Castlereagh complained, but too early, just as he had been too early when he called upon the Italians to take their independence. For that, their patriotism had to contain itself for almost half a century, until the bloody battle of Solferino.

Lord William Bentinck had then been dead for twenty years. But before he made his exit he undertook a further task, one which enabled him to bring great social and political benefits to the nation entrusted to his care.

17 • Lord William Bentinck, Governor-General of India

E VEN AFTER Castlereagh's suicide in 1822, Bentinck still had to wait for a more liberal ministry before being appointed to a post worthy of his ability. In 1819 he had been offered the same post in Madras from which he had been recalled twelve years before, but he turned it down. In 1822 he had hopes of the governor-generalship of Bengal, but as a friend of the philosophers James Mill and Jeremy Bentham he had no chance of taking up such a post under the ministry of Lord Liverpool, who rejected Catholic emancipation and persecuted Queen Caroline. Lord Amherst, who had been Bentinck's ineffective predecessor in Sicily and had done no better as a diplomat in China, was appointed to Bengal.

Amherst had to fight the first Burmese war (1824–6), which concluded with the English taking possession of Assam and parts of Burma. His administration was not totally unproductive, but it did give rise to considerable expense, not always justified. The East India Company was concerned enough to seize the opportunity of Lord Amherst's illness to replace him with Lord Bentinck just at the moment when George Canning formed his new ministry. Bentinck was therefore expected to avoid wars and to balance the budget.[1]

The new Governor-General reached Fort William in Calcutta in July 1828. After receiving letters of congratulation from the Emperor of Delhi, the Raja of Nepal and various chiefs of the Punjab and other Indian states, he set to work. The Company Court of Directors wanted to reduce or abolish the supplementary wages, or *batta*, paid to employees, which were sometimes justified by special missions or because normal salaries were set too low. The massive reductions demanded by the Court caused resentment against Bentinck, but the order was supported by the Duke of Wellington and he had to apply it, although he managed to halve the reduction.

Some of Bentinck's own economy measures proved effective. He suppressed the provincial appeal courts, which were notoriously inefficient, and abolished customs duties on the movement of domestic goods, thereby not only cutting down the number of company employees but increasing the volume of trade, so producing an overall gain much greater than the loss of customs revenue. Bentinck also made considerable savings by replacing many English functionaries with natives and appointing native magistrates. These measures were not passed purely for reasons of economy, and as well as balancing his budget the new Governor-General had improved relations with the Indian population.

From the outset of his career in Bengal the welfare of the Hindus was William Bentinck's chief objective. He felt that their attitudes and behaviour were subject to a number of social and moral evils linked with their religion, and although he did not wish to interfere with it he felt bound to remove some of the murderous practices involved. The customs he made up his mind to eradicate were attacks by 'Thugs' on travellers and caravans, self-immolation by widows on their husband's funeral pyre, known as *suttee*, and suicide by drowning of the incurably ill. The Thugs, so called from the Hindustani word for 'cheat', were also known as Phansigars, stranglers, after their practice of killing their victims with a scarf tied in a slipknot. They addressed their rites to the bloodthirsty goddess Kali and went about disguised as ordinary merchants or religious beggars. They would join caravans of travellers and choose their moment to strangle selected victims, usually during their prayers or ablutions.[2]

In the eighteenth century the Mogul Emperors had managed to dislodge the Thugs from Delhi but not to destroy them. The authorities in the small states, unable to suppress them, gave them protection in return for a share of the proceeds. In the time of Hastings and Amherst some were arrested, but the native tribunals did not dare to find them guilty. In 1829 Major-General Sleeman, Bentinck's agent in the territory of Narbada, received orders and special powers to act against the Thugs. Bentinck backed all actions against this powerful criminal organization, and when he left India six years later it had disappeared.

The abolition of *suttee* posed grave problems for the Governor-General. Although the people had approved of the suppression of the Thugs they opposed the British attempts to eliminate the ritual suicide of widows, which was considered a sacred act by model wives.

Lord Bentinck expressed his feelings in a minute to the Court.[3] His aim was to preserve hundreds of lives lost every year, often against the will of the innocent victims. Yet if his intervention were to provoke a revolt it might spread to the army and put millions of people at risk in an even greater disaster. Nor could Bentinck forget that at the time of the Vellore mutiny, while he had been governor of Fort St George in Madras, he had been accused of violating the religious customs of the sepoys. He knew that if he failed in his attempt to suppress *suttee* he could expect the same fate, or worse. Would he look after his own interest and tread in the cautious footsteps of his predecessors? He had no hesitation in rejecting any idea of a self-serving policy in a case which meant so much to humanity and civilization.

Extensive questioning of the English authorities in India revealed that there was little reason to fear an immediate uprising if *suttee* were to be suppressed, since the custom was most widespread in Bengal, where outbreaks of violence did not present such a threat as in the north. This time William Bentinck was not disowned by the Court, and less than a month after his Minute reached them the practice of *suttee* was declared illegal, on pain of severe penalties. In general the decision was respected. One flagrant violation, followed by a petition to the King alleging that suppression of *suttee* violated the right of the Indians, was counterbalanced by the views of figures respected by the natives themselves, such as Dwarakanath Tagore and Ram Mohun Roy.[4]

The custom by which a person suffering from leprosy or an incurable disease would put an end to his life in ceremonial fashion, generally by weighing himself down with sand and throwing himself off a boat into a river, also took a heavy toll of victims. It was William Bentinck's achievement to establish a plan for appropriate medical treatment, which was carried out under the direction of two capable doctors, Goodeve and O'Shaughnessy.[5] Major-General Sleeman considered that these medical advances made in the teeth of cruel superstitions were among the greatest benefits the British conferred on India.

In his political activities Lord Bentinck always held the welfare of the people in mind. He avoided wars, particularly wars of annexation. However in 1834 the Raja of Coorg, a small state on the western side of Mysore, in southern India, turned against the British and treated his own people so tyrannically that these proud hillmen appealed for protection. Lord Bentinck took personal charge of operations, and the Raja was exiled to England, where he died. It was the only annexation effected by Lord Bentinck and took place in response to the unanimous wishes of the people.[6]

Earlier, Bentinck had visited the far north of India, the Punjab, on the border of Afghanistan. He had a famous meeting with Ranjit Singh, the Lion of the Punjab, at Rupar, where he was greeted with great pomp and ceremony. The commercial agreement he obtained brought the Indus into the British sphere of influence, associated Sind and the Sikhs with its defence and improved relations with Afghanistan as a buffer state between India and any would-be aggressor.

In 1833 the charter of the East India Company was altered by the India Act. The power of the Governor-General of Bengal was extended to cover the whole of India, with corresponding responsibilities. On this occasion Lord Lansdowne paid tribute in the House of Lords to William Bentinck's hard work and judgement.

The poet and historian T.B. Macaulay was now appointed to the Governor-General's Council, and when he arrived he became president of the Committee of Public Instruction. Bentinck had to decide on India's official language, and Macaulay drew up a Minute recommending the adoption of English. For him the ancient oriental languages were a subject purely for academic study.[7] Bentinck did not hesitate and came down in favour of English rather than the Persian or Sanskrit which were no longer the spoken languages of the country and needed ten or fifteen years' study. There were so many local dialects that they varied from one district to the next and often from the village to the nearby town; these made consistent education impossible. Bentinck's decision was taken against the advice of the oriental scholars but was supported by Sir Charles Trevelyan and John Russell Colvin as well as Macaulay himself.

For the native population the adoption of English brought the great advantage that the highest administrative positions were opened to them. They were also able to make their views known in the English-language newspapers; indeed Lord Bentinck revoked the press regulation of 1823, which had permitted censorship.

Macaulay's Minute had been the concluding step in the controversy about the official language. The Governor-General and Commander-in-Chief had now fulfilled his task and prepared to leave. In a farewell reception the Vice-President of the Council said: 'I never met with the individual whose integrity, liberality of sentiment and delicacy of mind excited in a greater degree my respect and admiration.' The charm and kindness of Lady Bentinck were also keenly missed after her departure.

Admiration for the achievements of Lord William Bentinck lasted long among both Indians themselves and his former colleagues. Twenty years after his reforms in India Sir Charles Trevelyan stated before the Select Committee of 1853 that it had been Bentinck's great distinction to have acknowledged the principle that India ought to be governed for the benefit of the Indians and that the advantages derived by England ought to be subject to that rule.

Lord William Bentinck was sixty when he left the Indian sub-continent at the end of his seven-year tenure of office. Macaulay summed up the services he rendered in lapidary style on the monument erected to him in Calcutta by public subscription, shortly before he left India for Europe on 20 March 1835.[8] By sharing the expense the Indians recognized their debt to Bentinck's continued efforts on their behalf.

After these full and fertile years, William Bentinck declined a peerage and, in February 1836, shortly before his death, he was elected Liberal member for Glasgow. Among his most vital memories were those of Sicily and the vision of Italian unification. When he went to Paris he met the daughter of the forceful Queen Marie Caroline of Naples, Marie-Amélie, now Queen of France through her marriage to Louis-Philippe. Bentinck had not forgotten the encouragement he had received from the French King when he was Duke of Orleans. It was in Paris that Lord William Bentinck died in 1839, on one of those June days when Queen Marie-Amélie delighted in gathering bouquets in the garden at Neuilly with the Princess of Orleans.[9]

Mary, Lady Bentinck, survived her husband for a few years more and planned to write his biography, but unfortunately her notes have never been found.[10] Of those who knew him best, James Mill expressed the view that no one could match what he was and what he had achieved.[11] Even the historian of India Horace Hayman Wilson, who had opposed him over the abolition of cruel rites for fear of an uprising, felt bound to admit that he must occupy a place of honour among the statesmen entrusted with the sovereignty of the British empire in the East.[12] Nor have Italian historians forgotten the part he played as an early spokesman for their country's unity and independence.

18 • Lord George Bentinck, Champion of Religious Liberty, the Protection of Workers and Honesty on the Turf

L ORD WILLIAM BENTINCK's eldest brother, William Henry, inherited the family estates and became Duke of Portland in 1809. Their father had had the gardens at Bulstrode redesigned in a more natural form by the famous gardener Repton; he eradicated all traces of the bad taste of earlier times, employing a hundred children between the ages of ten and fifteen on the landscaping, so as to habituate them to healthy work. He also altered the façade and commissioned the architect Wyatt to build a monumental entrance which still stands as the 'Pigeon Tower'.[1]

Finding himself unable to meet all the expenses occasioned by the alterations at Bulstrode, Lord William's brother sold the estate bought in 1707 by his famous ancestor Hans Willem Bentinck but kept Harcourt House in Cavendish Square, Marylebone, near the church housing the Bentinck burial vaults, and Welbeck, the former residence of his Cavendish Harley ancestors. There he reared horses and schooled jockeys. His wife, the daughter of General Scott of Balcomie and sister of Lady Canning, gave him four sons and five daughters. The eldest son died very young, the second died without issue, whereupon the duchy passed to a nephew, then to a great-nephew of Lord William Bentinck.

The fifth Duke of Portland made ambitious improvements at Welbeck. The nine-gabled façade by the little lake survives as in the time of the Dukes of Newcastle. Near a more recent building in the Palladian style are the entrances to a vast system of underground vaults which the Duke of Portland had excavated, containing the biggest stable in Europe, after the Tsar's.[2]

Meanwhile his younger brother George developed his own remarkable gifts, although, unlike his brother, he did not study at Oxford. After a fairly rudimentary schooling he joined the Tenth Hussar Regiment as a cornet at the age of seventeen.

In 1822 George Bentinck was to have become military secretary to his uncle, George Canning, when he was appointed Governor-General of Bengal, but the sudden death of Lord Castlereagh kept Canning in London, where he became Foreign Minister. Five years later it was another of George's uncles who set out for Bengal.

After a brief period as Canning's private secretary, George gained a reputation in the sporting world as a powerful oarsman, daring rider and stylish huntsman. He was six feet tall, elegant without being showy and reserved in character. He might have made a fine manager for Welbeck, but the estate was reserved for his elder brothers.

Since he did not like the profession of arms and did not reveal any political gifts, George Bentinck turned to the Turf. He began with success and might soon have become involved with the underhand dealings common in the racing world at that time, except at Newmarket, where the Jockey Club was already in operation. Instead he became the most influential member of the Club and campaigned against the swindlers.[3] He was particularly severe towards jockeys who took money for pulling up their horses, and all his life he kept a special contempt for bribe-takers. He himself won all the big prizes except the Derby, which required too great an investment.

George's elder brother died young, in 1822. John, another brother, also older than George, inherited the title of Marquess of Titchfield but did not become Duke of Portland until after

H

the death of their father, who outlived George. John Bentinck also received the elder brother's seat in Parliament, but he preferred fox-hunting and continental travel and gave up politics in favour of George, who entered the House of Commons as the member for King's Lynn in 1826, at the age of twenty-four.

For eighteen years Lord Bentinck did not take an active part in the deliberations of the House, attending irregularly and rarely speaking.[4] He was never to be a great orator, but when he did speak it was after close study of the documents and statistics which had bearing on his chosen subject. This left him no time to drum up electoral popularity on secondary matters. As Disraeli put it, all the questions he took up were colossal questions.

In 1846 the Commons debates on the Corn Laws which had protected British production for centuries jerked George Bentinck out of his political lethargy. The law as it stood completely excluded foreign corn until home-produced corn exceeded a certain price-level. During his brief ministry George Canning made up his mind to introduce a scale of moderated customs dues, but his death prevented a satisfactory solution being reached. During Sir Robert Peel's ministry the shortage of corn caused by poor harvests in Ireland led various members of the so-called Manchester school of economic thought to advocate the importation of corn from abroad and the removal of tariff protection from England, Ireland and English colonies such as Canada. One of these members, Richard Cobden, managed to persuade Peel that the threat of famine necessitated the immediate repeal of the Corn Laws.

Although Peel was a Tory, he now ceased to follow the line of his own party. Lord Bentinck, who had no partisan bias, had no difficulty in perceiving that while Cobden was sincere in his wish for more and cheaper food in a moment of crisis he was overlooking an important part of the population, the domestic producers and farmers. He sensed a political manœuvre behind Peel's *volte-face*. In Bentinck's view, total free exchange would harm not just the landlords, as its advocates claimed, but all farmers; far from improving the state of affairs in Ireland, already suffering from harvest failures, it would destroy the value of what little corn was being produced. Lastly, Canada would be antagonized by not being protected against competition from the United States.[5]

From the moment when George Bentinck became convinced that the problems at issue in the House of Commons would to some extent affect the welfare of the whole country and the balance of power among its different parts, he decided to investigate them as fully as possible and help to resolve them. He threw all his abilities into the fray, to the point of exhaustion and an early death in the prime of life. He was not fighting for his lands, for he had none; nor was he defending his interests as a horse-breeder, since he could sell his horses more easily in a free economy. He wanted a sound economy for the whole of Britain, including its agricultural regions.

From then on Lord Bentinck was the first to arrive and the last to leave when the Commons met. In mid-career he abandoned all his former pleasures, often working an eighteen-hour day, taking no time for lunch and not dining until 2 o'clock at night. He did so not out of ambition but for the sake of principles arising out of genuine convictions and facts. When Peel finally succeeded in passing the repeal of the Corn Laws he did so as a general without an army. The Commons were no longer with him, and he was repudiated on the same day in a vote on the Coercion Bill which was meant to restore order in Ireland by force. Peel had to resign, to be succeeded by Lord Russell.

Lord Bentinck had to be dragooned into accepting the leadership of the so-called protectionist party, which was not in fact opposed to liberalization in the sense of a freer market. He accepted it only until such time as a more suitable candidate could be found.

George Bentinck was out of step with the majority of the protectionists on another issue. He was in favour of total religious freedom, which was not granted to Roman Catholics or Jews. Ever since entering Parliament he had voted to abolish the obligation to take part in the Anglican Communion as a condition of holding office; this disqualified Catholics. In addition Jews might not sit in Parliament, because members had to take an oath 'on the true faith of a Christian', which barred any practising Jew.

Lord Bentinck's application to the complexities of the Corn Laws was equalled by his researches into the problems and statistics of silk, as well as the domestic production of beet sugar in England and the colonies, which had run into severe competition from cane sugar produced by exploiting slave labour overseas. He also worked out a plan to develop a vast railway network in Ireland to bring in investment and employment, in the belief that 'capital, bringing industry, employment, wealth and contentment in its train, will effectually drive agitation from the shores of Ireland'.[6]

Late in 1847 the 'Jewish question' took concrete shape when the banker and philanthropist L.N. Rothschild was re-elected to Parliament; he remained unable to take his seat because his conscience would not allow him to pose as a Christian. Peel had always resisted emancipation, and now that he was no longer a member of the government Bentinck felt that the time had come to get rid of the oath-taking clause. He therefore delivered an eloquent speech in favour of religious freedom. He had already compromised himself in the eyes of some members of his party by requesting an endowment for Irish Catholic priests, and now his stance in defence of the Jews angered one faction of the protectionists, who collectively wrote a letter of protest. They must have forgotten or been too recently elected to remember the condition of religious freedom imposed by Bentinck when he became their leader. On his side, Bentinck did not realize the strength of the discontent inside his own party, and those who might have informed him were absent for the Christmas recess. He was the last man to dream of imposing his presence when he no longer enjoyed general support and made an irrevocable decision to resign the leadership in December 1847.

Thus, after making a speech which Disraeli considered one of the best he ever heard on the subject, George Bentinck gave up 'the leadership of the country gentlemen of England', although he believed that post to be an honour which any high-minded independent Englishman should consider superior to all the rewards in the gift of the crown.

His return to the opposition back benches never diverted Lord Bentinck from working to promote the prosperity of all classes in the British Empire, whether at home or in the colonies. By the following February he was already showing that he did not shrink from further burdens. At his request the Commons agreed to set up a committee of inquiry into the sugar and coffee plantations in British India, the West Indies and Mauritius, which was to study the measures necessary to assist these colonies. His mastery of the subject made him the obvious candidate for chairman, and six days after his appointment it started work.

The committee heard eighty-three witnesses in quick succession, and sixty-five of them were questioned by Lord Bentinck himself. Merchants, planters, brokers and distillers, as well as MPs and secretaries of state, answered more than seventeen thousand questions between them. By the end of March 1848 the extra-ordinary vigour and efficiency of the committee was the talk of circles well beyond Westminster itself.

The Commons debate on the measures recommended by Bentinck to relieve the distress of the sugar-planters in the Indies provoked violent attacks, especially when he rounded on the bureaucracy of the Colonial Office. Statesmen understood him better, even when they opposed him. The achievement of the committee impressed even an opponent such as Sir Robert Peel, who found time to read the proceedings. Peel recognized that a blaze of light had been shed on the situation of the West Indies, 'thanks to a chairman who brings to the execution of his task the assiduity, zeal and knowledge acquired by himself. . . .'[7]

Thanks to this success, Lord Bentinck scarcely regretted his sacrifice of his best racehorse, whose buyer had won the Derby – his own lifetime ambition. Even so he was heard to wonder to what end he had made his sacrifice.[8] He might also have wondered why he had devoted his energies, given his health and shortened his life with days and nights of researching and publicizing knowledge, if politics were to take precedence over progress, cleverness over sincerity, the immediate interest of one class over the ancestral tradition of agriculture. Not that he was necessarily right – it is very hard to judge whether subsequent events have always justified his expectations. But he felt that all the issues had not been foreseen nor all the facts considered.

George Bentinck's next undertaking was the thorny problem of the protection of navigation, but when, after a particularly arduous session of Parliament, he visited his father the Duke of Portland for a few weeks' rest his strength suddenly ebbed, drained by superhuman exertions. On 21 September 1848 he was setting out on a long walk to see a friend at Thoresby when a sudden heart attack struck him down. They found him by a rustic gate where he had leaned for a moment for support, still grasping his walking stick. Thus died a pioneer of the rights of the working man, who had given up all the comforts and pleasures of a patrician life to work eighteen hours a day in order to master and present to Parliament the social principles which he felt to be just.

19 • The Bentincks in Present-Day Europe: Adolphe Bentinck, Ambassador and Assistant Secretary-General of NATO

THIS BOOK cannot extend to the living, whose actions will be retraced by posterity. Before returning to the Dutch branch of the Bentincks, descended from a brother of Hans Willem Bentinck and hearing the testimony of witnesses who will evaluate the work of the Dutch diplomat Adolphe Bentinck, we must not forget the descendants of the third and fourth Dukes of Portland, who continued the tradition which has made the Bentincks a European family ever since the medieval knights of Gelderland.

Since none of Lord George Bentinck's brothers had married, the heir presumptive to the Portland title was Arthur Cavendish-Bentinck, born in 1819, the second cousin of the proprietors of Welbeck. Arthur embarked on a military career, became a lieutenant-general and commanded the seventh Guards regiment. But he died in 1877, before his cousin John, and never became duke. So it was a son of Arthur's first marriage to Sophie Elizabeth Hawkins-Whitshed, William John Arthur Charles James, who became sixth Duke of Portland. His son William Arthur Henry Cavendish-Bentinck is the present Duke, the seventh in the line. Decorated with the Order of the Garter, he was Chancellor of the University of Nottingham and a justice of the peace and now lives in retirement.[1]

Among the other present-day representatives of the English branch is the heir presumptive, Major Sir Ferdinand William Cavendish-Bentinck, whose father was related to the family of the Dukes of Somerset. He is descended from the fourth Duke of Portland. Sir Ferdinand held high office in the government of Kenya. His brother Victor, a former ambassador and delegate to international conferences, is an authority on the chemical industry. He remembers his visits to Bulstrode where he fished in the long pond which reminded Hans Willem Bentinck of his native Holland. Bulstrode was acquired by a Duke of Somerset, and Victor Cavendish-Bentinck stayed there as a guest of his mother's parents.

In addition, a brother of the fourth Duke of Portland and of Lord William Bentinck, Governor-General of the East Indies, William Charles Augustus Cavendish-Bentinck, married Anne Wellesley, daughter of Richard Wellesley and niece of the great Duke of Wellington, who was Governor-General of Bengal in 1807 when Lord William Bentinck commanded Fort-Saint-George at Madras. The grand-daughter of these Bentincks, Nina Cecilia Cavendish-Bentinck, married the Earl of Strathmore and became the mother of HM Queen Elizabeth the Queen Mother, and thus grandmother of HM Queen Elizabeth II, who was born at Nina Cecilia's London home in Bruton Street.

Returning to Holland, we find the descendants of Hans Willem's brother Eusebius, lord of Schoonheten. We have already encountered his descendant Rudolf Floris Carel, the present proprietor of Schoonheten, where he lives with his family.

R.F.C. Bentinck's great-great-uncle served in the Indian cavalry shortly after the return of Lord William Bentinck. This Hendrik Bentinck was the grandfather of Adolphe Bentinck, to whom the greater part of this chapter is devoted. Hendrik married one of his relations, the last descendant of the Bevervoerde branch, Baroness Adolfine Marie Franzisca Caroline Bentinck.

The history of the Beverwoerde branch goes back to the seventeenth century, when one of Eusebius Bentinck's sons,

Hendrik Adolf, became lord of Beverwoerde, burgomaster of
Maastricht and collector general of Brabant. Two of his daughters,
Mathilda Florentina Maria and Anna, died in a shipwreck in 1743
off the Scilly Isles. Their only brother, Willem Bentinck, lord of
Beverwoerde and Nijhuisen (which his father had bought from
Charles Bentinck), was Adolfine's great-great-grandfather.[2]

Adolphe Bentinck's father was therefore descended through his
father and mother from two branches of Bentinck barons, those
of Diepenheim and Schoonheten. After the death of his first wife
and his second marriage, to Maria Sigrid van Karnebeek, his son
Adolphe was born in 1905 in Ede, between Utrecht and Arnhem.
His sister Caroline Marie Claudine was born at The Hague in
1909, when their father was chamberlain to Her Majesty the
Queen of the Netherlands.

Adolphe Bentinck's mother was the daughter of Abraham
Pieter Cornelis van Karnebeek, who was vice-president of the
first peace conference of the Carnegie Foundation and then
president of the International Court of Justice. His wife, Adolphe's
maternal grandmother, was a Rochussen. One of Adolphe's
uncles, Herman Adriaan van Karnebeek, was colonial minister, a
cousin of the same name was President of the International Olympic
Committee, and another cousin was an official at the European
Economic Community's headquarters in Brussels.

After studying at Utrecht University, Adolphe joined the
Ministry of Finance at The Hague as a lawyer, after working in a
bank for a time. He seemed to have a bright future there,
and was about to be taken on to the permanent establishment
when he learned that a rival without private means had hoped
to obtain the post. He therefore withdrew his candidature.
This gesture determined his career. Soon afterwards he joined
the foreign ministry and was appointed chargé d'affaires in
Budapest.

On 1 September 1938, in the church of Castagnola by Lake
Lugano, Adolphe Bentinck married Gabrielle Wilhelmine
Hedwig Marie, Baroness Thyssen-Bornemisza von Kaszony.
Baroness Bentinck-Thyssen relieved him of as many family

responsibilities as she could and became his mainstay in his diplomatic career. Thirty-five years later the wife of a great French minister wrote to her: 'I know how great a contribution you and your husband made over the years towards rapprochement in Europe, and particularly between the Netherlands and France. . . .'

For most of the Second World War, Adolphe Bentinck was his country's representative to the court of King Farouk in Egypt. His colleagues were immediately impressed by his charm and ability as well as by his hard work. And on top of all his diplomatic activity and running the legation, he was not above helping a secretary to write out invitations to his brilliant garden parties. He was devoted to his staff and their interests.

Sometimes, on the occasion of a particularly fascinating ceremony such as the dispatch of the gold-embroidered black silk coverings for the Black Stone in Mecca, which he had already attended in a previous year, he would lend his own car to his staff so that they could be taken to the vast green and gold tent and watch the seven camels sway past with their precious burden between files of white-clad policemen, to the sound of music, before setting out into the desert. He won the heart of his staff by having a private letter taken to a devoted colleague one Sunday, because he had been without news for a long time, or by visiting a sick employee in a remote district of the city accompanied only by his dog Whisky.[4]

Adolphe Bentinck's superiors at The Hague soon took note of his exceptional diplomatic skill, and at the end of the war he was posted to London as minister-counsellor. There he established relationships and friendships which were very useful when he returned as ambassador. During his first posting to London, between 1945 and 1950, he renewed the links between the Dutch branch of the Barons Bentinck and that of the descendants of the Dukes of Portland. He met his cousin Victor Frederick William when he returned from his embassy in Poland in 1947 to pursue his interests in the chemical industry, and he also visited the Duke of Portland at Welbeck. Like Margaret, Duchess of

Portland, Rousseau's friend, Adolphe Bentinck had an interest
for natural science collections, and he himself collected
minerals.

After London, Adolphe Bentinck was appointed minister
plenipotentiary to Berne. The ministerial residence was surrounded by rhododendrons, which brought to mind the region
of Utrecht. In post-war Switzerland Adolphe Bentinck was able
to observe the slow evolution of a small nation which had been
spared hostilities but had been tested by perpetual mobilization
and privations in the midst of the belligerent nations. The seven-
hundred-year old Confederation sought to forge its links with
Europe once more without losing the benefits of neutrality for
itself and for its international humanitarian activities.

If the aftermath of the Second World War posed no territorial
problems for Switzerland, it was a different story for the industrial
regions closer to the river network of the Netherlands and
Luxemburg. Before it flows into the Meuse the River Saar runs
through the mining basin whose principal town is Saarbrücken.
The signature of the treaty between the Saar and France in 1955,
which returned Saarland to Germany, demanded the presence of
international officials to supervise this very delicate settlement.
Adolphe Bentinck was appointed to the Saar Referendum
Commission in 1955.

His skill in international negotiation and his diplomatic
experience then singled him out for the post of Deputy Secretary-
General of the North Atlantic Treaty Organization. At the time
of his appointment in 1956 the original twelve members had
grown to fifteen after the admission of Greece and Turkey in
1952 and the German Federal Republic in 1955. In addition to its
defensive aims it was working towards the development of
peaceful international relations by promoting stability and
prosperity and encouraging economic co-operation among its
members.

While Adolphe Bentinck was working for NATO in Paris the
organization was undergoing far-reaching changes. Stalin had
died, and the period of urgent defensive measures against the

USSR was over. Lord Ismay had been replaced as Secretary-General by the Belgian Paul-Henri Spaak, who laid great stress on the political significance of the Alliance. The Korean war showed that conflicts could also erupt outside the areas of NATO, and economic co-operation through the EEC was slowly developing.

It was as if Adolphe Bentinck were continuing his family's tradition when as knights of Gelderland they created Confederations recalling the old central state of Lotharingia, which once linked Lombardy to the North Sea and the Baltic by a network of roads and waterways. The European Coal and Steel Community, the Benelux, the Common Market, Switzerland with the International Bank in Basel, the International Red Cross and many other world organizations – these institutions cover the same area as the ancient kingdom.

As a native of Gelderland, a descendant of its medieval knights and a graduate of Utrecht University, Adolphe Bentinck was ideally situated to keep informed about preparations for and against Europe, in addition to being convinced that all the nations of Europe must come together. It followed that England was a natural partner, and in that belief Ambassador Bentinck was being faithful to centuries of Bentinck thinking, as embodied notably by Hans Willem Bentinck, first Earl of Portland, and by Willem Bentinck, Imperial Count and negotiator in London and Vienna.

In his work for NATO Adolphe Bentinck was in touch with many national representatives and was particularly close to his French colleagues, among them François-Didier Gregh, the Deputy Secretary-General of NATO, now Inspector-General of Finances in France. Gregh recalls that the humanity of his Dutch colleague continually reinforced his political activity.

In 1958 Adolphe Bentinck was appointed Dutch ambassador to London. More than two centuries had passed since Willem Bentinck's mission to King George II of England. England's European future was uncertain as he took up his post: the alternatives were to turn towards the United States or to strengthen ties with the European community. The Conservative government

opted for Europe, and, in 1963 Edward Heath was chosen to lead
the negotiations. In this year Adolphe Bentinck became Dutch
ambassador to Paris.

Joseph Luns, the Dutch Foreign Minister, found a convinced
interpreter of his European ideals in his London ambassador.
On his side, Edward Heath felt that unless England could
work hand in hand with Europe it had no other choice than
to become the fifty-first state of America. Like Edward Heath,
Adolphe Bentinck looked forward to increased production
in a wider market and to advanced technological development
with Great Britain as a partner. European security would also
be reinforced.[5]

During his embassy in London Adolphe Bentinck suffered a
first attack of the illness of which he was later to die in Paris. The
British authorities even diverted traffic into another street for
several days so as not to disturb his rest. He had barely recovered
when he resumed his taxing career first in London then in Paris.
Joseph Luns now held high office in NATO, and needed him as
ambassador in Paris.

The friendship between the Dutch ambassador and the British
statesman Edward Heath continued to grow; nor was it affected
by the difficulties caused by General de Gaulle's refusal to allow
Great Britain into the Market in 1963. As I was told by M.
Palewski, President of the French Constitutional Council, in an
interview in the Palais-Royal in February 1973: '. . . It was no
easy task to be Dutch ambassador in the time of General de
Gaulle: in its day-to-day aspects at any rate his country's European
policy was contrary to that of the statesman he was accredited to.
It is greatly to Bentinck's credit that this fundamental dissonance,
which was a source of all kinds of intrigues and complications, in
no way diminished the confidence he had inspired in General de
Gaulle, who was a good judge of men.'

This portrait is fully in keeping with the sentiments expressed
by Admiral Philippe de Gaulle when he wrote to Baroness
Bentinck of those 'two men with a great esteem for one another,
the late lamented Baron Bentinck and my father. . . '.

M. Couve de Murville, General de Gaulle's Prime Minister during Adolphe Bentinck's ambassadorship in Paris, has his own memories of his good will and intelligence. He told me that Bentinck was in every sense 'an excellent diplomat', and went on in a more personal vein to say that he was also 'a very kind man', leaving no doubt about his genuine regret at his premature decease.

It was in Paris too that Adolphe Bentinck re-established his cordial relationship with Edward Heath, who in 1965 became leader of the Conservative Party. Their contacts made so valuable a contribution to his own policy of European *rapprochement* that when Mr Heath learned that this book was being written he offered of his own accord to take time off from his duties to receive the author.

When I met Mr Heath, my own prepared questions became superfluous. He drew an unerring, fascinating portrait of Adolphe Bentinck.

'In the Sixties,' Mr Heath recalled, 'when I was head of the Cabinet division with responsibility for European affairs, Adolphe Bentinck was the Dutch Ambassador in London, after being deputy secretary-general of NATO in Paris, first at the Palais de Chaillot and then in the Bois de Boulogne.'

From their earliest acquaintance, Mr Heath found in Adolphe Bentinck a friend of both his country and himself. As a representative of one of the Benelux countries he helped him with ideas and advice even when the European climate was unfavourable for Great Britain.

'He was always able to consider problems from their central aspect, irrespective of the cares of the day, and to discern their long-term future. He applied that gift in both his professional and his family life. He was a philosopher.'

I realized then that Mr Heath had seen in him something of the same patience – valued by the British as much as the Dutch – which William the Silent voiced in the saying often attributed to him: 'There is no need of hope in order to strive, nor of success in order to persevere.'

The Prime Minister continued:

'Ambassador Bentinck wanted Great Britain to be part of the European Community. He saw it rather as a *rapprochement* with the Benelux, and realized that there were difficulties ahead from the French side. In any case things were going much the same way between the Netherlands and France. For years the Dutch had been exasperating the French in the matter of Great Britain. Adolphe Bentinck kept his temper.'

'Once Adolphe Bentinck was appointed,' Mr Heath told me, 'I used to visit him often in Paris. I always found him well informed. I was well aware that at the Quai d'Orsay they were more willing to talk to him than to my own ambassador.'

This remark of Mr Heath's seems more readily understandable if examined in conjunction with his previous comment about Adolphe Bentinck's long-term view of affairs. Diplomats talked frankly to him because they recognized that his guiding principle was the welfare of Europe. Mr Heath's tribute was specific: 'He gave us information which proved accurate. He was a skilled, an admirable diplomat. He had very good judgement. He justly inspired confidence.' And he added a touch of humour by continuing: 'All that makes a very good combination.'

In his concern for complete objectivity, Mr Heath concluded by saying: 'We only once had a difference of opinion, and that was on the question of Indonesia.' But he stressed the unique nature of the disagreement and hastened to add: 'A few years afterwards we came to the conclusion that we had both been partly right. And he never allowed that disagreement to influence our friendly relations.'

It is to Edward Heath's friendship with Adolphe Bentinck that I owe the opportunity to understand the nature of the help he gave to the statesmen of his time. In this respect he continued the tradition of Hans Willem Bentinck and Lord William Bentinck, but in a manner more peaceful than that of earlier days.

If in Paris the political ideas of Adolphe Bentinck sometimes departed from those of his contemporaries, they were in harmony with the philosophy of Montesquieu, the immortal author of

De l'Esprit des lois, who 'would regard as a crime what might be of service to his own country but prejudicial to Europe and the human race'.[6]

In order to know Adolphe Bentinck one must also know the views of the great exponents of the European idea. *The European Idea* is the title of a book published in 1966 by Lord Gladwyn, one of several he has written on this vast subject. I was privileged to meet him to discuss the life and career of Adolphe Bentinck shortly after my conversation with Mr Heath. Like Adolphe Bentinck, Lord Gladwyn has made European unity his chief preoccupation. Like him, he envisaged international institutions which would have room for men of political calibre sufficient to follow an independent line of conduct and to remain in-different to popularity inside their own country if the interests of Europe so required.[7]

It is the recognition of a higher supra-national element which aligns the beliefs of the late ambassador of Queen Juliana, like his ancestors before him, with those of Lord Gladwyn, whether it is a matter of preventing an unjust war or improving diplomatic and human relations. On Adolphe Bentinck's abilities in this field, Lord Gladwyn expressed himself categorically: 'Yes, Adolphe Bentinck can be said to have been a good European.'

One of the most attractive aspects of Adolphe Bentinck's personality was his gift for arousing the respect even of those who, in strict logic, should have kept their distance, either because their own ideas would have deferred certain forms of European integration or because they belonged to a country recently at war with his own. In Paris as in London, his eclectic brand of diplomacy rendered outstanding services to the cause of European reconciliation.

In Paris I saw the German ambassador, Herr von Braun, on two occasions. He had found in the person of Adolphe Bentinck a friend and mentor. Herr von Braun echoed the general opinion that Adolphe Bentinck had an instinct for telling truth from falsehood and a tried and tested gift for assessing men and events.

Yet no one could assess the work of Adolphe Bentinck better

than his own chief, the Dutch Foreign Minister Joseph Luns, now Secretary-General of NATO. In a recent message to Baroness Adolphe Bentinck Luns wrote of the combination of modesty and humour which won him countless friends in the world of diplomacy. In Luns' view, Adolphe Bentinck's last posting to Paris was crowned with the utmost success:

His experience, his tact, his good humour, his quick brain and his great affection for France earned him an exceptional position in the capital of France.

Moreover the Dutch Embassy became the meeting place of leaders in the political, artistic and intellectual life of the City. With the help of his wife, the guests were accorded there a welcome and hospitality in the grand style . . .[8]

Everybody felt at ease with the 'highly intelligent diplomat with his unusually balanced, pleasant character and exquisite sense of humour'. This tribute comes not from a diplomatic acquaintance but a lifetime friend of Adolphe Bentinck and fellow-Gelderlander, Baron E.B.F.R.G. Wittert van Hoogland. They had known each other since boyhood and saw each other several times in Paris in later years.

Baron Wittert van Hoogland then lived at the Embassy, and Adolphe Bentinck was a master of the art of discarding his cares on those evenings when there were no diplomatic receptions to attend, after long days of exertion on behalf of his countrymen and of international affairs. On such evenings he would take his friend out into the city in search of relaxation and entertainment. They would stroll past the Étoile and along the avenue Wagram to the rue Rennequin, where in an auberge they would dine on pike, washed down with a Muscadet from the banks of the Loire.

Baroness Bentinck's insight showed her at once the value of the informal friendship between the diplomat and the noble captain of industry from Velp. It was with deep emotion that among the host of official figures at her husband's funeral ceremony she saw Baron Wittert van Hoogland paying his last respects to the man who was as much a loss to his boyhood friends as to those he subsequently made throughout Europe and beyond.

It was no mere chance that linked Adolphe Bentinck with the magistrate whose duty it is to watch over the observance of the French Constitution. The entire political history of the Bentinck family has been bound up with the inviolability of constitutions. M. Gaston Palewski, holder of the high office of President of the French Constitutional Council, paid homage to Adolphe Bentinck in a letter written after he had spoken to me of the friendly atmosphere in which these problems had been approached at the Dutch Embassy, 'that charming residence in the rue de Grenelle which Jonkeer Loudon had formerly acquired from the heirs of the Avray family, and whose exquisite taste and wonderful paintings, together with his wife's tireless exertions, made it one of the most popular places in Paris.'

Scholars of Dutch history were made very welcome in the intimately furnished rooms of the Dutch Embassy. Baron Bentinck frequently mentioned the book on William the Silent being written by M. Yves Cazaux, the author of *Marie de Bourgogne*. When this masterly work at length appeared, Yves Cazaux came to present it to Adolphe Bentinck in person, but too late.

Struck down by death in mid-career, Adolphe Bentinck was torn from all his plans and separated from a steadfast wife. She too has her vision of a broader Europe and devotes herself to working for the European Parliament in Strasbourg. At the same time he was taken from children who still needed the love and advice of a man who had so often gone out of his way to guide the young into interesting careers. His friends and colleagues everywhere lamented his unexpected death, which was also felt in his home in Holland.

Adolphe Bentinck has passed into the history of the Bentinck family. Before he left this world, did he too build a dream of a united Europe, as Hans Willem Bentinck dreamed of a Europe without the War of the Spanish Succession, as Lord William Bentinck dreamed of a free, united Italy, and as the brothers

Alexander and Philip saw a Netherlands uniting North and South four centuries before the creation of Benelux?

They all lighted the way. They were the friends of William III of Orange and Maria Theresa, of George I and of the Prime Minister of Queen Elizabeth II. They conversed with Louis XIV, Marshal Boufflers and General de Gaulle.

Jean-Jacques Rousseau corresponded with them. Handel played the harpsichord in the Countess of Portland's Whitehall drawing-room. Whether as dukes at Welbeck or as lords of centuries-old estates in Gelderland, they have handed down from generation to generation the banner that bears their fine motto, *Craignez honte*, and have done honour to their arms, the moline cross, the liberating cross of the Bentincks.

Notes

CHAPTER I

1 Wicherus Bentinck, whom we shall mention again as a witness of the foundation of Zwolle.

2 Willem Bentinck, *Oratio de Constantia Romanorum Publice Recitata*, Utrecht, 1696.

3 *Nederland's Adelsboek*, 1905. Cf. *Stammtafel des Mediatisierten Hauses Bentinck*, 1894.

4 *Bijdr. tot de Gesch. v. Overijssel*, I, p. 28, quoted in W. A. Beelaerts van Blockland, 'De afstaming van het Geslacht Bentinck', in *De Nederlandsche Leeuw*, XIV, August 1926.

5 W. Wijnaendts van Resandt, 'De eerste generaties van het geslacht Bentinck', in *De Nederl. Leeuw*, XLVII, September 1929.

6 *Leenaktenboeken van Gelre.* Cf. Wijnaendts v. Resandt, 'De eerste generaties'.

7 *Genealogisches Handbuch des Adels Bd.* VI, 1961.

8 Nijhoff, *Gedenkwaardigheden uit de Geschiedenis v. Gelderland*, part III, no. 31.

9 Beelaerts v. Blockland, 'De afstaming'.

10 Nijhoff, *Gedenkw.*, p. 28.

11 The pact was signed and sealed on the day of Epiphany, 6 January 1377. It is known to us from a copy dating from the late fourteenth

century, preserved in the Provincial Archives of Arnhem and reproduced in toto by Nijhoff, *Gedenkw.*, p. 28 ff. The names of 'Jan Bentinc, Gossen Bentinc, Gerit Bentinc' appear on p. 30.

12 Wijnaendts van Resandt, 'De eerste generaties', col. 260, from documents from Vornholz Castle in Westphalia, then in the Rijksarchiev van Gelderland.

13 Beelaerts van Blockland, 'De afstaming', col. 306.

14 Wijnaendts van Resandt, 'De eerste generaties', col 268.

15 The whole text of the Nijmegen quarter is reproduced, with parts of the other texts where they differ (signatures, etc.).

16 Sismondi, *Histoire des républiques italiennes au moyen age*, 1809–18; Norman King, 'Chevalerie et liberté', communication to the Colloque International sur Sismondi Européen, Geneva, 1973.

17 Nijhoff, *Gedenkw.*, VI, I, 229; *Reg. leenaktenb. van Geldre en Zutphen*, Veluwe 245; *Nieuw Nederlandsch Biografisch Woordenboek*.

18 Alexandre Henne, *Histoire du règne de Charles-Quint en Belgique*, Brussels, 1858, vol. I, p. 267.

19 On the alliance of W.Z.Bentinck with Sophia Teijssen, cf. H.H. Roell, in *Maandblad*, August 1926, cols. 231 & 233.

20 *Allg. Deutsche Biographie*, vol. 31, Leipzig 1875–1900.

21 Archives of Simancas, State Papers 590, quoted in *Acte des Etats Généraux de 1600*, collected by M. Gachard, Brussels, 1894, p. LXIV.

22 Gachard, *Actes*.

23 Gachard, *Actes*, p. 128.

24 Gachard, *Actes*, p. 400.

25 Gachard, *Actes*, pp. 399 ff.

26 Gachard, *Actes*, p. 762.

27 Gachard, *Actes*, p. 133.

28 Gachard, *Actes*, p. 328.

29 Document of 10 October 1607, reproduced in 'Geschiedenis van de Heerlijkeid en Herren van Obbicht', in *Publ. Soc. Hist. dans le Limbourg*, Maastricht, 1883, p. 235.

CHAPTER 2

1 Luc Hommel, *Marguerite d'York*, Paris, 1959.

2 Max Bruchet, *Marguerite d'Autriche, Duchesse de Savoie*, Lille, 1927, pp. 72 ff.

3 Reiffenberg, *Appendice à l'histoire des ducs de Bourgogne*, vol. x, p. 255, cited by A. Henne, *Le règne de Charles-Quint en Belgique*, pp. 389 ff.

4 J.Duverger, 'Lucas Cranach en Albrecht Dürer aan het hof van Margareta van Oosterrijk', in *Jaarboek 1970 Kon. Museum voor Schone Kunsten*, Antwerp, pp. 7 ff., and M.J. Schoutreten, 'Iconographie de Marguerite d'Autriche', in *Publications du Centre européen d'études burgondo-médianes*, no. 9, 1967, pp. 88 ff.

5 Archives du Nord, LM No. 41.270, cited in Bruchet, *Marguerite*, p. 75.

6 Marie-Caroline Murray, *Éloge et mémoire . . . sur la vie de Jean de Carondelet, Seigneur de Champvans Sobre sur Sambre, Chancelier de Bourg*, Brussels, 1786.

7 Lebroussart, *Éloge de Jean de Carondelet*, 1786.

8 Président Clerc, *Mémoire de l'Abbaye de Montbenoit et sur les Carondelet, premiers restaurateurs de l'art en Franche-Comté*, Besançon, 1868.

9 Bruchet, *Marguerite*, p. 182: Codicil of 28 November 1530.

10 M.Gachard, *Analectes belgiques*, vol. i, p. 457.

11. E.Quinsonas, *Matériaux pour servir à l'histoire de Marguerite d'Autriche*, Paris, 1860, vol. i, p. 384.

12 Victor de Mestral Combremont, *La sculpture à l'église de Brou*, Paris, n.d.; Victor Nodet, *L'église de Brou*, Paris, 1911.

CHAPTER 4

1 *Correspondentie van Willem III en van H.W.Bentinck*, ed. N.Japikse, s'Gravenhage, 1927, p. 164 ff., 'Portland aan Mevrouw van Ittersum 30 Maart 1691'.

2 Paul Zumthor, *La vie quotidienne en Hollande au temps de Rembrandt*, Paris, 1959, p. 127.

3 *Nieuw Nederlandsch Woordenboek*, art. Duyn, Adam van der.

4 Japikse, *Correspondentie*, p. 4.

5 Japikse, *Correspondentie*, p. 8.

6 Japikse, *Correspondentie*, p. 8.

7 *Mémoires de Jacques II*, vol. ii, Paris, 1824.

8 Japikse, *Correspondentie*, p. 8.

9 *Mémoires de Jacques II*, pp. 195 ff.

10 Japikse, *Correspondentie*, p. 8.

11 Cited in *Dictionary of National Biography*, vol. xix, p. 522, art. W. Temple.

12 Japikse, *Correspondentie*, p. 5.

13 *Mémoires de Jacques II*, vol. ii, p. 200.

14 Henry Sidney, *Diary of the Times of Charles the 2nd*, ed. R.W. Blencove, London, 1843.

15 Japikse, *Correspondentie*, p. 15.

16 Ludwig von Pastor, *Geschichte der Päpste*, vol xiv, Pt 2, p. 901, Freiburg/Br., 1930.

17 Burnet, *History of My Own Times*, The Hague, 1735, vol. i, p. 467.

CHAPTER 5

1 B.M., Add. Ms. 32.681, Letters to H. Sidney.

2 John Dalrymple, *Memoirs of Great Britain and Ireland*, London, 1773, pp. 228–31.

3 *Verschickung Hr. Rath von Fuchs nach Zelle*, Staatsarchiv Berlin.

4 Burnet, *History of My Own Times*, London, 1753, vol. ii, p. 485.

5 *Letters and Memoirs of Mary, Queen of England, wife of William III*, collection of documents preserved in the archives of the counts of Aldenburg–Bentinck, The Hague, 1880, p. 2.

6 Japikse, ed., *Correspondentie . . . Bentinck*, p. 58.

CHAPTER 6

1 These last messages from Bentinck to his sick wife were piously preserved by the Bentinck family and eventually donated to the British Museum Library, together with many other papers, by a descendant of Elizabeth Bentinck, wife of the Hon. Henry Egerton, Bishop of Hereford: B.M., Mss Egerton, 1705 A.

2 Constantijn Huygens, *Journaal*, Utrecht, 1876–88, p. 15.

3 Huygens, *Journaal*, p. 24.

4 Francois Guizot, *Études biographiques sur la révolution d'Angleterre*, Paris, 1851, p. 295.

5 Japikse, ed., *Correspondentie . . . Bentinck*, p. 49.

6 F.A. Mazure, *Histoire de la révolution de 1688 en Angleterre*, Paris, 1825, vol. iii, p. 197.

7 *Letters and Memoirs of Mary* . . ., pp. 88, 89, 92 ff.

8 Henry Clarendon, *The State papers* . . . *during the reign of King James the 2nd & his Lordship's diary for the years 1687–1690 from the originals* . . . Oxford, 1763, vol. II.

9 Clarendon, *State papers*, p. 104.

10 L.Ranke, *Englische Geschichte*, vol. VI, p. 46.

11 Burnet, *History of My Own Times*, p. 824.

12 Mazure, *Histoire*; vol. III, p. 356.

13 Col. Sir Thomas Butler, *The Crown Jewels and Coronation Rituals*, London, 1973.

CHAPTER 7

1 Burnet, *History of My Own Times*, vol. II, p. 46.

2 C.E.Engel, *Figures et aventures du XVIIème siècle*, Paris, 1939, p. 112.

3 Abbé Prevost, *Les campagnes philosophiques ou Mémoires de M. de Montcal*, Amsterdam, 1741–, vol. I, Pt I, p. 21 f.

4 Nicolas Chevalier, *Histoire de Guillaume III, Roy d'Angleterre, d'Écosse et d'Irlande, prince d'Orange* . . . *par médailles, inscriptions, arcs de triomphe*, Amsterdam, 1692, p. 158.

5 Japikse, ed., *Correspondentie* . . . *Bentinck*, p. 163 f.

6 Japikse, *Correspondentie*, p. 169.

7 Auersperg, Report, 16 August, cited in Onno Klopp, *Der Fall des Hauses Stuart*, Vienna, 1879, vol. VI, p. 335.

8 T.B.Macaulay, *The History of England*, London, 1889, vol. II, p. 530.

CHAPTER 8

1 Klopp, *Der Fall des Hauses Stuart*, vol. VII, p. 378.

2 Klopp, *Der Fall*, vol. VII, p. 389 ff.

3 Klopp, *Der Fall*, vol. VII, p. 447.

4 Letter from Louis XIV to the Marquis d'Harcourt, 19 February 1698, quoted in C.Hippeau, *Avènement des Bourbons au trône d'Espagne*, vol. I, p. 13.

5 Saint-Simon, *Mémoires*, vol. I.

6 Macaulay, *The History of England*, vol. V, p. 74.

7 Saint-Simon, *Mémoires*, vol. I.

8 Torcy's account of a report from the Marquis d'Harcourt, 17 March 1698, quoted in Hippeau, *Avènement*, vol. I, p. 15.

9 Hippeau, *Avènement*, vol. I, p. 49.
10 Japikse, ed., *Correspondentie . . . Bentinck*, p. 297, letter of 20 March 1698.
11 Japikse, *Correspondentie*, 2 April 1698, p. 274.
12 Japikse, *Correspondentie*, p. 297, letter of 20 March 1698.
13 Klopp, *Der Fall*, vol. VIII, p. 83. Cf. Grimblot, vol. I, p. 447.
14 Hippeau, *Avènement*, vol. I, p. 50.

CHAPTER 9

1 Louis XIV to d'Harcourt, 15 September 1698, quoted in Hippeau, *Avènement des Bourbons . . .*, vol. I, p. 199.
2 8 February 1699, quoted by Hippeau, *Avènement*, vol. II, p. 20.
3 Japikse, ed., *Correspondentie . . . Bentinck*, p. 347.
4 Klopp, *Der Fall des Hauses Stuart*, Vol. VIII, p. 553.
5 Pastor, *Geschichte der Päpste*, vol. XIV, Pt. 2, 1165–6.
6 Memoir of Nicolas de Sainctot. Cf. R.Maindron, *La France aux XVIIe et XVIIIe siècles*, Paris, 1970.
7 Louis XIV to d'Harcourt, 17 November 1700, quoted in Hippeau, *Avènement*, vol. II, p. 306.
8 Japikse, *Correspondentie*, vol. I, p. 352.
9 Document of 1707.

CHAPTER 10

1 Burke, *A Genealogical and Heraldic Dictionary of the Peerage and Baronetage*, London, 1901, p. 244.
2 B.M., Add. Mss 22. 676.
3 B.M., Egerton Mss 1717.
4 Egerton Mss 1710.
5 R.W.Goulding, 'John Achard. A Duke's tutor & friend', in *The National Review*, September 1913, vol. LXII, p. 85.
6 Antoine Jean d'Ailly Jr., *Willem Bentinck van Rhoon . . . gedurende de laatse Jaren voor den Vrede van Aaken*, Amsterdam, 1890, p. 6.
7 B.M., Egerton Mss 1711.
8 Egerton Mss 1711.
9 Egerton Mss 1711.
10 Egerton Mss 1711.
I

11 Egerton Mss 1711.
12 Cf. the letter from Lord Sandwich to the Duke of Newcastle, dated 17 October 1747, B.M. Add. Ms. 32810: '. . . His first appearance is, I think, not to his advantage, but he has very good parts, is a scholar, thoroughly honest, in the strictest friendship and connection with his brother and is one that I can safely assure you, you may venture to trust.'
13 W.C. van Huffel, *Willem Bentinck van Rhoon 1725–1747*, s'Graven-hage, 1923, p. 16.
14 Ibid.
15 J.J. Bonnet, former Syndic, grandfather of the naturalist and philosopher Charles Bonnet, a correspondent of Charles Bentinck.
16 B.M., Egerton Mss 1711.
17 Journal of Willem Bentinck, B.M., Egerton Mss 1712. This manuscript is used several time in the following pages.
18 C. van Huffel, *Willem Bentinck*, p. 77.
19 B.M., Egerton Mss 1712.
20 A. Beer, *Holland u. der oesterreichische Erbfolge-Krieg*, vol. VIII, pp. 89 ff.; H. de Vries, *W. Bentinck van Rhoon*, Amsterdam, 1898, p. 9 n.
21 C. Gerretson and P. Geyl (ed.), *Briefwesseling*, p. 260; Journal of Willem Bentinck B.M., Egerton Mss 1712.
22 B.M., Add. Ms. 32809.
23 B.M., Add. Ms. 12811 ff., cited by A.J. d'Ailly, *Willem Bentinck*, p. 12.
24 V. de Broglie, *La paix d'Aix-la-Chapelle*, Paris, 1892, p. 266.
25 B.M., Add. Ms. 12811.

CHAPTER II

1 A. Beer, *Aufzeichnungen des Grafen Willem Bentincks über Maria Theresia. Einl. über die öster. Politik 1749–1755*, Vienna, 1871, p. III.
2 Note dated 22 October 1749, Beer, *Aufzeichnungen*, p. 28.

CHAPTER 12

1 Réaumur and A. Trembley, *Correspondance inédite*, pub. M. Trembley, Geneva, 1943.
2 Réamur, *Correspondance*, p. 63; P.F. Geisendorf, *Les Trembley de Genève de 1552 à 1846*, Geneva, 1970.

3 J.R.Baker, *Abraham Trembley of Geneva*, London, 1952, p. 25.
4 *Philosophical Transactions*, vol. XLII, 1742–3.
5 Manuscript letter, Library of Leyden University.
6 *Philosophical Transactions* T.42.
7 Charles Bonnet, *Mémoires autobiographiques*, Paris, 1948, p. 220.

CHAPTER 13

1 Public Library of Geneva, Charles Bonnet MSS 70.
2 Cf. Paul-Emile Schazmann, *La Comtesse de Boufflers*, Paris–Lausanne, 1933, pp. 19 ff.
3. J.J.Rousseau, *Correspondance générale*, ed. Dufour and Plan, Paris, 1931, vol. X, p. 200.
4 B.M., Egerton Mss 1714 (1744).
5 Letter published in P.E.Schazmann, 'La Comtesse de Boufflers, première adepte d'*Emile*', in *Revue d'histoire littéraire*, July 1937, p. 404.
6 Paul-Emile Schazmann, *La Comtesse de Boufflers*, Paris 1933.
7 British Museum, letter published in P.E. Schazmann, *La Comtesse de Boufflers*, p. 405.
8 Doorwerth had belonged to Willem Bentinck's father-in-law Anton, Count von Aldenburg. Until 1837 it belonged to the Aldenburg–Bentinck family. The gateway of the castle still bears the arms of the La Trémoïlle Aldenburgs. The castle now contains a museum.
9 Manuscript letter, Library of Leyden University.
10 W.C.van Huffel, *Willem Bentinck van Rhoon, zijn Personlijkeid en leven, 1725–1747*, s'Gravenhage, 1923. p. 150.
11 J.Fransen, 'Rousseau directeur de conscience d'une comtesse Bentinck', in *Revue de Hollande*, Paris–The Hague, June 1916, pp. 1380–2.
12 Aubrey Le Blond, *Charlotte-Sophie, Countess Bentinck*, London, 1912, vol. II, p. 69.

CHAPTER 14

1 A.S.Turberville, *A History of Welbeck Abbey and Its Owners*, 1938.
2 *The Diary of Humfrey Wanley, 1715–1726*, ed. C.E. and Ruth C. Wright, London, 1966, vol. II, pp. 222, 236, 256.

3 Horace Walpole, *Correspondence*, 1751.

4 B.M., Egerton Mss 1721.

5 Mary Wortley-Montagu, *The Letters and Works*, ed. Lord Wharncliffe, London, 1837, vol. I, p. 63.

6 Delany, *Letters*, vol. I, p. 68.

7 John Lightfoot, *Flora Scottica or a systematic arrangement in the Linnean methods*, London, 1777.

8 Thomas Pennant, 'Some account of the author', in Lightfoot, *Flora Scotticia*, preface.

9 Delany, *Letters*, vol. I, p. 68.

10 Delany, *Letters*, vol. I, pp. 70, 79.

11 Delany, *Letters*, p. 71.

12 Rousseau, *Correspondance générale*, vol. VI, p. 43.

13 Rousseau, *Correspondance*, vol. XVI, p. 101.

14 Rousseau, *Correspondance*, vol. XVI, p. 293.

15 Rousseau, *Correspondance*, vol. XVI, p. 293.

16 Rousseau, *Correspondance*, vol. XVII, p. 40.

17 Rousseau, *Correspondance*, vol. XVII, p. 262.

18 Janssen, *J.J.Rousseau als Botaniker*, Berlin, 1895, p. 112.

19 Rousseau, *Correspondance*, vol. XIX, p. 172.

20 Jacques-Annibal Claret de la Tourrette, *Voyage au Mont Pilat*, Avignon, 1770.

21 Delany, *Letters*, vol. I, p. 542.

22 Stanhope, *Life of Pitt*, vol. IV, p. 249, quoted in *Dictionary of National Biography*, vol. II, art. Bentinck.

CHAPTER 15

1 *Lykrede ter gedachtenisse van Wolter Jan Gerrit Baron Bentinck. Met eene genealogie dezer Familie*, Amsterdam, 1781.

2 K. Jaeger, *Die Münzprägungen der deutschen Staaten*, Basle, 1954.

3 State Archives, Vienna. Published by Dard in *Revue des deux mondes*, Paris, 15 January 1934, p. 417. Dard wrongly believed that this letter referred to the 'Count Bentinck' who commanded in Sicily. Lord William Bentinck was in Madras in 1807, and was not appointed to Sicily until 1811.

4 The branch of the Counts von Altenburg–Bentinck has continued thanks to the sons of Carel Anton and his wife Mechtild.
One of their sons, Count Carl Philipp Otto, was the father of
Willem Fr.Ch.H., Count von Altenburg-Bentinck (d. 1958). He was
the father of Countess Sophie Mechtild, born at Middachten in
1924, the wife of Don Enrico Gaetani dell'Aquila d'Arragona, of the
House of the Dukes of Laurenzana; her sister, Countess Isabelle
Adrienne, is the wife of the agronomist Aurel, Count van Ortenburg, who is rebuilding Middachten Castle.

Another son of Carel Anton, Count Godard Jan George, born
at Middachten in 1857, had two sons by his wife, née van Bylen;
both died without male issue. The daughter of the second son,
Countess Louise Adrienne Jacoba, is the wife of the art expert
George Léon Alexandre de Brauwere. They preserve the memory
of the family of the counts of the Holy Roman Empire in the
imposing castle where their charming children are already proud
of their noble ancestry.

5 Mme de Staël, *Carnets de voyage*, Geneva, 1971.
6 Mme de Staël, *Dix années d'exil*, Paris, 1966.
7 Norman King in *Cahiers Staëliens*, new series, no. 16, June 1973,
p. 3.

CHAPTER 16

1 Antonio Capograssi, *Gl'Inglesi in Italia durante le campagne Napoleoniche*, Bari, 1949, p. 48.
2 Philip Longworth, *The Art of Victory. The Life of Generalissimo
Suvorov*, London, 1965.
3 William Bentinck, Address to Wellesley, May 1804. Cf. Demetrius
C.Boulger, *Rulers of India, Lord William Bentinck*, Oxford, 1892,
p. 22.
4 Giovanni Aceto, *Della Sicilia e dei suoi rapporti con l'Inghilterra
nell'epoca della Costituzione del 1812*, Palermo, 1970, p. 85.
5 Capograssi, *Gl'Inglesi*, p. 48.
6 Capograssi, *Gl'Inglesi*, p. 55.
7 Aceto *Della Sicilia*, pp. 91 ff.
8 Capograssi, *Gl'Inglesi*, p. 56.

9 Capograssi, *Gl'Inglesi*, p. 96.
10 Capograssi, *Gl'Inglesi*, p. 98.
11 J.Gomez de Arteche, *Guerra de la indipendenza*. Cf. Napier, *History of the Peninsular War*.
12 3 December 1813. Archivio storico Casa reale Borbonica, destroyed in Naples in 1943 but reproduced in part by Capograssi, *Gl'Inglesi*, p. 156 ff.
13 *Letters and Dispatches of H. Visc. Nelson*, selected and arranged by J.K. Laughton, London, 1886.
14 Capograssi, *Gl'Inglesi*, p. 201.
15 Proclamation of William C. Bentinck, Livorno, 14 March 1814. Archives of the State of Bologna. Cf. Capograssi, *Gl'Inglesi*, p. 196.
16 Capograssi, *Gl'Inglesi*, p. 188.
17 Report of the Duke of Vicenza to Napoleon, Paris, 27 November and 30 December 1813. Cf. Weil, *Le Prince Eugène et Murat*, vol. III, pp. 137, 139.
18 Capograssi, *Gl'Inglesi*, p. 188.

CHAPTER 17
1 *Dictionary of National Biography*, art. Amherst.
2 *The Gazetteer*, vol. II, Calcutta, new edn, 1928, p. 498.
3 Minute by Lord William Bentinck, 8 November 1829.
4 Boulger, *Rulers of India*, p. 92.
5 Major-General W. H. Sleeman, *Rambles and Recollections of an Indian Official*, London–Oxford, 1915, p. 571.
6 Boulger, *Rulers of India*, p. 169.
7 Macaulay, memorandum to the Council of 2 February 1835, in reply to the letters from the Orientalists dated 21 and 22 January 1835.
8 Boulger, *Rulers of India*, p. 203.
9 Imbert de Saint-Amand, *Marie-Amélie et l'apogée du règne de Louis-Philippe*, Paris, 1894, p. 40.
10 *Dictionary of National Biography*, art. William C. Bentinck.
11 Alexander Bain, *Life of James Mill*, London, 1882.
12 H.H.Wilson, *History of British India*, vol. III, London, 1867.

CHAPTER 18

1 G.C.Edmonds, *A History of Chalfont St Peter & Gerards Cross.* Cf. Humphrey Repton, *Landscape Gardening*, London 1840, p. 141.
2 English Homes No. xxxviii, Welbeck Abbey, in *Illustrated London News*, 3 August 1895; Arthur S. Turberville, *A History of Welbeck Abbey and Its Owners*, 1938.
3 M.Seth-Smith, *Lord Paramount of the Turf*, London, 1971.
4 B.Disraeli, *Lord George Bentinck*, London, 2nd ed., 1905, p. xxxiv.
5 Cf. introduction to Disraeli, *Lord George Bentinck*, by Ch.Whibley, p. xxxiv.
6 Hildegard Herr, *Das Arbeitsbeschaffungsprogramm Lord George Bentincks 1847*, Lörrach, 1958, p. 61.
7 Disraeli, *Lord George Bentinck*, p. 356.
8 Disraeli, *Lord George Bentinck*, p. 351.

CHAPTER 19

1 Cf. *Porträt-Album van den Nederlandschen Adel*, The Hague, 1937.
2 This title was confirmed by decision of the King of Holland, William I, on 10 June 1919.
3 Cf. *Stammtafel des Mediatisierten Hauses Bentinck*, tables x & xi.
4 Letter from Esphir Sack.
5 E.Heath, *Old World, New Horizons*, Harvard, 1967, pp. 11 f.
6 Montesquieu, *Cahiers*, Paris, 1941, p. 9.
7 Lord Gladwyn, 'Britain in Europe', in *New Europe*, May 1972.
8 Joseph Luns to Baroness Bentinck, guest of honour at the *Yorkshire Post* literary luncheon, 1974.

Bibliography

GENERAL WORKS

Nieuw Nederlandsch Biografisch Woordenboek, ed. Molhuysen and Block, 10 vols, Leyden, 1911–37

Dictionary of National Biography, ed. Leslie Stephen and S.Lee, vols 1–21, London, 1921–2

Ludwig van Pastor, *Geschichte der Päpste*, 14 vols, Freiburg im Breisgau, 1930

T.B.Macaulay, *The History of England*, London, 1889

L.Ranke, *Englische Geschichte*, Berlin, 1859–69

Kunstreisboek voor Nederland, Amsterdam, 1969

Paul Zumthor, *La vie quotidienne en Hollande au temps de Rembrandt*, Paris, 1959

J.Balteau, J.Barroux, M.Prevost, *Dictionnaire de biographie française*, Paris, 1933–

Neue Deutsche Biographie, ed. von der Bayer, Akademie der Bayer, Akademie der Wissenschaften

Allegemeine Deutsche Biographie, Leipzig, 1890

Allg. Geschiedenis der Nederlanden, Utrecht, 1949–58

Allg. Lexikon der bildenden Kunstler, ed. U.Thieme, F.Becker (since 1923 ed. Hans Vollmer), 36 vols, Leipzig, 1907–47

H.H.Wilson, *History of British India*, vol. III, London, 1867

Albert Malet, *Histoire Moderne* (1498–1715), Paris, 1914
J.C.de Jonge, *Verhandelingen betr. de Geschiedenis der Nederlanden*, 2 vols, Delft, 1825–7

MEMOIRS, PUBLISHED CORRESPONDENCE, DOCUMENTS
Wilhelm Bentinck, *Oratio de Constantia Romanorum*, Utrecht, 1696
Actes des Etats Généraux de 1600, coll. M.Gachard, Brussels, 1894
E.Quinsonas, *Matériaux pour servir à l'histoire de Marguerite d'Autriche*, Paris, 1860
Correspondentie van Willem III en van H.W.Bentinck, ed. N.Japikse, s'Gravenhage 1927
Lettre écrite à L.Seldenus . . . sur la guerre présente entre la France et la Hollande, Diarium Europaei XXVI, Frankfurt am Main, 1673
Mémoires de Jacques II, Paris, 1824
Gilbert Burnet, *History of My Own Times*, The Hague, 1735 and London 1753
John Dalrymple, *Memoirs of Great Britain and Ireland*, London, 1773
Letters and Memoirs of Mary, Queen of England, collection of documents preserved in the archives of the Counts of Aldenburg–Bentinck, The Hague, 1880
Constantijn Huygens, *Journaal*, The Hague, 1873
Henry Clarendon, *The State Papers . . . During the Reign of King James the Second and His Lordship's Diary for the Years 1687–1690*, from the originals, Oxford, 1763
Nicolas Chevalier, *Histoire de Guillaume III, Roy d'Angleterre, d'Ecosse et d'Irlande, prince d'Orange . . . par médailles, inscriptions, arcs de triomphe*, Amsterdam, 1692
Lettres de Madame de Sévigné, ed. Bossange, Paris, 1806
Hippeau, *Avènement des Bourbons au trône d'Espagne*, Paris, 1875
Saint-Simon, *Mémoires*
Journal of the Extraordinary Embassy of H.E. the Earl of Portland in France, ed. G.D.J.Schotel, The Hague, 1851
Mémoires de Charlotte-Amélie de la Trémoille, comtesse d'Altenbourg 1652–1719
W.Bentinck, *Briefwisseling*, ed. C.Gerretson and P.Geyl, Utrecht, 1934
Aufzeichnungen des Grafen Willem Bentinck über Maria-Theresia, ed. A.Beer, Vienna, 1871

J.J.Rousseau, *Correspondance générale*, ed. T.Dufour and P.P.Plan, Paris, 1924–34

The Diary of Humfry Wanley 1715–1726, London, 1966

Horace Walpole, *Correspondence*, London, 1903–5

Mary Wortley-Montagu, *The Letters and Works*, ed. Lord Wharn-cliffe, London, 1837

Granville, Mrs Delany, *The Autobiography and Correspondence*, London, 1862

Voltaire, *Correspondence*, ed. Th. Besterman, Geneva and Paris, 1953 ff.

Mme de Staël, *Carnets de voyage*, Geneva, 1971

Mme de Staël, *Dix années d'exil*, ed. S. Ballayé, Paris, 1966

Letters and Dispatches of H.Viscount Nelson, selected and arranged by J.K.Laughton, London, 1886

William C.Bentinck's Proclamation at Livorno, 14 March 1814, Hansard, 1847

BIOGRAPHIES, MONOGRAPHS, SPECIAL HISTORIES

Is. Ant.Nijhoff, *Gedenkwaardigheden de Geschiedenis van Gelderland*, Arnhem, 1839

Alexandre Henne, *Histoire du règne de Charles-Quint en Belgique*, Brussels, 1858

Luc Hommel, *Marguerite d'York*, Paris, 1959

Max Bruchet, *Marguerite d'Autriche, Duchesse de Savoie*, Lille, 1927

Président Clerc, *Mémoire de l'Abbaye de Montbenoit et sur les Carondelet*, Besançon, 1868

Victor de Mestral-Combremont, *La sculpture à l'église de Brou*, Paris, n.d.

Victor Nodet, *L'église de Brou*, Paris, 1911

F.A.Mazure, *Histoire de la révolution de 1688 en Angleterre*, Paris, 1825

Marion E.Grew, *William Bentinck and William III Prince of Orange*, London, 1924

Mrs Aubrey Le Blond, *Charlotte Sophie Countess Bentinck, Her Life and Times, 1715–1800*, 2 vols, London, 1912

Barozzi and Berchet, *Le relazioni degli stati europei al senato degli amb. Veneziani*, vol. III, Venice, 1877

François Guizot, *Etudes biographiques sur la Révolution d'Angleterre*, Paris, 1851

Onno Klopp, *Der Fall des Hauses Stuart*, Vienna, 1875–88

A. Beer, *Holland und der Oesterreichische Erbfolge Krieg*, Vienna, 1871

V.de Broglie, *La paix d'Aix-la-Chapelle*, Paris, 1892

R.A.Réaumur and A. Trembley, *Correspondance inédite*, Geneva, 1943

P.F.Geisendorf, *Les Trembley de Genève de 1552 à 1846* Geneva, 1970

J.R.Baker, *Abraham Trembley of Geneva*, London, 1952

Jean Rostand, *Un grand biologiste, Charles Bonnet*, Paris, 1966

A.J.d'Ailly Jr., *William Bentinck van Rhoon . . . gedurende den laatse Jaren voor den Vrede van Aaken*, Amsterdam, 1890

W.C.van Huffel, *Willem Bentinck van Rhoon 1725–1747*, s'Gravenhage, 1923

Paul-Emile Schazmann, *La comtesse de Boufflers*, Paris–Lausanne, 1933

A.S.Turberville, *A History of Welbeck Abbey and its Owners*, London, 1938

John Lightfoot, *Flora Scottica* (with an 'Account of the Author' by Thomas Pennant), London, 1777

J.J.Jansen, *Rousseau als Botaniker*, Berlin, 1895

J.A.Claret de la Tourrette, *Voyage au Mont-Pilat*, Avignon, 1770

A.Capograssi, *Gl'Inglesi in Italia durante il campagne Napoleoniche*, Bari, 1949

P.Longworth, *The Art of Victory, the Life of Generalissimo Suvorov*, London, 1965

D.C.Boulger, *Rulers of India, Lord William Bentinck*, Oxford, 1892

G.Aceto, *Della Sicilia e dei suoi rapporti con l'Inghilterra nell'epoca della Costituzione del 1812*, Palermo, 1970

John Rosselli, *Lord William Bentinck and the British Occupation of Sicily 1811–1814*, Cambridge, 1956

M.H.Weil, *Le Prince Eugène et Murat*, Paris, 1902

Major-General W.H.Sleeman, *Rambles and Recollections of an Indian Official*, London–Oxford, 1915

G.C.Edmonds, *A History of Chalfont St Peter and Gerards Cross*, London, 1972

M.Seth-Smith, *Lord Paramount of the Turf*, London, 1971

Benjamin Disraeli, *Lord G.Bentinck* (with Introduction by C.Whibley), 2nd ed., London, 1905

Hildegard Herr, *Das Arbeitsbeschaffungsprogramm Lord George Bentincks*, Lorrach, 1958

Edward Heath, *Old World, New Horizons*, Harvard, 1967

E.W.Moes and K.Sluyterman, *Nederlandsche Kastelen en hun historie*, Amsterdam, 1912–15

A.W.J.Mulder, *Het kasteel Amerongen en zijn bewoners*, Maastrict, 1949

Geoffrey Cotterell, *Amsterdam*, Boston, 1972

Niccolo Palmieri, *Saggio storico e politico sulla Costituzione del Regno di Sicilio infino al 1816*, Lausanne, 1847

Frank Cundall, *The Governors of Jamaica in the First Half of the Eighteenth Century*, The West India Committee, London, 1937

J.C.de Jonge, *L'Union de Bruxelles, année 1577*, Rotterdam, 1829

J.K.J.de Jonge, *Geschiedenis van de diplomatie gedurende den Oostenrijkschen successie-oorlog*, Leyden, 1852

Horace Walpole, *The Duchess of Portland's Museum*, with an introduction by W.S.Lewis, New York, 1936

Catalogue of the ornamental furniture works of art, and porcelain at Welbeck Abbey, privately printed 1897

The Victoria History of the County of Buckingham, vol. III, London, 1925

Imperial Gazeteer of India, Oxford 1892

GENEALOGIES AND GENEALOGICAL WORKS

Nederland's Adelsboek, 1905–

Stammtafel des Mediatisierten Hauses Bentinck, 1894

Genealogische Reportorium, Jhr E.A.van Beresteyn, 2 vols, The Hague, 1972 (contains an extensive bibliography)

Genealogisches Handbuch des Adels., Limburg au der Lahn, 1952–75

E.B.F.F.Wittert van Hoogland, *Porträt-Album van den Nederlandschen Adel*, The Hague, 1937

De Nederlandsche Leeuw, monthly review of the Genealogisch Genootschap, s'Gravenhage.

Adelsarchiv, Jaarboek voor den Nederlandschen Adel, ed. D.G.van Epen, s'Gravenhage–Brussels, 1901

B.Burke, *A Genealogical and Heraldic Dictionary of the Peerage and Baronetage*, 36th ed., London, 1901

Genealogisches Handbuch des Adels, Fürstl. Häuser, vols IV, VI, IX; *Gräfliche Häuser*, Glücksburg

J.van Doorninck, *Geslachtkundige aanteekeningen ten aanzien van de gecommitteerden ten landdage van Overijssel sedert 1610–1794*, Deventer, 1871–

Lijkrede ter gedachtenisse van Wolter Jan Gerrit Bentinck, met eene genealogie dezer familie, Amsterdam, 1781

PRINCIPAL PERIODICALS CONTAINING ARTICLES CONCERNING THE HISTORY OF THE BENTINCKS

Publications de la Société d'Histoire et d'Archéologie dans le Limbourg, Maastricht, 1864

Publications du Centre européen d'études burgondo-médianes, Basle, 1957 ff.

Jaarboek Kon. Museum voor Schone Kunsten, Antwerp

Hansische Geschichtsblätter, Weimar, 1871 ff.

Philosophical Transactions, London 1742

Revue d'histoire littéraire de la France, July 1937

Revue de Hollande, Paris–The Hague, 1916

Revue des deux mondes, Paris, 1934

The Imperial Gazetteer, Calcutta, new edn, 1957 ff.

New Europe, 1972

Cahiers Staëliens, Paris

Annales de la Société J.J. Rousseau, Geneva, 1905 ff.

Index

147-8; received by Francis I and Maria Theresa, 148-9, 150; his success at Imperial court, 151-3; and regency for William v of Orange, 153-4; Curator of Leyden University, 155; patron of Abraham Trembley, 156-9; and the 'Leyden Jar', 160; his encouragement of learning 161-2; death of his son, 164; defends Rousseau, 165; receives Diderot, 166; his ideas on education, 166; expressed admiration for Rousseau, 167; agrees to burn letter for Rousseau, 168; and his son John, 169; 170; birth of his granddaughter Sophie-Henriette, 172; affinities with England, 173; corresponds with Duchess of Portland, 175; further reference, 220

Bentinck, Willem (son of Eusebius I), 33, 35, 183

Bentinck, Willem (nephew of E. of Portland), 33

Bentinck, Willem (son of E. of Portland), 62, 122, 185

Bentinck, Willem Friedrich Christian, 186

Bentinck, Willem Zuylen, 13

Bentinck, William (2nd Duke of Portland), 127-9

Bentinck, William (3rd Duke of Portland), 173, 175

Bentinck, Lord William (1774-1839); his birth, 180; early military career, 189; campaigns with Suvarov, and marriage, 190; first experience in India, 191; and Napoleonic Wars, 192; in Sicily, 193-4; and Sicilian Constitution, 195; in Spain, 195-6; returns to Sicily, 196; foresees unification of Italy, 197-9; continued concern with Sicily, 199-

200; his views vindicated after his death, 201; appointed Governor General of Bengal, 202; career in India, 203; struggles to suppress 'Thugs' and end 'Suttee', 203-5; an annexation of Coorg, 205; becomes Governor-General of India, 206; his achievements, refuses peerage, his death, 207; retrospective references, 208, 216, 223, 226

Bentinck, William (Vice-Admiral), 170, 187, 188

Bentinck, William Arthur Henry Cavendish (7th Duke of Portland), 215, 218

Bentinck, William Henry Cavendish (4th Duke of Portland), 181-3, 208, 210, 214-15, 216

Bentinck, William Henry Edward (Archdeacon of Westminster), 181

Bentinck, William John Arthur Charles James (6th Duke of Portland), 215

Bentinck, William John Cavendish Scott (5th Duke of Portland), 209-210, 215

Bentinck, Wolf Goswin, 35

Bentinck, Wolter Jan Gerrit, 183-5

Bentinck, Zeger, 30

Bentinck, Zeno Arend, 31, 33

Bentinck-Thyssen, Baroness Gabrielle Wilhelmine Hedwig Marie (wife of Adolphe Bentinck), 217, 224-6

Berka, Count von, 89

Berkel, van, Burgomaster of Delft, 143-4

Berkeley, John, of Stratton, 93, 116, 123

Bernadotte, Marshal Jean-Baptiste, later King Charles xiv of Sweden, 187

260

Index

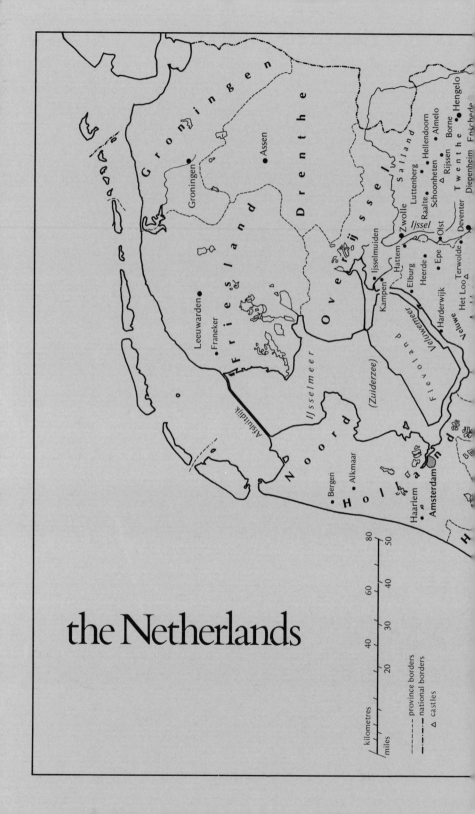

the Netherlands

kilometres

miles

------ province borders
-·-·- national borders
△ castles

Groningen

Assen

Groningen

Drenthe

Overijssel

Salland

Almelo
Hellendoorn   Borne   Hengelo
Luttenberg   Rijssen   Enschede
Raalte   Schoonheten   Twenthe
Zwolle   Olst   Deventer   Diepenheim   Enschede
IJssel

Friesland

Leeuwarden
Franeker

IJsselmuiden
Hattem
Elburg   Heerde   Epe   Het Loo   Terwolde
Kampen   Harderwijk   Veluwe

IJsselmeer

(Zuiderzee)

Afsluitdijk

Flevoland   Veluwemeer

Noord

Bergen   Alkmaar

Holland

Haarlem   Amsterdam

H